Attack at Chosin

ATTACK at CHOSIN

The Chinese Second Offensive
in Korea

Xiaobing Li

UNIVERSITY OF OKLAHOMA PRESS : NORMAN

Publication of this book is made possible through
the generosity of Edith Kinney Gaylord.

Library of Congress Cataloging-in-Publication Data

Names: Li, Xiaobing, 1954– author.
Title: Attack at Chosin : the Chinese second offensive in Korea / Xiaobing Li.
Description: First. | Norman, OK : University of Oklahoma Press, 2020. | Includes
    bibliographical references and index. | Summary: "Explores the role of command and
    control, technology, and combat effectiveness from the point of view of the Chinese,
    and examines the cooperation and friction between Beijing and Pyongyang during the
    Battle of Chosin Reservoir"—Provided by publisher.
Identifiers: LCCN 2019050468 | ISBN 978-0-8061-6499-1 (hardcover)
Subjects: LCSH: Korean War, 1950–1953—Campaigns—Korea (North)—Changjin Reservoir. |
    Korean War, 1950–1953—Participation, Chinese.
Classification: LCC DS918.2.C35 L53 2020 | DDC 951.904/242—dc23
LC record available at https://lccn.loc.gov/2019050468

The paper in this book meets the guidelines for permanence and durability of the Committee
on Production Guidelines for Book Longevity of the Council on Library Resources, Inc. ∞

1 2 3 4 5 6 7 8 9 10

For my parents,
Li Weiying and Zhang Xiaoyi

Contents

Abbreviations

AMS   Academy of Military Science (PLA)
AWM   Australian War Museum
BCT   battalion combat team
CCP   Chinese Communist Party
CMAG   Chinese Military Advisory Group (in Vietnam)
CMC   Central Military Commission (CCP)
CPVF   Chinese People's Volunteer Force (PLA)
DGPT   Department of the General Political Tasks (PLA)
DPRK   Democratic People's Republic of Korea (North Korea)
DRV   Democratic Republic of Vietnam (North Vietnam)
ECMR   East China Military Region (PLA)
GAAA   General Advanced Army Academy (PLA)
GMD   Guomindang (or Kuomintang, KMT)
NEBDA   Northeast Border Defense Army (PLA)
NEMR   Northeast Military Region (PLA)
NKPA   North Korean People's Army
PLA   People's Liberation Army
PLAN   PLA Navy
PRC   People's Republic of China
RAR   Royal Australian Regiment (UNF)
RCT   regimental combat team
ROC   Republic of China (Taiwan)
ROK   Republic of Korea (South Korea)
UNC   United Nations Command

UNF   United Nations Force
USAF   U.S. Air Force
USMC   U.S. Marine Corps
WRUSAK War to Resist the United States and Aid Korea (*Kangmei yuanchao zhanzheng*)

Note on Transliteration

For Chinese terms and names of people and places, I have used the *Hanyu Pinyin* romanization system. This is also used for the titles of Chinese publications. Chinese names are written in the Chinese way with the surname first, such as Mao Zedong. Some names of people in *Hanyu Pinyin* romanization are followed by the names in Wade-Giles romanization at first mention, such as Jiang Jieshi (Chiang Kai-shek). The same is true of some place-names, such as Guangzhou (Canton).

The romanized names of most Korean people follow the traditional East Asian practice of putting the surname first, as Kim Il-sung. If a place-name has different spellings in English and Korean literature, the English spelling appears in parentheses at the name's first appearance—for example, Hagaru-ri (Hahwaokri).

Acknowledgments

Many people at the University of Central Oklahoma (UCO) have contributed to this book and deserve recognition. First, I would like to thank Provost John F. Barthell, Dean of the College of Liberal Arts Catherine S. Webster, and Chair of the Department of History and Geography Katrina Lacher. They have been very supportive of the project over the past years. The UCO faculty merit-credit program sponsored by the Office of Academic Affairs, as well as travel funds from the College of Liberal Arts, provided funding for my research and trips to conferences. The UCO Research, Creative, and Scholarly Activities (RCSA) grants sponsored by the Office of High-impact Practice, led by Director Michael Springer, made student research assistants available for the project during the past four years.

I wish to thank my Chinese colleagues and collaborators at the PLA Academy of Military Science (PLA-AMS), China Academy of Social Sciences (CASS), Military Archives of the PLA, National Defense University (NDU), Peking University, East China Normal University, China Society for Strategy and Management (CSSM), China Foundation for International and Strategic Studies, Logistics College of the PLA, Nanjing Political Academy of the PLA, and provisional academies of social sciences and history museums in Heilongjiang, Jilin, and Liaoning. They made the many arrangements necessary for interviewing PLA officers and retired generals in 2010–17. I am grateful to Major General Chen Zhiya, Senior Colonel Ke Chunqiao, Li Danhui, Liu Zhiqing, Niu Jun, Shen Zhihua, Major General Wang Baocun, Senior Colonel Wang Zhongchun, Major General Xu Changyou, Yang Dongyu, Yang Kuisong, Colonel Yang Shaojun, Zhang Baijia, and Zhang Pengfei for their help and advice on my research in China. This volume is also supported by the Fundamental Research Funds for the

Central Universities (Project #19JNYH03), under Shao Xiao at Ji'nan University in Guangzhou, Guangdong.

Thanks also to the staff of the China Reunification Alliance and the Veteran Administration of the Republic of China (ROC), Taipei, Taiwan. They provided financial assistance and arranged many interviews with the Chinese prisoners of war during my several trips to Taiwan in 2012–14 and 2017. Colonel Ming-Hsien Chuang (ROC National Defense University) also offered research assistance in Taiwan.

Special thanks to Hampton Sides, who read the manuscript. Chen Jian, Bruce A. Elleman, Steven I. Levine, Allan R. Millett, David Shambaugh, Harold M. Tanner, David Ulbrich, Peter Worthing, Yafeng Xia, Shuguang Zhang, and Xiaoming Zhang made important comments on earlier versions of some chapters. Stanley J. Adamiak critically reviewed and edited the manuscript. Brad Watkins prepared all the maps. Heidi Vaughn and her Laboratory of History Museum at UCO reproduced all the images. UCO graduate students Ann Riley-Adams and Travis Chambers proofread all the chapters. Other graduate and undergraduate students traveled with me to meet the veterans, transcribe the interviews, and provide technical support. They are Maj. Phred Evans (USA, ret.), TSGT Charles D. Heaverin (USAF, ret.), Captain Alex Zheng Xing (PLA, ret.), Michael Molina, SrA Oliver Pettry (USAF), Blake Taylor, and 1st Lieutenant Jimmy Xiangyao Xu (PLA, ret.).

I also wish to thank the four anonymous readers for the University of Oklahoma Press, who offered many valuable suggestions and criticism on both the proposal and the manuscript. Adam C. Kane and the staff at the University of Oklahoma Press patiently guided the production of the book. Any remaining errors of facts, language usage, and interpretation are my own.

During the research and writing period over the past twenty years, my parents encouraged my interest in the Korean War and helped me with the contacts, interviews, and translation in China. I dedicate this book to them. My wife, Tran, and our two children, Kevin and Christina, got used to my working weekends and holidays and shared with me the burden of overseas traveling. Their understanding and love made this book possible.

Introduction

Chinese Military Strategy and Operations

On a hot summer day in 2015, two old soldiers sat in a restaurant and reminisced about their foreign war experience. Ironically, more than sixty-five years before, both men faced each other as enemies in the Korean War. Harold Mulhausen, a U.S. Marine veteran, met Wu Donglai, a Chinese army veteran, in Oklahoma City.[1] In the summer of 1950, the United States sent troops into South Korea as part of a United Nations Command (UNC) to check the North Korean invasion of South Korea. After repelling the invasion, the UN Force (UNF) crossed the 38th parallel on October 1 and approached the Yalu River, the Chinese–North Korean border. Leaders of the People's Republic of China (PRC) saw the UNF as a threat to the newly founded Chinese Communist regime. Beginning on October 19, the Chinese government sent more than 3 million troops of the People's Liberation Army (PLA) to North Korea to drive the UNF out of the Korean Peninsula in what Mao Zedong (Mao Tse-tung), president of the PRC and chairman of the Chinese Communist Party (CCP), labeled as the "War to Resist the United States and Aid Korea" (WRUSAK, or *Kangmei yuanchao zhanzheng* in Chinese).

Wu was a mortarman in the 172nd Regiment, 58th Division, 20th Army, 9th Army Group of the Chinese People's Volunteer Force (CPVF). "We were actually the regular Chinese troops assigned to the Korean War. We still wore the same PLA's uniforms, but no Chinese badges and no Red Star cap insignias in Korea." Wu put down his chopsticks and told Harold, "We didn't know we were going to Korea until we arrived at the Yalu River!" Harold, a corporal in the 7th Regiment of the 1st Marine Division, understood Wu's feeling and said that, even though he was excited about being a marine, he didn't want to go to war. He thought that the war probably wouldn't last very long anyway. Neither expected a prolonged three-year conflict. While the two veterans reconciled with each other at the dinner table, I couldn't help but think about Chosin, where they might have met on the battleground in Korea. When the waitress brought the crispy fish as the last entrée, I asked both veterans: "What about Chosin?"

Chosin (*Changjin* in Chinese), a mountainous area in the northeastern part of the peninsula, includes two large lakes and a reservoir. On November 27, 1950, the CPVF 9th Army Group launched a large-scale offensive campaign aimed at destroying the 1st Marine Division and U.S. Army 7th Infantry Division at the Chosin Reservoir. "It was very cold," Harold muttered while looking at the whole fish from head to tail in the sweet-and-sour sauce. "It was so cold that a hot meal would be frozen before you could even find a place to sit down." Wu looked at the fish eyes (the fish always faces the guest at a Chinese dinner), answering that "many people died at Chosin. Of course, many died of frostbite because of the cold weather." There was a long silence before the fortune cookies were served. I wondered what they had recalled about the bloody battle, and why Wu hesitated to talk about his experience at Chosin.

Although the UNF defense has been extensively documented in the West, much less is known about the Chinese perspective in their attack against the UNF in November–December 1950. What was the Chinese campaign strategy? How did their operational tactics affect the battle? Had the UNC underestimated the combat effectiveness of the Chinese army? History students, Asian studies teachers, and concerned readers in the West also have some broader questions about the impact of China's intervention in Korea: Does the study of the Chosin campaign provide a better understanding of the Chinese strategic culture?

This book examines the Chinese attack at Chosin, as part of the Second CPVF Offensive Campaign in November–December 1950. Based on Chinese sources, the study attempts to answer these pivotal questions by looking into the relatively neglected PLA battle stories. The untold stories of the rank and file provide unique insights into the internal weaknesses and behavior of those who fought against the UN/U.S. armed forces in Korea. The exploration of their strategic thinking, combat and operational behavior, and political values reveals the military culture of the Chinese army, which has defined the PLA's characteristics both during and after the war. As a relatively young army in Asia, the PLA acted according to its traditional system and its consistent logic in military affairs. The views depicted here offer a better understanding of Chinese military organization, doctrine, and leadership. This book also identifies some general patterns demonstrated by Chinese commanders, who faced the most powerful militaries in the world for three bloody years.

Western Perspectives

After Chinese forces entered North Korea on October 19, 1950, the CPVF command organized five major offensive campaigns against the UNF. From November 25 to December 24, the CPVF launched its second campaign against General Douglas MacArthur's "home-by-Christmas" offensive toward the north. While 240,000 Chinese troops attacked the U.S. 8th Army on the west, the CPVF 9th Army Group, totaling 150,000 men, attacked the U.S. X Corps, including the 1st Marine and 7th Army Divisions, at the Chosin Reservoir in the east on November 27. Peng Dehuai (P'eng Te-huai), commander in chief of the CPVF, believed that "this crucial campaign will determine the war situation in Korea."[2]

At the Chosin area, the Chinese attacked from the surrounding hills and often established roadblocks to cut off the retreating American troops. The 1st Marine Division put up a strong defense. This fierce fighting, combined with the bitter cold, made Chosin one of the worst battles of the Korean War for both sides. On November 29, MacArthur, commander in chief of the UNF, warned the Joint Chiefs of Staff at Washington, "We face an entirely new war," while he planned a general withdrawal of the UNF troops facing an all-out Chinese attack in North Korea.[3] The marines retreated southward, fighting through Chinese roadblocks. Those engaged in this retreat, including Mulhausen—"The Chosin Few," as they now call themselves with pride—endured unbelievable hardships. Maj. Gen. Oliver P. Smith, commander of the 1st Marine Division, gave his well-known explanation of the retreat, in response to a reporter's question: "Retreat, hell—we're attacking in another direction." Making headlines in the United States, Smith has been forever associated with the marines at the Chosin Reservoir.[4] General Matthew B. Ridgway, then commander of the U.S. 8th Army and later the commander of the UNF after MacArthur's dismissal, complained in his memoir about the misleading reports on the UNF retreat: "actually they had performed a magnificent withdrawal in the face of unremitting attacks by overwhelmingly superior forces—and thanks to some extremely gallant fighting, particularly by the 1st Marine Division and the U.S. 2nd Division, had kept their losses to a minimum."[5]

Meanwhile, the CPVF suffered heavy casualties, 80,000 men in less than three weeks. Mao Anying, one of Mao Zedong's sons, was killed on November 25 in a U.S. air raid against CPVF headquarters.[6] The Chinese attacks at Chosin failed to achieve their campaign objective of destroying the 1st Marine and 7th Army Divisions. During their attacks, the CPVF 9th Army Group lost 40,000 men and was forced to abolish three infantry divisions because of their heavy losses, a subject Wu Donglai tried not to talk about during the interview. Some of the Chinese commanders were punished after the Battle of Chosin. On December 17, the badly depleted army group was recalled to China. One of MacArthur's objectives was to stop the Chinese in the North. He might have missed an opportunity to lure the CPVF into the South and destroy its main strength by further exploiting its problems with transportation, communication, supply, and air protection. Nevertheless, the battle had changed the American attitude toward the Chinese army from dismissing and ignoring it to taking the Chinese intervention in the Korean War seriously, since "the UN command in the last week of 1950 found itself in full retreat before this 'bunch of Chinese laundrymen.'"[7]

Most Western histories cover Chosin as a "celebrated battle" with an emphasis on the UNF's operations and successful retreat.[8] Their perspective on Chinese failure is based on the analysis of the UNF's superior firepower, tactical air support, airlift, and combat effectiveness as the reasons for the Chinese casualties, not the inability of the CPVF itself. Among some insightful assessments are those of Stephen Taaffe, Stanley Weintraub, David Halberstam, Edwin H. Simmons, Patrick C. Roe, Roy E. Appleman, Billy Mossman, Russell A. Gugeler, Martin Russ, and Max Hastings.[9] Their works rarely conflict in the major interpretations, in part because many proponents of this method of historical research base their works on Western documents and memoirs. There is an absence, however, of a perspective from the "other side of the hill." There is no solid operational history of the Chinese army from other than a "faceless enemy conducting human wave attacks" standpoint in the Korean War, and no literature on the CPVF's Second Phased Offensive.

The Battle of Chosin had tested the limits of Chinese military power and exposed the huge gap between the PLA and U.S. armed forces. Due to a lack of readily available Chinese sources for Western researchers, English-language accounts evince a significant shortcoming in their limited explanation of Chinese operational problems. Moreover, the lessons learned from the Second Offensive Campaign substantially transformed the perceptions of Chinese military leaders with respect to strategic and operational goals throughout the war. Western historians have been largely unable to provide a thorough analysis of the Chinese assessment of Chosin and thus have drawn only the broadest of conclusions concerning an evolution of Chinese operations because of the paucity of Chinese documents and archives available. Certainly, the Chinese government is still far away from "free academic inquiry."

Among the recent scholarly works, which have included newly available Communist sources, are those by Chen Jian, Allan R. Millett, Russell Spurr, and Shu Guang Zhang. They offer objective surveys and some fresh interpretations by analyzing the CPVF problems both in China and on the Korean front. As "the single most authoritative work,"[10] Millett's work identifies Chinese planning flaws since Mao micromanaged the campaign by "war on the map" in Beijing and "proved unable to accept military realities" on the battleground.[11] It became even worse when there was no one to question Mao's miscalculations, either in the high command or on the front. Millett also questions the overconfidence of Peng Dehuai and generalship of Song Shilun (Sung Shih-lun), commander of the 9th Army Group, while pointing out that the CPVF's "principal sources of trouble had been the cold, the lack of appropriate clothing and food, limited medical care, and the lack of active air defenses, either anti-aircraft artillery or interceptor aircraft."[12]

Russell Spurr, a British reporter and war historian, presents the negative impacts these serious problems had brought to the CPVF troops. Through individual interviews of ordinary soldiers, Spurr explains how the Chinese tried to deal with the problems to survive. His oral history collection in the early 1980s, however, did not intend to reconstruct a Chinese campaign history; as he states, "even then it was not always easy to establish verifiable facts, owing to a lack of documents and the participants' difficulty in recalling details from half a lifetime ago."[13] Chen Jian and Shu Guang Zhang use Chinese sources to provide a new treatment of Beijing's war strategy, carefully constructing a framework to present effectively the Chinese leaders' concerns that American historians might have overlooked. They put individual leaders and commanders within the context of Chinese tradition and view their war-fighting ideas through their historical experience, domestic politics, and military culture. However, the scale and focus of these works do not allow either author to provide a day-to-day operational account of the Chinese attack at Chosin.[14]

Chinese Perspective: Doctrine, Strategy, and Tactics

When the Second Offensive Campaign was over by mid-December 1950, both the CPVF and the 9th Army Group claimed victory at Chosin. Beijing was also pleased with the campaign's outcome. Mao Zedong cabled Peng Dehuai on December 17 that "this campaign operated by the 9th Army Group under extremely difficult conditions on the eastern front has accomplished a great strategic task."[15] The

1st Marine Division's retreat has become a part of USMC lore, but it was still a retreat, not a victory. Marshal Peng states later in his writing that "the Second Campaign was a big victory."[16] General Hong Xuezhi, CPVF deputy commander, points out in his memoir that, after "the First Campaign stabilized the front line, the Second Campaign turned the war situation around in Korea. We fought so well and the campaign was very successful."[17] Strategic analyst Bin Yu points out that the Second Offensive Campaign "represented the peak of CPVF performance in the Korean War."[18] Within less than three weeks, the CPVF pushed the battle line back to the 38th parallel, recaptured Pyongyang, capital city of North Korea, and inflicted 36,000 UNF casualties, including 24,000 Americans, according to the Chinese field reports.[19] Peng explains how the CPVF won the battle by emphasizing that "the Chinese Volunteers fought bravely and pushed forward so that the enemy was forced into complete disarray. Unexpected and unprepared for our attack, the enemy troops had never experienced this kind of battle before." He concluded, "Surprise is the combat tactic that guaranteed our victory in the Second Campaign. There was no better way to win it."[20]

First, the Chinese strategic culture demonstrates a characteristic emphasis on secrecy, deception, and organization of unorthodox troops, an emphasis that permeates the Chinese combat experience. The Chinese generals successfully used their familiar tactics from previous wars: surprise attacks, close combat, and night operations for a very short period from late October to early December. The CPVF operations and tactics reflected the Chinese view of war. Some of their methods were holistic, effective, flexible, and as successful as those of the West. The PLA grew from guerrillas in the Red Army in World War II, between 1937 and 1945; they could still appear suddenly, attack, and then steal away to safety. While it was possible for the Chinese to have armies of 150,000 troops appear at Chosin unexpectedly, it was the Chinese army's ability to preserve their forces that may have been its greatest advantage. The irregular warfare fought by the CPVF in Korea has become synonymous with a Chinese approach to war.

These very traditional strategies from the military classics helped in maneuvering the 9th Army Group's divisions to a point where they could obtain the best advantage in the offensive campaigns.[21] During the battle, the CPVF lacked the air force, the tanks, and the heavy artillery necessary for a successful campaign against more powerful and mechanized U.S. troops. Zhang comments, "The Chinese leaders were convinced that they had achieved the first victory not by sheer good luck but by superior strategy and tactics. After the initial battles, the belief that 'we can defeat American armed forces' became increasingly prevalent among the commanders."[22] Rather than relying on technology to win, Chinese forces sought victory through a military advantage achieved by deception and application, and Chinese commanders and soldiers believed that their "fighting spirit" would lead them to victory. Thus, U.S. superiority in Korea was in the categories of technology, firepower, and mobility, while the Chinese army relied on human factors.

Another important characteristic of the PLA is its emphasis on the human component in war. Mao firmly believed that a weak army could win in a war against a strong enemy because he was convinced that a man could beat a weapon. "Weapons are an important factor in war, but not the decisive factor," Mao wrote. He explicitly made the distinction that "it is people, not things, that are decisive."[23] Mao's confidence in a human being's "subjective capability" to determine defeat or victory in war made sense to the PLA officers and soldiers. Shaped by a military culture and communist ideology, the Chinese belief in human superiority over technology suggests their contradictory attitude toward war and combat. The idea that a soldier or a warrior, because of his godliness and virtue, can vanquish stronger opponents has a long tradition. Based on Mao's perception of "man vs. weapon," the Chinese officers and soldiers developed a fighting system around a weak army's strategy and tactics workable for the defense of North Korea.

Third, active defense became conceptualized as a new strategy for China's national security in the 1950s. After the founding of the PRC in 1949, the PLA transformed itself from a "liberation army" into a two-pronged national force with two new goals: to repel foreign invasions in the global Cold War, and to repress internal threats to the new regime. In 1950, Korea was the major Chinese security concern. Mao believed the U.S. war plan aimed to destroy the one-year-old People's Republic in its cradle by attacking it from Korea, Taiwan, and Vietnam. He made it clear at the CCP Politburo meeting on August 4 that "[we] will take back Taiwan, but now can't just sit by and watch Vietnam and Korea."[24]

A successful defense against international imperialist attacks could be achieved by stopping foreign invading forces outside of China. Mao telegraphed his new strategy to Zhou Enlai (Chou En-lai) on October 14, 1950, when the Chinese premier was visiting Moscow. Mao asked him to explain this to Stalin: "We do it in such way to advance the national defense line from the Yalu River to the line of the Tokchon-Nyongwon and areas south of it. This is absolutely possible and beneficial [to us]."[25] Mao considered the UNF/U.S. northward advance in North

Korea as an immediate threat to China's national security and viewed Chinese intervention as necessary to stop a perceived U.S. invasion of China.

According to Mao, the new Chinese defense line was more than 100 miles south of the Yalu in North Korea. The new strategy changed China's approach to warfare from fighting an enemy at the Chinese border to defeating a potential invader in its neighboring country. Mao's active defense made sense to the Chinese generals who remembered Japan's invasion of China and eight bloody years of the resistance war against the Japanese army in the country at the cost of 3 million Chinese military dead and 10 to 12 million more civilians. Mao's strategy led to China's intervention in the Korean War in 1950 and in the Vietnam War in 1965.

Mao claimed that his military strategies drew on ancient military classics. Scholars in the West have studied 2,500 years of Chinese warfare and military thinking, including Sunzi (Sun-tzu)'s classic *The Art of War* and Maoist doctrine.[26] John Fairbank identified a few points of Chinese war-fighting, including a Confucian ruling ideology of neither using military force nor glorifying military actions, a tradition of defensive land warfare, and using geography to either wear down or pacify enemies as an alternative to annihilating or attacking the enemy.[27] Some historians have described it as the Chinese "way of war" (WOW) when they contrast the Chinese military doctrine with that of the West.[28] Comparing Chinese and Western approaches to war is a popular topic of discussion between military experts and the general public.[29] Some historians draw a line between the Western WOW and Chinese WOW. Victor Davis Hanson and Geoffrey Parker argue about distinctions in the Western WOW—particularly in the areas of superior military technology, discipline and training, continuity and flexibility, the goal of total defeat and annihilation of the enemy, and organization for war.[30]

The findings in this book suggest that in comparison to the Western experience in the Korean War, the Chinese experience offers a mixed picture. Countless parallels can be drawn between the PLA and Western armies in the war. In the ongoing debate, some scholars have questioned the perspective of the Chinese WOW as more Chinese military writings have become available. Among the dissenters are Peter Lorge, Kenneth M. Swope, Harold M. Tanner, William Thompson, and Hans van de Ven, who state that, while a comprehensive and holistic set of Chinese principles exists to deal with war, they do not describe a separate, distinct, and mutually exclusive WOW.[31] These scholars contend that the Chinese invented or adopted many of the supposed Western ways of warfare. David Graff and Robin Higham point out that Chinese military history has been overly typified by the use of the Confucian tradition. This sort of contrast is the result of the WOW historians' failure to see similarities between Western armies and their Chinese counterparts.[32]

Chinese war strategy and tactics have evolved over time. One PLA general considered Mao's active defense as a theoretical innovation of Sunzi's idea "to win a defensive war without fighting the enemy in our country."[33] Although Mao's military strategies drew heavily on ancient classics, he had adapted to the post-WWII international environment. Having been actively involved in military actions through the late 1940s and 1950s, Mao developed the new strategy for China's defense in the global Cold War, when traditional military theories failed to meet the demands of modern warfare. Active defense, or stopping the invader outside the gate, sounded reasonable and achievable for the PLA generals in Korea, who consistently recognized the original form or traditional style of Chinese warfare.[34]

Shaped by a military culture and communist ideology, nevertheless, Mao's new strategy suggests a contradictory policy toward war since proactive defense is certainly offensive and aggressive in nature. It goes beyond an apparent homeland defense, a tendency to avoid war by caution and delay, or winning without fighting. China's intervention in Korea seemed a successful application of the new strategy by stopping the UNF in South Korea, preventing a North Korean collapse, and securing China's northeastern border. The Chinese generals recalled their fighting in Korea as a heroic defense and a continuity of their own struggle against world imperialism. Chinese history books portray China as a "beneficent victor" of the Korean War. Peter Gries observes, "To many Chinese, Korea marks the end of the 'Century of Humiliation' and the birth of 'New China.'"[35]

Chosin Revisited: What Has China Learned?

This work focuses on the "lessons learned" aspect of the evaluations of the Chinese campaigns at Chosin. It finds that reasons for the CPVF's heavy casualties lay not in the abilities of the UNF but in the challenges and problems the Chinese commands faced on the Korean front. I aim to answer the following questions: Did the Chinese make mistakes or simply encounter unforeseen problems? Did miscalculations lead to the military disaster at Chosin? Why did a large force, holding the initiative and outnumbering the UNF, suffer such huge casualties? What kind of lessons, if any, has the Chinese army learned from the Battle of Chosin?

At the conclusion of the Second Offensive Campaign, the CPVF Command had learned that its campaign strategy and combat tactics were out-of-date and inflexible, often resulting in heavy casualties.[36] Its strategy of mobile warfare—using numerical superiority (usually outnumbering the enemy two or three times), engaging the enemy in mobile operations to encircle one or two UN/U.S. divisions, and trying to destroy an entire U.S. division—employed in Korea from November 1950 to May 1951, had been tried with success in the Chinese Civil War in 1946–49. Unfortunately for the Chinese Communist forces, Korea was not China, and the UN and U.S. forces were much different from the Chinese GMD or Japanese troops they had fought before. Mao's strategic drawbacks far outweighed their advantages. The 9th Army Group, his main force for a planned attack on Taiwan, never got a full recovery after losing more than 40,000 men in the Battle of Chosin. Thereafter, the invasion of Taiwan never materialized. While in Korea in August 1952, Song Shilun was surprised to receive an order of his new appointment as the superintendent of the PLA Advanced Infantry Academy in Nanjing. He had to leave the post he had held for twenty-three years as battlefield commander of the 9th Army Group.

In the meantime, after the spring of 1951, the Chinese war-fighting strategy began to evolve, and positional warfare rose to the point of replacing some of the previous mobile warfare. The CPVF adopted more cautious and realistic strategies, including maintaining a relatively stable front line; increasing CPVF air force, artillery, and tank units; and beefing up logistical support. The Korean War began China's military modernization and professionalism in terms of command, organization, technology, and training. By the end of the war, the CPVF emphasized the role of technology and firepower. Having learned differing ways of war, the PLA respected its technologically superior opponents. In order to narrow the technology gap, China purchased enough weapons and equipment from the Soviet Union to arm sixty infantry divisions in 1951–53.[37] Thereafter, Chinese weaponry became standardized. The Soviets also transferred technology for production of rifles, machine guns, and artillery pieces. The CPVF improved its logistics and transportation by establishing its own logistics department in Korea in the spring of 1951. The new system improved CPVF logistical capacity at the regiment and battalion levels and increased frontline troops' combat effectiveness.

In retrospect, China had learned a hard lesson and paid a huge price at Chosin. Nevertheless, Chinese military historians remained unmoved for fifty years on their stand on the Battle of Chosin. A 1990 official PLA history of the Korean War continued the government position that "the Second Offensive Campaign was the most successful and excellently executed operation the CPVF had fought in the Korean War."[38] In the 2000s, however, a different opinion began to challenge the official conclusion regarding the battle by asking whether the 9th Army Group actually won the battle.[39] Major critiques of the official position include that the army group command failed to employ the reserve troops in a timely manner and did not pay enough attention to logistics, and that the 26th Army delayed its southward movement and lost an opportunity to engage the 1st Marine Division. In addition, Chinese division and regiment commands did not provide efficient combat training, transportation vehicles, and air protection for their troops.[40]

In the 2000s, historians and scholars in China reopened the objective research and academic debate over this decisive battle, departing from the official position. Untold stories emerged with evidence of misinformation, miscalculation, broken communication, and unpreparedness. The new inquiries may have resulted from recent changes in international relations, such as the rapid collapse of the Soviet Empire in the 1990s, and China's twenty-first-century ascendance. Whether a rising China and the United States will go to war again is a perennial question in strategic analysis and foreign-policy circles. Chinese military historians and strategists now want to learn more from Chosin instead of merely continuing to glorify it politically. Yu states, "The Korean War is the only meaningful reference point for sustained PLA contingency operations beyond China's border. The Korean War is also the only real experience, no matter how outdated, that the PLA has had in operating against the U.S. ground forces."[41] The Korean War has become one of the most discussed subjects in China.[42]

China's renewed interest in the lessons of the Korean War has also resulted in many sources becoming available, both government documents and private recollections, which has spurred many recent publications. For political reasons, however, Chinese historians still have a long way to go before they can publish an objective account of the history of the Second Offensive Campaign in their home country. The present study is supported by primary Chinese sources only made available in recent years, including party documents, government archives, and military materials.[43] It is vital to note, however, that during most of the PLA's history, strategic and even tactical decisions were micromanaged by the Political Bureau (Politburo) of the CCP Central Committee. The primary sources used in this book include selected and reprinted party documents of the Central Committee, Central Military Commission (CMC), and CCP regional bureaus, and the writings, papers, and memoirs of Chinese Communist leaders.[44] While Mao was the undisputed leader in both theory and strategy throughout most of the PLA's history, China's military leaders worked together and made the majority of important decisions within the CMC. Their papers are fundamental for study of the PLA.[45] In addition, some PRC government documents have been released in recent years.[46]

The book's main focus is the Chinese operational experience. It examines the CPVF's battle plans and preparations, campaign organization and execution, tactical decisions, combat problem solving, technology application, political indoctrination, and performance evaluation in 1950–51. It provides some insights into Chinese operations by illustrating the CPVF's chain of command at different levels, including the CPVF General HQ, 9th Army Group and three army commands, and twelve division and thirty-six regiment commands. The interviews, memoirs, and writings by retired generals and field commanders describe their command skills, combat effectiveness, and problem solving.[47] Their experiences and tremendous difficulties highlight new and penetrating insights into the Chinese attacks at Chosin. No matter how politically indoctrinated they might have become, the generals are culturally bound to cherish the memory of the past. More importantly, they have only recently felt comfortable talking about their experiences and allowing their recollections to be recorded, written, and even published. The 2010s brought a considerable number of military and war memoirs to Chinese readers through books, journal articles, and printed reference studies for restricted circulation only.[48]

This book also examines the everyday life of the men who fought the battle and encountered the UNF troops. I conducted more than two hundred interviews, collecting direct testimony from Chinese soldiers themselves. Many discussed their combat experience in great detail, thus making a remarkable contribution to this study by adding a soldier's perspective. Recollections and interviews of CPVF soldiers and junior officers indicate the various issues they faced—from massive air raids to endless bombardment, from ammunition shortages to hunger. Breakdowns in discipline ranged from frequent refusals to follow orders to shooting officers from behind.[49] Soldiers' accounts reveal the challenges the Chinese army faced and illustrate key differences between the Chinese army and U.S. armed forces. I also had opportunities to interview several former CPVF prisoners of war who had not returned to China, but instead went to Taiwan after the Korean Armistice Agreement was signed in July 1953. They are very critical of the Chinese operations in Korea and believe they made the right decision in coming to Taiwan rather than being repatriated to the mainland. These sources add a valuable view of the Chinese perspective, which reinterprets a series of fundamental issues crucial to an understanding of the Chinese military.

This book covers the chronological development of the Chinese 1950 Second Offensive Campaign. Chapter 1 clarifies the high command's debates and decisions in the fall of 1950 concerning intervention in Korea. It discusses the 9th Army Group's mobilization, war preparation, and battle formation through an examination of Chinese strategic culture. Chapter 2 examines the operational culture by studying the campaign planning, debates over the Second Offensive in November 1950, and the political culture of the chain of command. The chapter also identifies some advantages and disadvantages facing Chinese troops in Korea. Chapter 3 reconstructs the first part of the Chinese offensive on the eastern front from November 27 to 29. The 9th Army Group launched a major attack committing six divisions, totaling 70,000 men, against the 1st Marine and 7th Army Divisions. Chapter 4 explores the second phase of the Chinese offensive at Chosin on November 30–December 2, when the 9th Army Group concentrated its troops to attack the 7th Division. Chapter 5 explains why the CPVF failed to stop the 1st Marine Division's withdrawal from the Chosin Reservoir through the Hungnam (Heungnam) Port to South Korea from December 2 to 23. Chapter 6 analyzes the recovery and reengagement of the 9th Army Group in the war after the Battle of Chosin from December 1950 to October 1952. The conclusion indicates that the lessons learned in 1950 had a strong impact on the evolution of China's strategic culture and on subsequent development of the country's power status in Northeast Asia.

Despite having only been founded in October 1949, the People's Republic of China proved its great power status in Asia as a new Communist state. Not only was China capable of fighting the world's most powerful country to a draw, the conflict also proved that Chinese society was secure enough to withstand a terrible war. Those factors brought first the Soviet Union and then, following the Sino-Soviet split, the United States to seek Beijing's favor. Even now, the world's most powerful nations measure their standing in Asia by their relations with China. While today most of the world dimly remembers the Korean War as a relatively minor conflict, it was a formative moment in Chinese history. It gave Beijing immense political and military power. Mao used the war to declare an independent and powerful nation and to cement Communist control over its state and society in the following decades. The Chinese strategic culture that evolved from the Korean War took an active role in Asia, leading to the Taiwan Strait crises in 1954–55 and 1958, a border clash with India in 1962, participation in the Vietnam War from 1965 to 1970, border conflict with the Soviet Union in 1969–73, and the invasion of Vietnam in 1979.[50] The Chinese army became a modern force with a strategy of active (or aggressive) defense through the Cold War.

Today, China still faces a technologically superior force, the United States, in the Asia-Pacific region. Its weak army's strategy—proactive defense and asymmetric operations—can still play a significant role in addressing the disparity with respect to the PLA's inferiority in technology. Hu Jintao, PRC president in 2002–12, explained to PLA chiefs the *National Defense Project 998* (NDP 998), which emphasizes asymmetric strategies in dealing with a "new threat" from the United States: for at least the next ten years, China will "not be intimidated by a military superpower," and China's foreign policies will "not be constrained by its military weakness."[51] Xi Jinping emphasized in his speech at the Sixtieth Anniversary Celebration of the CPVF's Participation in the War to Resist the United States and Aid Korea in 2010 that the tremendous impact and historical significance of the war "will never fade away with time."[52] The war contributed to the transformation of the Chinese military from a peasant rebellion force to a modern army with new technology, strategy, and tactics. In 2012, Xi became president of the PRC and the new commander in chief in 2012. Even if the war has been largely forgotten in America, it is by no means forgotten in China.

1

From Taiwan to Chosin

On June 25, 1950, the North Korean Army, or the North Korean People's Army (NKPA), launched a surprise attack on South Korea, starting the Korean War. In China, Song Shilun, commander of the PLA 9th Army Group, was surprised when he heard a different account from China Central Radio the next day: that South Korea (the Republic of Korea, or ROK) had attacked North Korea (the Democratic People's Republic of Korea, or DPRK). Two days later, Song was relieved when the 3rd Field Army headquarters passed down the CMC briefing that North Korea "had launched successful counterattacks and moved the front line into South Korea." Beijing soon openly supported North Korea's "counterattacks" and then its "national liberation."[1]

While winning the Chinese Civil War in 1949, the PLA had enthusiastically supported the Communist militaries in neighboring countries such as Vietnam, Laos, Myanmar (Burma), and North Korea. In May 1949, for example, the PLA high command accepted North Korea's requests and allowed Chinese soldiers of Korean origin to return to North Korea.[2] By April 1950, three PLA infantry divisions of ethnic Korean troops had been transferred to North Korea with weapons and equipment, including the 163rd (10,821 men), 164th (10,320 men), and 165th (14,000 men) Divisions.[3] In April, the CMC ordered its armies to select experienced and educated officers with at least nine years of education, or a middle school certificate, in order to qualify for the Chinese Military Advisory Group (CMAG) sent to Vietnam.[4] In May, hundreds of officers reported to CMAG, including commanders and officers at division level or higher.[5] On June 27, two days after the Korean War broke out, Mao, CCP chairman, and Zhu De (Zhu Teh), PLA commander in chief, met high-ranking CMAG officers at Zhongnanhai.[6] Mao told them, "It is President Ho Chi Minh who has asked me for [your assistance]. The chairman added, "Who would have thought our revolution would succeed first? We should help them. This is called internationalism."[7]

What really shocked Song Shilun and the Chinese officers was not the outbreak of war between North and South Korea, but the U.S. shift from a "hands-off" policy to a "hands-on" commitment regarding the security of Taiwan (or Formosa; the Republic of China).[8] On June 27, President Harry S. Truman announced that the U.S. Seventh Fleet would be deployed in the Taiwan Strait to prevent a Chinese Communist attack on Taiwan. Under the presidential directive, for the first time the United States committed its armed forces to the defense and security of the ROC government, signaling a shift in American strategy on Taiwan from noninvolvement to military commitment.

At that moment, Song and his 9th Army Group were ready to launch a large-scale landing campaign against the Chinese Nationalist (Guomindang/GMD; or Kuomintang/KMT) troops on Taiwan. The Seventh Fleet's presence in the Taiwan Strait marked a turning point in the cross-strait situation. On June 30, 1950, Song was told to halt all of his offensive operations against the GMD-held islands off the mainland's southeastern coast. On August 8, Beijing postponed the Taiwan campaign, at least until 1952. On September 20, the 9th Army Group was ordered to terminate its amphibious preparations and move to the north. Mao summoned Song to Beijing on October 23 and discussed his new assignment in the Korean War. In November, the 9th Army Group, totaling 150,000 men, crossed the Yalu River and attacked the U.S. forces at Chosin. General Song later confessed, "Our armies were not ready yet when we attacked the Americans in Korea."[9]

This chapter examines Chinese leaders' debates and decision in July–September 1950 concerning a strategic shift from invading Taiwan to intervening in Korea. It explains why the 9th Army Group had to rush from Fujian (Fukien) and Zhejiang (Chekiang) Provinces to Korea without basic preparation, necessary training, and with only minimum logistics. It will identify some major problems of the 9th in transportation, communication, intelligence, weaponry, and winter clothing. The 150,000 troops, dressed in light canvas shoes and quilted cotton uniforms, had been prepared to invade Taiwan about 200 miles south—not Korea, more than 1,500 miles to the north. They were not ready to face the bitter cold Korean winter after they crossed the Yalu. The 9th Army Group lost nearly 30,000 men to frostbite in the Battle of Chosin from November 27 to December 14. Mao had

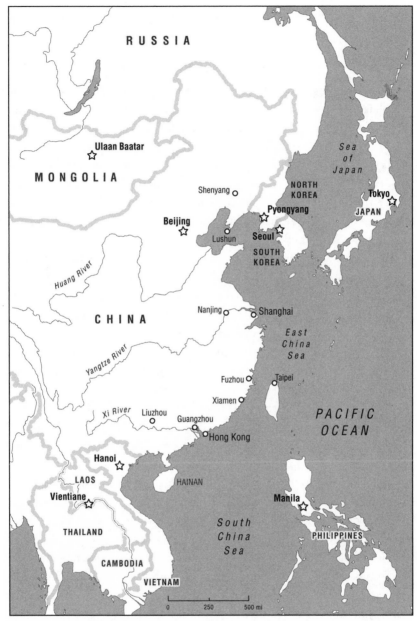

East Asia.

Map by Erin Greb Cartography.

to recall the badly depleted army group to China on December 17, and the 9th was thus no longer an able force for the invasion of Taiwan.[10]

Plan Change: No Landing on Taiwan

After the founding of the PRC on October 1, 1949, Mao's first priority was to consolidate the new state by eliminating all remnants of Jiang Jieshi's Nationalist forces of 1 million fighters on Taiwan and other offshore islands.[11] Therefore, from October 1949 through June 1950, China's military strategy was focused on its southern and coastal regions. According to Mao's instructions, in late 1949 the PLA's 3rd Field Army (1 million troops in the southeast) and 4th Field Army (1.2 million strong in the south) actively prepared for amphibious operation campaigns against the GMD-occupied islands to draw to an end the Chinese Civil War.[12]

The 3rd Field Army was established in early March 1949, when the CCP's armed forces were officially designated the People's Liberation Army. The field army's commander and political commissar was Chen Yi (Ch'en Yi).[13] The deputy commander of the 3rd Field Army was Su Yu, one of the most experienced commanders of the PLA after Lin Biao (Lin Piao), commander of the 4th Field Army.[14] In 1949, the 3rd Field Army consisted of four subordinate units, the 7th, 8th, 9th, and 10th Army Groups. The 9th was the 3rd Field Army's main strength, with Song Shilun as commander and political commissar.[15]

By September, the PLA occupied most of the country except for Tibet, Taiwan, and various offshore islands. In late 1949, Jiang moved the seat of his government to Taiwan. At Taibei (Taipei), the ROC's new capital, Jiang prepared for the final showdown with Mao in the last battle of the Civil War while concentrating his troops on four major offshore islands: Taiwan, Hainan, Zhoushan (Chou-shan), and Jinmen (Quemoy).[16] Taiwan lies 120 miles away from the mainland, and had a population of some 4 million in 1949. Jiang concentrated 200,000 troops on Taiwan. Hainan Island had a population of 1 million, and Jiang deployed 100,000 men in its defense. Jinmen, with a population of 40,000 at that time, is not in the open ocean, but lies in Xiamen (Amoy) Harbor and is surrounded by the mainland on three sides, less than two miles away from Xiamen. With 60,000 troops, Jinmen was also prepared to defend against attack.[17]

For the PLA, the offshore operations became an important and difficult issue in late 1949, because of the lack of amphibious experience and a naval force. After taking over Xiamen on October 17, the 10th Army Group of the 3rd Field Army ordered its 28th Army to attack Jinmen Island on October 24. As the first wave of 10,000 troops landed, they found themselves tightly encircled by the GMD garrison and suffered heavy casualties at Guningtou, a small fishing village on the island.[18] With no boats, the 10th Army Group, 150,000 strong, could not reinforce the Jinmen landings. The 28th Army lost 9,086 landing troops, including more than 3,000 prisoners, while the GMD lost only about 1,000 defenders.[19] ROC General Jiang Weiguo (Chiang Wei-kuo), son of Jiang Jieshi, recalled that the Battle of Guningtou not only boosted the ROC troops' morale but also convinced his father that the GMD government could survive on these islands by building up a strong defense.[20]

Shocked, Mao drafted a circular with a warning to all PLA commanders, "especially those high-level commanders at army level and above," that they "must learn a good lesson from the Jinmen failure."[21] Mao suggested that all concerned armies take time to train for cross-strait operations in order to have their troops better prepared for future landings. Mao directed his coastal army commanders to "guard against arrogance, avoid underestimating the enemy, and be well prepared."[22] In early November, Mao instructed Su Yu to postpone the attacks on the islands in the East China Sea.[23] In the meantime, Su also warned the high command that it would be "extremely difficult to operate a large-scale cross-ocean amphibious landing operation without air and sea control."[24]

To better prepare an amphibious campaign, in December the high command established the PLA Navy (PLAN) with Xiao Jinguang (Hsiao Kin-kuang) as its commander.[25] Xiao became vice minister of defense in 1954 and was promoted to grand general in 1955. It is important to note that at this time the PLAN was numerically and technologically inferior to the GMD navy.[26] The GMD navy had a total tonnage of 100,000 at that time, while the PLAN had fifty-one small warships, landing crafts, and support vessels, totaling 43,000 tons.[27] Since the PLA did not have a modern navy, it would require Soviet aid.

Mao paid a state visit to the Soviet Union on December 16, 1949, hoping to get the military assistance China desperately needed through an alliance between the PRC and the USSR. Stalin tried to engage the PRC in the Cold War ideologically and geographically. Whether it was the symbolic significance of a shared Communist ideology that bound China to show its duty, or simple nationalistic interest, China needed to make at least some commitment to support the Soviets in the Cold War. Though Mao was unhappy with Stalin's demand, he understood the Soviet leader's intention and agreed to share "the international responsibility." Chen Jian points out that "in an agreement on 'division of labor' between the Chinese and Soviet Communists for waging the world revolution, they decided that while the Soviet Union would remain the center of international proletarian revolution, China's primary duty would be the promotion of the 'Eastern revolution.'"[28] In February 1950, Mao and Zhou Enlai, China's premier and foreign minister, signed the Sino-Soviet Treaty of Friendship, Alliance, and Mutual Assistance with Stalin in Moscow.[29] The alliance between Beijing and Moscow was the cornerstone of the Communist international alliance system in the 1950s.[30] This military alliance marked the beginning of a new stage of the Cold War in Asia. As part of the agreement, Mao and Zhou also signed a major naval pact. The Soviet Union agreed to arm a new Chinese naval force with warships and equipment worth $150 million, half the total aid package granted through the treaty.[31] In the meantime, Beijing also purchased two retired British cruisers (displacing 7,000 tons each), five destroyers, and four mine-sweepers through some business middlemen in Hong Kong.[32]

Returning from Moscow in February 1950, Mao called a meeting of the PLA high command. During the discussions, Mao instructed Nie Rongzhen (Nieh Jung-chen), acting chief of the General Staff, along with Su, to plan attacks on Jinmen and Taiwan, with an emphasis on training airborne forces and preparing an additional four divisions for amphibious maneuvers.[33] On March 11, Su met Xiao to discuss the first detailed plan, in which the 3rd Field Army and the navy would deploy 500,000 troops to attack Taiwan. The army would send its 7th and 9th Army Groups, totaling 300,000 troops, as the first landing wave on Taiwan. Its 10th Army Group plus the other three armies, totaling 200,000 troops, would be the second landing wave.[34] The 13th Army Group of the 4th Field Army remained as a reserve for the attack. The 19th Army Group would deploy its three armies along the coast as a mobile force. Total forces for the invasion of Taiwan would include nearly 800,000 men. In April, the CMC approved the Su-Xiao plan. The 9th Army Group then began landing training along the southeastern coast near Shanghai.[35]

In May, the 9th Army Group defeated 120,000 GMD defenders on the Zhoushan Island group in the East China Sea and occupied the islands. In early June, the army group landed on the GMD-occupied Dongshan and Wanshan Island groups and took over forty-eight small islands. In the summer of 1950, people on both sides of the Taiwan Strait expected an imminent PLA attack on Jinmen and Taiwan.[36]

When the CCP held its Third Plenary Session of the Seventh Congress at Beijing on June 6–9, Mao urged the liberation of Taiwan and Tibet (Xizang) as the party's central tasks. Su reported on PLA preparations for invading Taiwan. The Party Center agreed that its first priority was to liberate Taiwan and Tibet.[37] At the same session, to mobilize the local resources for successful offensives, the CMC reorganized the 3rd Field Army into the East China Military Region (ECMR) with Chen Yi as commander and Rao Shushi as political commissar. The ECMR continued the preparation for the Taiwan campaign. Under the ECMR Command, Su and Song were ready to launch their well-prepared landing on Taiwan. However, the Korean War broke out on June 25, altering their plans.[38]

The Communist Chinese leaders considered the presence of the U.S. Seventh Fleet as both an intervention into the Chinese Civil War and a direct threat to the new state. The central government held an emergency meeting in Beijing at 5:00 P.M. on June 28, the day after Truman's order. Zhou Enlai briefed the top officers and the PLA high command. On the same day, Zhou denounced the move as "armed aggression against the territory of China in total violation of the United Nations Charter." Zhou continued, "no matter what obstructive action U.S. imperialists may take, the fact that Taiwan is part of China will remain unchanged forever" and "all the people of our country will certainly fight as one man and to the end to liberate Taiwan."[39] Later the same day, at a government meeting, Mao echoed this statement and denounced the U.S. action as an "open exposure" of its "imperialist face."[40]

Beijing watched Washington closely as the American military presence and support to Taiwan's defense increased on a daily basis. After June 28, for example, more than a dozen American warships and supply ships from the Seventh Fleet arrived at Jilong (Keelung, or Chi-lung) and Gaoxiong (Kao-hsiung), two major seaport cities of Taiwan. In July, the American warships began their patrol in the Taiwan Strait. Meanwhile, American diplomats and military strengthened their ties with the ROC government. On July 31, MacArthur led a U.S. military delegation, including sixteen generals, to visit Taiwan to strengthen the island's defense and bolster GMD morale.[41] Then, Vice Adm. Arthur D. Struble, commander of the Seventh Fleet, visited Taibei and met Jiang. Later Maj. Gen. Howard M. Turner, commander of the U.S. Thirteenth Air Force, and Rear Adm. Francis P. Old, commander of the USN in the Philippines, discussed the defense of Taiwan with top GMD military officials. On August 4, the first combat group of American fighters and bombers from the Thirteenth Air Force arrived at the Taibei air base.[42] David M. Finkelstein argues that Truman's order to the Seventh

Fleet was intended not only to keep the Communists from invading Taiwan, but also to keep the GMD from attacking the mainland, and thus widening the war beyond Korea. Finkelstein makes it clear that "Taiwan was neutralized for purely military-strategic reasons. Washington could not allow the island to be occupied by enemy forces while U.S. ground troops were committed to a land war in Korea."[43]

Truman's order secured the ROC by preventing a planned PLA landing on Taiwan by the end of June 1950.[44] With Washington's direct involvement in the Taiwan Strait, the PLA now faced a serious challenge.[45] An amphibious campaign against U.S. forces in the Taiwan Strait in the summer of 1950 could have been a military disaster for the PLA. MacArthur said that a Chinese Communist attack on Taiwan that summer would face "such a crushing defeat it would be one of the decisive battles of the world—a disaster so great it would rock Asia, and perhaps turn back Communism."[46] The Seventh Fleet's presence in the Taiwan Strait totally changed the balance of military power in the Chinese Civil War. The Communist leaders faced a serious challenge—America's direct involvement transformed the conflict into an international confrontation.

On June 30, Zhou made it official that the PLA would postpone its operations against Taiwan.[47] Beijing's point of view can be best understood through one of Mao's speeches. Before June 1950, liberating Taiwan was the PLA's primary task against Nationalist forces. After June, Mao stated, "The American armed forces have occupied Taiwan, invaded Korea, and reached the boundary of Northeast China. Now we must fight against the American forces in both Korea and Taiwan."[48] Later the CMC cabled Chen Yi, commander of the ECMR, that there would be no attack on Taiwan until 1952 at the earliest. In November, after the Chinese troops intervened in the Korean War, Mao ordered the ECMR to put off all offshore offensive operations. Before the end of December, the CMC issued another order to all coastal army group commanders that there would be no operations offshore until the Chinese People's Volunteer Force achieved a decisive victory in Korea.[49]

Truman's order drew a line between the CCP and GMD forces in the Taiwan Strait. The policy was to disengage the Chinese from their hot civil war while engaging them in the global Cold War. What had been merely part of the Chinese civil struggle was now linked to geopolitics. The Truman legacy was keeping military conflict "cold" in the Taiwan Strait and creating the foundation and opportunity for political, civil, and international competition in which both Chinese parties could find alternatives to their civil struggle.[50] Truman never intended to bring either Chinese party into the Korean conflict. Since late June, the NKPA had driven the ROK forces into a pocket around the southeasternmost city of Pusan. Here the UNF stopped the NKPA's offensive.

The 9th Goes North

The Communist Chinese leaders, however, had their own understanding of the Taiwan problem. Militarily, they believed that the Korean War had caused the American military intervention in China. Even though Korea was apparently less important politically and emotionally than Taiwan, the war in Korea had brought the Seventh Fleet into the Taiwan Strait. The armed occupation of Taiwan appeared to be part of a U.S. war plan in Asia aimed at destroying the one-year-old People's Republic in its cradle by attacking it from both the north and the south. The Chinese leaders believed that China must counter the expected invasion and defend itself, especially Northeast China, which shares a border with North Korea. Mao made it clear at the Politburo meeting on August 4, 1950, that "[we] will take back Taiwan, but now can't just sit by and watch Vietnam and Korea."[51]

Mao later explained his strategic shift from the south to the north and, in his speech at the Chinese People's Political Consultative Conference, justified fighting against the United States: "Chinese people would not have fought America if the US forces had not occupied our territory of Taiwan, not invaded the DPRK, and not brought the war to our Northeastern border."[52] Historians in China agree that, up to July 1950, none of these war preparations, including the later organization of the CPVF, could be construed as anything but strategically defensive. The Chinese defense strategy can be best understood in historical terms by three elements underlying Mao's intent at that moment: political legitimacy for the new regime, a global political context formed largely by the opposition of the United States and the Soviet Union in the Cold War, and military resources available for national defense.

According to Mao's Cold War theory, there would be a clash between the two countries sooner or later. In the 1950s, the United States intruded in and threatened China's security in three areas: Korea, Vietnam, and the Taiwan Strait. Concerned with the geopolitics, regional economy, and transportation capacity of these three conflicts, the Chinese believed America's intervention in Korea was the most critical threat to the new regime. Mao described American involvements in the three areas as three knives threatening China: America in Korea was like a knife over her head; America in Taiwan was one around her waist, and Vietnam was one at her feet.[53] Thus Korea, rather than Taiwan, was considered the most immediate threat. Moreover, China stood a far better chance for victory in Korea, since it might have a better odds of winning a land war. Later, Zhou explained this at a meeting of CPVF commanders:

> It is inevitable for us to have a showdown with the American imperialists. The question is how to choose a place for this fight. Although it is certainly up to the imperialists, we do have a choice at the moment. When the imperialists chose Korea as the battleground, it favors us. So we decided to resist America and aid Korea. Let us think about these three possible battlegrounds. No matter which part of the war you are talking about, you can see the differences. If the war-fighting had taken place in Vietnam, no need to mention a naval war over the offshore islands, it could have been much more difficult than our fighting here [in Korea].[54]

Thus, in early July, Chinese leaders made a significant shift in strategy: instead of landing at Taiwan, they were now defending Manchuria.[55] On July 1 and 2, Mao, Zhu, Zhou, PRC vice president Liu Shaoqi, and other top leaders met and discussed the military situation in Korea. After the meetings of the CCP high command, Zhou briefed Russian ambassador Nikolai Rochshin in Beijing on the second evening. According to Rochshin's telegram to Moscow, the Chinese leaders were not optimistic about Kim's advance in the South. They were worried about U.S. military intervention and a possible U.S. landing in the rear area of the NKPA.[56] Beijing believed it necessary for China to bolster forces in Northeast China along the Chinese–North Korean border. It was only after the Korean War broke out that China's military began to see significant strategic changes, from focusing on attacks on GMD-held islands to protecting the mainland. The concept of national defense against a possible Western invasion became the cornerstone of China's new strategic culture and its military modernization in the 1950s.

On July 7, when the United Nations Security Council adopted a resolution calling for all possible means to aid the ROK, the Truman administration announced it was sending in U.S. forces. The CMC, at Mao's suggestion, held the first national defense meeting in Beijing. Chaired by Zhou, the meeting included Zhu, Nie, Lin, Luo Ronghuan (Lo Jung-huan), and chiefs of all the services along with heads of all the general departments of the PLA. Luo Ronghuan served as political commissar of the 4th Field Army in the Chinese Civil War and became director of the Department of the General Political Tasks of the PLA after the founding of the PRC. The high command assembly decided to establish the Northeast Border

Defense Army (NEBDA, *Dongbei Bianfangjun*) to forestall any emergency that might arise along the Chinese-Korean border.[57] The NEBDA would include three strategic reserve armies in Central China and one army in the Northeast. Zhou submitted the meeting minutes to Mao, covering NEBDA commanding officer candidates, organizational structure, mobilization, deployment, logistics, and transportation. Mao approved the minutes and wrote on Zhou's report, "Agree; carry it out accordingly."[58]

On July 10, after Mao's approval, the CMC named Su Yu as the NEBDA commander and political commissar, along with Xiao Jinguang, chief of the PLA Navy, as its deputy commander, even though Mao's best generals had been ready for an amphibious attack on Taiwan.[59] However, for different reasons, neither reported to his position. At the time, Su was admitted into a hospital for a health problem, and Xiao was busy with the newly established PLAN.[60] On July 13, the CMC issued the "Decision on Northeastern Border Defense" to all the PLA general departments and army headquarters. The high command began transporting its best troops from Central China to the Northeast. By late July, the 38th, 39th, 40th, and 42nd Infantry Armies, and 1st, 2nd, and 8th Artillery Divisions, totaling 260,000 troops, arrived in Manchuria under the NEBDA command.[61]

It is important to note that Mao escalated China's war preparation in early August from a "border defense in China" to "a proactive defense in Korea" by planning an intervention to "assist the Korean people."[62] On August 4, after the UNF had halted North Korea's invasion, Mao called a Politburo meeting to discuss preparation for possible involvement in the conflict. Mao told the top leaders that the American imperialists would be even more aggressive and threatening to China if they won the war; thus, China must assist Korea more effectively.

Mao explained the new strategy in a telegram to Zhou, who was to meet with Stalin in Moscow later that year. Omitted in the reprinted text of Mao's manuscript are two important sentences: "We do it in such way to advance the national defense line from the Yalu River to the line of the Tokchon-Nyongwon and areas south of it. This is absolutely possible and beneficial [to us]."[63] Mao considered the UNF an immediate threat to China's national security, and Chinese intervention was necessary to stop a perceived UNF northward advance or even an invasion of China. Thus, the Chinese defense line was more than 100 miles southeast of the Yalu in North Korea. Mao's plan changed the approach of China's national defense from fighting an enemy force along the Chinese border to fighting a potential invader within its neighboring country's territory. Mao's

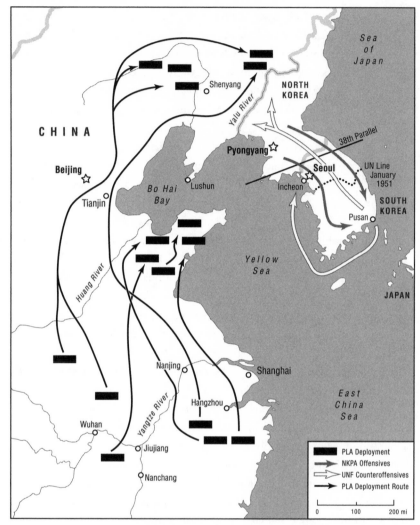

PLA Deployment, July–October 1950.
Map by Erin Greb Cartography.

proactive defense, however, would certainly become more offensive and aggressive in nature. The new strategy led to Chinese entry in the Korean War in October.

To justify China's military involvement, Mao suggested at the August 4 meeting that the Chinese troops in Korea should use a "volunteer" name, and that Chinese military leaders could of course decide the timing of the intervention.[64] The four NEBDA armies would "change to volunteer uniform and use volunteer flags" to assist the Korean people and to participate in the Korean War. The next day, Mao ordered the armies "to get ready for fighting in early September" in Korea.[65] At a mid-August meeting, most of the army commanders believed that the best time for the Chinese to take action was after the UNF had crossed the 38th parallel, but before they had "established a foothold" in North Korea.[66] All these considerations reveal an important strategic shift of the PLA high command, moving from a defensive position to an intervention. Mao had determined by mid-August to send troops to Korea. From that point on, China began mobilizing more troops for an intervention in Korea, as the high command realized that four armies were not enough.

On August 18, Mao decided that the 9th Army Group would serve as the second echelon of the volunteer force. Song's armies should be transferred in September from Fujian and Zhejiang Provinces on the southeastern coast, where they had been preparing for the invasion of Taiwan, to the Shandong (Shantung) Peninsula, where the forces could be quickly moved by sea or rail to northeastern China. In late August, following Mao's instructions, Zhou chaired several CMC meetings on how to transport these armies from the Southeast to Manchuria.[67]

Mao confidently explained his thoughts on how to defeat U.S. forces in Korea to national leaders at the Ninth Plenary of the PRC Central Government on September 5, saying, "You [the United States] fight in your way, while I fight in mine. You can use nuclear bombs, and I use my hand grenades. I will find your weakness and chase you all the way. Eventually, I can defeat you."[68] Mao's optimistic attitude toward a potential war against the United States had a contagious effect upon Chinese political and military leaders during the early stages of the Korean War.[69] At the meeting, Mao talked to Chen Yi, commander of the ECMR, about the new assignment for the 9th Army Group. According to Mao, Song's armies would have two months of training and preparation for combat readiness in October–December.

After his return to Shanghai, Chen held an emergency meeting of the 9th Command on September 7 and briefed the army commanders of the CMC's decision that the Taiwan landing training would be terminated, and that all the armies would be assembled immediately and made ready to move north to Shandong for war preparation in Korea. Under Song's command, the 9th Army Group had three infantry armies, including the 20th, 26th, and 27th. Zhang Yixiang was the commander and political commissar of the 20th Army with Liao Zhengguo as his deputy commander. Zhang Renchu was the commander of the 26th Army with Li Yaowen as the political commissar and Zhang Zhixiu as deputy commander. Peng Deqing was the commander of the 27th Army with Liu Haotian as his political commissar and Zhan Da'nan as deputy commander. Each army had three divisions in a regular formation, totaling about 30,000–35,000 troops.

To fight the foreign war in a better position, Chen reinforced the three armies with additional troops after the commanders meeting. The ECMR transferred the 89th Division from the 30th Army to the 20th Army; added the 88th Division to the 26th Army; and transferred the 94th Division from the 32nd Army to the 27th Army. Thereafter, each army had four divisions rather than three. In mid-September, the ECMC also sent to the 9th 15,000 former GMD troops of Jiang's 16th Army Group, which rose in revolt in Sichuan against the GMD regime in 1949. After these reinforcements, each division had 10,000 men, and each army 50,000. In sum, the 9th Army Group had twelve divisions, totaling 150,000 troops.

On September 20, Chen ordered the 9th Army Group to move north to the Shandong Peninsula; the 27th Army got on the train first, followed by the 20th and finally the 26th. Since the Chinese government had kept secret its sending of forces to Korea until October 25, the troops thought there would be another landing exercise before their invasion of Taiwan. They did not know until November that they were preparing a foreign intervention to save the North Korean regime from UNF counterattacks.

On September 15, 1950, MacArthur successfully landed UN/U.S. troops at Inchon, on South Korea's west coast, which rapidly changed the military situation in Korea. Informed by periodic reports from their agents in Pyongyang, the Chinese leaders watched these developments with growing dismay. After the UNF's Inchon landing, Kim's army did not respond quickly enough to prevent Seoul from being retaken in late September. Nor could Kim halt the collapse and retreat of the NKPA back across the 38th parallel. Facing a military disaster, Kim rushed representatives to Moscow and Beijing asking for additional military aid.

On October 1, the ROK 3rd Division crossed the 38th parallel, the first unit of the UNF to enter North Korea in order to liberate the country from the Communist regime. The goals of the UN/U.S. forces in Korea changed from a rescue mission to save the South Korean government to an expeditionary mission to end Kim's control of North Korea. Stalin telegraphed Mao on October 1 suggesting that China "should send at once at least five to six divisions . . . so that our Korean comrades will have an opportunity to organize a defense of the area north of the 38th Parallel under the screen of your troops." These Chinese soldiers could be "considered as volunteers" and remain under Chinese command.[70] Mao's early decisions and foresight to establish the NEBDA in July and to concentrate five armies in Manchuria in August made such an intervention possible.

Mao's Decision and Song's Rush to Korea

Nevertheless, China's final decision to enter the Korean War was not an easy or rapid process, particularly since Mao found it difficult to get other Chinese leaders on board. When the Politburo met on October 2, there were still divergent views. The Politburo members, as Mao's most influential and important advisers, also held positions on the CMC. Most expressed deep reservations about any military intervention in the Korean War. The chairman confessed to his comrades that dispatching Chinese troops to the Korean War was one of the most difficult decisions in his political life.[71] Mao believed that China had no alternative to military intervention.

First, Mao recognized the UN advance into North Korea as a direct, immediate threat to China. Pang Xianzhi and Li Jie point out that Mao had a "bottom line," which "was whether American troops would cross the 38th parallel."[72] In a later conversation with the Soviet delegation, the Chinese chairman said, "Should American imperialists intervene, and would not cross the 38th parallel, we would not intervene; should they cross the 38th parallel, we would certainly send troops to Korea."[73] In the meantime, Mao also considered the Sino-Soviet relationship.[74] Mao worried about Stalin's distrust of the CCP. He feared that the Soviet Union might intend to isolate New China from the socialist and communist camp. Finally, Mao wanted to prevent the Soviet Union from sending troops to Northeast China.[75]

Since the Politburo did not reach any decision on military intervention on October 2, Mao called an expanded meeting (*kuodahui*) of the Politburo on the 4th in order to break the deadlock. Twenty-two political and military leaders attended the meeting on October 4–5. To bring in more political supporters from outside Beijing, Mao sent an airplane to Xi'an (Si'an), northwestern Shaanxi (Shensi) Province, to pick up Peng Dehuai, vice chairman of the CMC and commander of the Northwest Military Region, for the enlarged meeting. With Zhu De, he was one of the PRC's most dedicated and experienced marshals.[76] Peng arrived at about 4:00 P.M. on October 4, when the participants were focusing on the disadvantages of sending troops to Korea. Mao, unhappy with the "reasonable and logical" discussions of the majority, said, "When we, however, are standing on the side, just watching other people who are undergoing a national crisis, we feel terrible inside, no matter what we may pretend."[77] Peng expressed no opinions during the afternoon discussions. With all these issues on the table, Peng could not sleep that night. Mao's words were reverberating through his mind. Peng understood why Mao needed him there.[78]

When the Politburo meeting continued its discussion in the afternoon of October 5, Peng strongly supported Mao's idea, arguing: "Sending the troops to aid Korea is necessary. . . . If the American military places itself along the Yalu River and in Taiwan, it could find an excuse anytime it wants to launch an invasion."[79] Many participants at the meeting were impressed by Peng's firm stand.[80] His support convinced the majority to send troops to aid North Korea and to resist American aggression. By the end of the day, the CCP Politburo had decided that China would send troops to Korea.[81]

Mao's decision to send Chinese troops into North Korea has remained controversial since the end of the Cold War. Most Chinese military historians argue that Mao made a rational, correct, and necessary decision.[82] China's intervention secured its northeastern border, strengthened Sino-Soviet relations, and saved the North Korean regime. China acted as a major military power for the first time since the Opium War against Britain in 1840. However, some historians in China, and many more in America, challenge this "wise decision" argument and condemn Mao for gross misjudgments and an "idiosyncratic audacity" that cost the lives of hundreds of thousands of Chinese soldiers.[83] Still others hold a middle position in which Mao had few political alternatives in his effort to achieve full acceptance in the Communist world and to assume leadership of Asian Communist movements in 1950.[84]

On October 7, Mao formally informed both Kim Il-sung and Stalin of Beijing's final decision to send troops to Korea.[85] The next day, Mao issued orders reorganizing the Northeast Border Defense Army into the Chinese People's Volunteer Force (CPVF, *Zhongguo Renmin Zhiyuanjun*) and appointing Peng as its commander in chief and political commissar.[86] According to Mao's order, the CPVF included four infantry armies (formerly NEBDA) and three artillery divisions, nearly 260,000 men. At a meeting with Kim in Beijing twenty years later in October 1970, Mao recalled China's defense mobilization in July and told the North Korean leader that Chinese forces could have had more advantage "if we could have had seven armies rather than five armies at that time."[87] It seemed to Mao that the more armies China sent to Korea, the better chance it might have of winning the war.

Despite the name, the troops of the CPVF were simply the same Chinese troops that had been assigned to the Korean border. The CPVF command was actually the PLA's front command. By using the term "volunteers," as Stalin agreed, Mao expected to convince the world that Chinese volunteers, not the Chinese government itself, organized the CPVF and therefore to avoid open war with the United States and the sixteen other nations that had joined the UNF in Korea. Peng once joked about being a "volunteer" in the CPVF HQ on the Korean front. "The volunteers, indeed," he jested. "I am not a volunteer . . . it is my chief who sent me here."[88]

On October 8, Song Shilun received the order from the CMC that the 9th Army Group should assemble in Shandong immediately for war preparation, and that the army group would move north to the Yalu River along the Sino-Korean border as the CPVF's strategic reserve. When the 9th Army Group received the order from Beijing high command to go to Korea on October 8, all its three armies were still in training along the southeastern coast around Shanghai for an amphibious attack on Taiwan. The next day, the army group changed its name from the "PLA 9th Army Group" to the "CPVF 9th Army Group." On October 14, Mao telegraphed Chen Yi, commander of the ECMR, to order the 9th to leave Shanghai for Shandong for foreign-war reorganization in preparation for leaving the country.[89] The plan for the 9th included combat training, weapons inspection, and reorganization in Shandong for two months. On October 17, the troops of the 9th boarded trains and assembled in the area of Yanzhou, Shandong Province, with a scheduled entry into Korea in December.

In late October, however, Lt. Gen. Edward M. Almond, commander of the U.S. X Corps, deployed the 1st Marine on the left, the 7th Division in the middle, and the ROK 1st Army on the right along the coastal line to march north. The Capital Division of the 1st Army went farther north to Jeju and Mincheon.[90] The X Corps rapidly advanced north along the eastern coast toward the Yalu River and Kanggye, which was made the wartime capital of North Korea after Kim Il-sung withdrew his government from Pyongyang on October 19.

Mao had to change the prewar preparation plan for the CPVF 9th Army Group. On October 23, Mao cabled Chen Yi again to summon Song Shilun to Beijing immediately. In his telegram, Mao urged that the 9th "must speed up its political mobilization and combat training. One of the armies should move to Northeast [China] first."[91]

On October 23, Mao and Zhou summoned Song in Beijing. Mao told Song, "We are currently trying to turn the war situation around, and striving for a strategic initiative in Korea." "The Changjin Lake is on the eastern front, but behind the CPVF on the western front. [We] must draw a line there, and never allow the 'UNF' to cross this line." The campaign objective of the 9th "is to stop the enemy there and then push it back." The chairman emphasized, "Your first priority is to attack the U.S. 1st Marine Division, or at least to destroy two of its regiments. . . . You are in command of the eastern front." Mao also explained why the high command had chosen the 9th as the second echelon of the CPVF. "Your army group is one of our best-known defensive forces and capable of fighting tough battles in the [Chinese] Civil War."[92] At the meeting, Mao also asked Song to continue his war preparation in Shandong, while Zhu De, PLA commander in chief, would visit the 9th in Shandong; and Nie Rongzhen, acting chief of the General Staff, would discuss issues such as troop transportation, weapons and equipment, and winter clothing with Song in Beijing. Song promised the chairman that he and his army group would accomplish the mission by winning the Battle of Chosin and thus making China's first engagement in the Korean War a success.

On October 25, 1950, the Chinese government announced it would send the Chinese People's Volunteer Force to Korea to fight the war, or "*Kangmei yuanchao, baojia weiguo zhanzheng*" [War to Resist the United States, Aid Korea, Defend the Country, and Safeguard the Homeland], or in short: "War to Resist the United States and Aid Korea" (WRUSAK).[93] In fact, Chinese troops had already crossed the Yalu River and entered North Korea on October 19. The first echelon of the CPVF consisted of six armies, including eighteen infantry divisions, three artillery divisions, and 7,000 support troops—in all about 300,000 men.[94]

Thereafter, the Korean War essentially became a conflict between China and the United States. China surprised the world when its troops launched a massive offensive south of the Yalu in early November. This was only the beginning of Chinese involvement. This rapid and unexpected deployment took place without discovery by American intelligence and air reconnaissance. The Chinese high command hoped its superior numbers would offset its inferior equipment and technology. It seemed rational to the high command that a larger force would be a decisive factor in their favor.[95] At home, the CCP rallied the nationwide "Great Movement for Resisting America and Aiding Korea" to mobilize the entire country for the war effort.

On October 27, Mao telegraphed Peng: "It has been decided that the 9th Army Group will be transported by train on November 1 to the Meihekou area for training and reorganization."[96] Thereby, Mao changed the location of the

9th Army Group's prewar training from the East to Northeast China along the border areas.

Unready Armies Cross the Yalu

By October 28, after Song's return from Beijing, all of his armies had moved into their assembly positions in Shandong with the 27th in Tai'an, the 20th in Duizhou, the 26th in Teng County, and the army group headquarters at Qufu, the birthplace of Confucius. On October 29, Mao telegraphed Peng again: "Song Shilun's army group must be surely used and deployed on the eastern front where the U.S. 7th Division and ROK Capital and 3rd Divisions are very likely to make northward attacks from Hamhung (Hamheung). It will help us to seize the initiative. Or it would cause negative effect on the whole situation."[97] After being in Shandong for only one week, the troops of the 9th were back on the train and traveling north in late October. There they would conduct war preparations in the border areas for two months.

On October 29, Commander in Chief Zhu De came to Qufu and delivered a mobilization speech to the PLA commanders at and above the regimental level of the 9th Command. Zhu told the officers that the American imperialists had ignored China's warning, crossing the 38th parallel in Korea and approaching the Chinese border, and that the United States was conspiring to invade China's northeast. We could not let it happen without any response, he said. Zhu issued the call: "to defend the motherland and support our friendly neighbor, we have a glorious mission and responsibility. We should win the war with international support."[98] The officers had just realized how close and serious the Korean War was, when their chief told them that, if the 9th Army Group failed to stop the Americans, they might have to stay in Korea for a prolonged guerrilla war.

On October 31, Mao changed the 9th's plan again. He issued an urgent order to Song to begin entering Korea on November 1. The chairman's telegram reads, "This army group (with three armies and twelve divisions) will come under command of the CPVF general headquarters. It must set up its goals as to seek opportunities to annihilate the ROK Capital Division, ROK 3rd Division, the U.S. 7th Division, and the U.S. 1st Marine Division one by one."[99] Mao was not aware of the problems the 9th Army Group faced in Northeast China, including insufficient transportation and inadequate winter clothing.

Song cabled Mao and the CMC in October asking the Northeast Military Region to provide the heavy coats, shoes, and hats for Korea's winter "since the East China Military Region does not have any experience in making the heavy winter clothing."[100] There was no reply from Beijing. The documents show that the ECMR reported to Nie Rongzhen, acting chief of the PLA General Staff, that the ECMR had already issued the "winter clothes" to the 9th Army Group before its departure on November 1. In fact, the ECMR ignored the differences between the "light winter cloth" issued by the ECMR in South China and the "heavy winter cloth" requested by Song for the Korean winter. Nie reported this to Mao, who believed that the troops of the 9th had received their winter uniforms.[101]

On October 31, the 9th Command received Mao's cable to move up its date for entering Korea from late December to November 15.[102] According to the original plan from the CMC, the 9th Army Group should have conducted training, reorganization, and logistical preparation for at least one month until December before it would move north to the border areas. However, during the CPVF's First Offensive Campaign from October 25 to November 7, Mao realized that the CPVF's troops on the eastern front (only two divisions of the 42nd Army) were far from adequate to deal with the U.S. X Corps (three U.S. divisions and two ROK divisions). Mao telegraphed Peng Dehuai, who had arrived in Korea on October 19, "We have decided to assign Song's army group to be responsible for the directions of Kangil and Changjin [Chosin]. Its main objective of engagement is to lure enemy forces deep in and seek opportunities to annihilate them one by one. Thereafter, the army group will be under your direct command and we will not control it from a distance."[103]

On November 5, Mao ordered the 9th Army Group to enter Korea immediately. Song called his commanders at 1:00 P.M. to end their very short one-week training in Shandong and to start boarding trains to move to the Sino-Korean border. On November 7, Chinese news media began to report the CPVF's operations in the Korean War, when all of the 9th armies reached the border areas of Andong (Dan-dong), Fushun, and Ji'an (Chi-an) along the Yalu River.

The 9th was hastily thrown into combat without proper preparation. The one-week training had not included weapons inspection, tactical drills, attack practice, defensive exercises, and, most importantly, air defense and protection. The officers had no idea about the American armed forces, and the men knew nothing about Korea. In addition, it was even worse that they were confident of defeating the Americans and winning the war. Through the ranks, the 9th was still influenced by the many victories they had won against the Japanese Army in 1937–45 and then the GMD Army in 1946–49. Overconfident and optimistic about their mission in Korea, some officers believed that it was going be a "short war" with a "quick victory." Some even scheduled their weddings for the following summer.[104] But the U.S. Army was not the Japanese or GMD Army. The 150,000 men of the CPVF 9th Army Group were marching into a military disaster.

The CPVF 20th Army was under the command of Zhang Yixiang, who also served as the political commissar, with Liao Zhengguo as the deputy commander and Yu Binhui as chief of staff.[105] In early November, Zhang received the order to move north from Shandong to Meihekou, Jilin Province, for war preparations, including training, reorganization, and resupply. At that time, he commanded the 58th, 59th, 60th, and 89th Divisions, totaling 50,569 men with 442 artillery pieces, 1,073 machine guns, 3,516 automatic weapons, and 5,150 rifles.[106] On November 5, the 59th Division boarded trains at Shandong and traveled to Meihekou as the vanguard of the 20th Army. On the 6th, when the first train passed through Huanggutun, Liaoning Province, the commander of the 59th Division received the new order that no one was to leave the train, and that the army would be entering Korea immediately from Ji'an and Linjiang (Lin-chiang).[107]

At the train station of Shenyang, He Jinnian, deputy commander of the NEMR, found out that the troops of the 59th Division were dressed in light canvas shoes and quilted cotton uniforms, light winter clothing from the south, and that they were not prepared for the bitter cold Korean winter. He rushed back to the NEMR headquarters and asked all the staff in the offices to donate their winter clothes to the CPVF troops. He brought back 641 winter coats to the 59th's officers.[108] Obviously, it was far from enough.

On November 7, the 59th Division crossed the border and arrived at Kanggye by train that night. Thereafter, the 58th, 60th, and 89th Divisions marched from Ji'an into Korea by foot without stopping at the border. According to NEMR logistics records, the regional command was able to provide 15,090 new and old coats to the 20th Army on November 8–12. Less than 30 percent of the troops received their winter clothing before they crossed the border.

The CPVF 27th Army was under the command of Peng Deqing with Liu Haotian the political commissar, Zhan Da'nan the deputy commander, and Li Yuan the chief of staff.[109] In fact, the 27th Army had crossed the Yalu at the southern border city of Andong on November 4, and was ordered to engage with the British 27th Brigade in the west. On November 7, however, the army was ordered to return to Andong and travel north to join the 9th Army Group since Peng Dehuai, commander in chief of the CPVF, had requested the critical participation of the 9th on the eastern front. When the army reentered Korea from Linjiang on November 12, it had 50,501 men with 635 artillery pieces, 1,422 machine guns, 4,413 automatic weapons, and 13,448 rifles.[110] The army commanded the 79th, 80th, 81st, and 94th Divisions. According to NEMR logistics records, the Northeast Military Regional Command delivered 22,980 winter coats to the 27th Army.[111]

The CPVF 26th Army entered Korea after the 27th. The 26th Army was under the command of Zhang Renchu with Li Yaowen the political commissar, Zhang Zhixiu the deputy commander, and Feng Dingshan the chief of staff.[112] When the army crossed the Yalu, Zhang had 48,894 men with 477 artillery pieces, 1,141 machine guns, 4,353 automatic weapons, and 13,504 rifles.[113] He commanded the 76th, 77th, 78th, and 88th Divisions in the Battle of Chosin. According to NEMR statistics, the regional command delivered 33,000 old coats to the 26th Army on November 13.

The 9th Army Group had received 72,000 new or old winter coats as its entered Korea. More than 65 percent of its troops did not receive winter coats, 60 percent did not have winter shoes, and no one had winter gloves.[114] Mao emphasized the importance of the 9th's combat readiness and preparation for the cold winter in his telegram to the CPVF and NEMR commands on November 9. "Please ask Gao [Gang] and He [Jinnian] to try everything possible to guarantee the supply of food, ammunition, and cloth (against the cold weather) for both the western and eastern fronts."[115] Unfortunately for the soldiers, the 9th's armies did not have time to prepare before they arrived at Chosin because Mao rushed them to the eastern front. It was too late to provide any help for the troops when Mao emphasized the decisive nature of the Battle of Chosin on November 12: "Since this battle is of such vital importance, please study and analyze the battle plan attentively and carefully. Make sure all armies are adequately prepared."[116]

2

A Deception with Three Problems

On November 7, 1950, the 173rd Regiment, 58th Division, 20th Army, crossed the Ji'an Bridge at the upper reaches of the Yalu River as the first combat troops of the CPVF 9th Army Group to enter Korea. All the men had removed any Chinese army insignia from their uniforms to maintain their claim of being "volunteers" as the first echelon, which had left the country in late October. On November 12, all the 20th Army's troops entered Korea.[1] In fact, the CPVF 27th Army had crossed the Yalu at the lower reaches of the river at Andong on November 4 and was ordered to engage with the UNF British 27th Brigade. On November 7, the army returned to Andong and traveled north to join the 9th Army Group. On November 17, the 27th Army reentered Korea from Linjiang at the northern border and marched toward the Chosin Reservoir.[2] As the second echelon of the Chinese forces, the 9th Army Group, including the 20th, 26th, and 27th Armies, totaling twelve divisions with 150,000 troops under the command of Song Shilun, moved into the eastern front of the Korean War.

By late November, China had dispatched thirty-three divisions, totaling 450,000 soldiers, to Korea. Peng Dehuai, commander in chief of the CPVF, had 240,000 men on the western front against 130,000 troops of the U.S. 8th Army, and another 150,000 men on the eastern front against 90,000 troops of the U.S. X Corps, a ratio of nearly 2:1.[3] With superior manpower, both Mao and Peng expected a major victory over the UNF in the next offensive campaign. Mao had a strategic intention to completely turn around the military situation in Korea. Peng planned an "in-house" operation to lure the UNF into the northern areas—and then strike.[4] This large-scale attack with a deception became known as the Second Offensive Campaign of the CPVF and lasted from November 25 to December 24.

In its design and preparation, the Second Offensive Campaign consisted of two phases: the first was along the Chongchon River on the western front against the 8th Army from November 25 to December 2, and the second in the east against the X Corps at the Chosin Reservoir from November 27 to December 24. Some of the PLA's tactics familiar from the Chinese Civil War were employed in the campaign, including outnumbering the UN Command whenever possible, engaging the enemy in mobile operations, and achieving surprise through night movements and operations. In nine days, the CPVF pushed the battle line back to the 38th parallel and recaptured Pyongyang, the capital city of North Korea. The Second Offensive Campaign "represented the peak of CPVF performance in the Korean War."[5] Because of this success, in early December PRC representatives to the UN refused to accept "a compromise peace" to end the Korean conflict through negotiations.

It should be understood, however, that the offensive campaign was an imbalanced attack between well-prepared armies in the west and ill-prepared forces in the east. This chapter will explore three major problems the 9th Army Group faced at Chosin. First, the troops of the 9th were hastily thrown into combat without proper training and with inadequate supplies. The 9th left Shandong in mid-October and arrived at the Korean border in early November. Its original plan was to conduct reorganization and war preparations for two months. On October 31, however, Mao and the CMC ordered the army group to enter Korea immediately to stop the X Corps and save the government of North Korea at Kanggye.[6] The men were not ready, and the officers did not know much about the situation in Korea. Most of the Chinese generals did not know who General Douglas MacArthur was, and nobody knew the name of 1st Marine Division commander Gen. Oliver Smith.[7] Second, Song Shilun's intelligence reports were flawed, and he did not have accurate information on either American division. Therefore, he underestimated the UNF's firepower and made the decision to attack all six American regiments (three of the 1st Marine Division, two of the 7th Infantry Division, and an artillery regiment) on the eastern front at the same time. His troops were overstretched, missed the weaker link of the marine defense, and failed to reach his campaign goal of destroying the 1st Marine Division. Third, the troops were not prepared for the bitterly cold Korean winter, which hit the army group exceedingly hard in late November. About 28,950 Chinese casualties in the Battle of Chosin were related to the weather.[8] The 9th Army Group paid the full price of unreadiness.

Peng's Trap: Destroy More UNF Divisions

On October 25, 1950, the CPVF launched its First Offensive Campaign, which lasted for thirteen days. The First Campaign was not well planned, as the UNF moved much faster and farther north than the Chinese had expected. The CPVF commanders considered the first phase of the campaign as a meeting engagement or contact battle. Peng instructed the CPVF to engage the ROK troops first, in order to gain some experience, before dealing with the more powerful U.S. units.[9] In fact, some Chinese troops tried to avoid U.S. troops.[10] By the end of the campaign, the CPVF did not reach its goal, which was to eliminate at least two ROK divisions. To Mao and Peng, it was a great relief that the first echelon of the CPVF had built up a foothold in North Korea and stabilized the front line at Chongchon River by November 7.[11]

Peng and his deputies at the CPVF Command knew that the overall situation had not substantially changed, and the CPVF had yet to control the battleground in Korea. Their first surprise attack did not weaken or cause any serious damage to the UN/U.S. forces. In the meantime, Peng and his senior commanders found the situation favorable to the CPVF, since MacArthur and the UNC still believed there were no major Chinese forces against the UNF, and that the volunteers might number about only 50,000 men rather than nearly 400,000 Chinese troops already in Korea.[12]

On November 4, Peng suggested to Mao that he lure the UNF into preset "traps" as far north as possible so that UNF divisions with extended supply lines might be more easily isolated and destroyed.[13] Mao immediately agreed with Peng's proposed strategy with a specific emphasis that "in the meantime, the 9th Army Group will take a full responsibility for military operations in the Kanggye-Changjin areas with its full strength. Its strategy is to lure the enemy in deep, and see opportunities to wipe out the enemy [divisions] one after another" to reverse the tide in the east.[14] Kanggye had become the wartime capital of North Korea after Kim Il-sung lost Pyongyang to the UNF in mid-October. Mao seemed to consider the next offensive campaign as an opportunity to turn the war situation around in Korea by destroying more American troops.

On November 7, when the CPVF troops stopped their attacks, MacArthur's objective was to return to the offensive: drive the Chinese back to the Yalu and complete the reunification of Korea. He ordered the 8th Army north along the western front and the X Corps in the east to stage an all-out, or perhaps final, counteroffensive on November 15. PLA historian Major General Xu Yan points

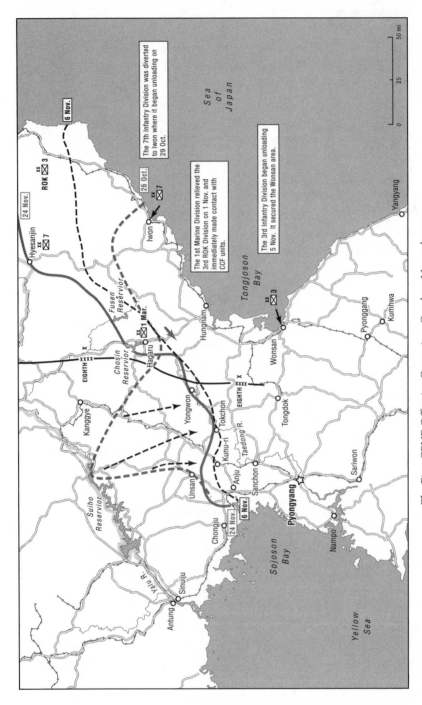

The First CPVF Offensive Campaign, October–November 1950.

Map by Erin Greb Cartography.

The 7th Infantry Division was diverted to Iwon where it began unloading on 29 Oct.

The 1st Marine Division relieved the 3rd ROK Division on 1 Nov. and immediately made contact with CCF units.

The 3rd Infantry Division began unloading 5 Nov. It secured the Wonsan area.

out that the biggest military mistake MacArthur made in the face of the initial setback from the first major engagement with the CPVF was ignoring the gap between his 8th Army in the west and X Corps in the east. The gap presented an unusually good opportunity for the Chinese commanders to plan penetration and deep encirclement operations to the rear of both groups.[15] Peng Dehuai saw a good opportunity to send his armies through the middle and penetrate into the 8th Army's right flank and rear, if MacArthur extended his dispersed forces further into CPVF predesignated ambush areas.[16]

Mao quickly approved Peng's plan and emphasized the need to "strive to launch one or two campaigns respectively on the eastern and western fronts from this month to early December. Annihilate seven or eight regiments of the enemy in total, and push the fronts forward to the area around the Pyongyang–Wonsan railroad line. Thus, our army will basically win the war."[17] Apparently, Mao considered the next campaign to be the decisive battle for the Chinese forces.

On November 13, the CPVF held its first expanded party committee meeting at Taeyu-dong to evaluate the First Campaign and plan for the Second.[18] At that meeting, CPVF leaders decided that, since their forces lacked adequate air, artillery, and armor support, they would conduct mobile warfare, trading territory for UNF casualties. The next campaign would lure the UNF into a deep trap, where Chinese troops could encircle and eliminate UNF units one by one. Thereafter, the CPVF Command withdrew its armies back into the mountainous areas of central North Korea to lure the UNF north and wait in preparation for the next attack.

Peng made clear his intentions regarding the western front at the November 13 meeting: "The enemy must be lured deep into our controlled areas from a campaign point of view. It will require assembling of superior forces and firepower to cut apart the enemy troops, encircling them and destroying them one by one."[19] Therefore, all the CPVF armies continued their withdrawal between November 17 and November 20. Peng's mobile tactics, pretending that the Chinese were weak, enticed the UNF to advance faster and deeper. The meeting encouraged each army to devise plans to destroy at least one or two UNF regiments in this Second Offensive Campaign.[20] Peng's plan worked because his deception continued to make UNF commanders feel overconfident and underestimate the CPVF's strength and fighting capabilities. By November 21, all the UNF frontline forces in the west had reached their final offensive line, less than ten miles from the Chinese armies. MacArthur made the first of several optimistic statements when he visited the 8th Army headquarters with Gen. Walton H. Walker, perhaps partly in jest, that if the troops advanced fast enough, "maybe some of them could be home by Christmas."[21]

Peng's deceptive offensive, however, was imbalanced, with a well-prepared attack along the Chongchon River on the western front against the 8th Army, but an unprepared attack in the east against the X Corps at the Chosin Reservoir. In early November, while there were more than 240,000 men of the CPVF in the west, there were as yet only 20,000 Chinese troops in the east. Two divisions of the 42nd Army faced five UNF divisions, totaling more than 90,000 troops, of the X Corps.[22] The X Corps, under the command of Maj. Gen. Edward "Ned" M. Almond, included the 1st Marine Division and U.S. Army 7th Division; the corps moved north toward the Chosin-Kanggye area.

It appeared to Mao that the X Corps would drive Kim and his government out of North Korea and cut off the CPVF from behind. To protect the CPVF's left flank and rear, Mao deployed Song Shilun's 9th Army Group from East China to Korea to stop the X Corps. Mao canceled the 9th's preparation plan and issued an urgent order to Song to begin entering Korea on November 1. Mao cabled Peng: "This army group (with three armies and twelve divisions) will come under command of the CPVF general headquarters. It must set up its goals as to seek opportunities to annihilate the ROK Capital Division, 3rd Division, the U.S. 7th Division, and the 1st Marine Division one by one."[23]

Mao's new plan for the 9th Army Group was to attack the X Corps at Chosin. After receiving Mao's telegram, Song issued his Army Group Operation Order No. 7 to the commands of his three armies on the same day.[24] Thus, Mao had to move up Song's entry date to Korea three times to keep up with Peng's plan.[25] The 9th had little time for preparation, which had been reduced from two months to a revised one-month plan, and then down to only one week before the troops entered Korea. Some of the troops did not even leave their train at all from East China all the way to the Korean border, covering about 1,500 miles in five to seven days. The officers told the men on the train what was happening in Korea from the local newspapers at the train stations and tried to explain why they were in such a big hurry to fight against the Americans.[26]

Song was worried because of the limited rail transportation capacity between Shandong and the Korean border. Song asked Mao to postpone the entry schedule until November 15, the earliest possible date for the 9th to cross the Yalu River. Mao was not happy with Song's bargaining request. Without accepting or rejecting the request, Mao replied to Song on November 2 that the 9th should "enter Korea on their arrival" at the border.[27] Mao also informed Peng on November 5 about the objective of the 9th Army Group. "It should be decided that Song's army group will take care of the Kanggye-Changjin [Chosin] area with its full strength. Its strategy is to lure the enemy in deep, and seek opportunities to annihilate the enemy one after another. After that, the army group will be under the direct command of your headquarters," Mao telegraphed. "One army of the 9th Army Group should advance to Kanggye directly, and then move on to Changjin promptly."[28] In less than two weeks, the 9th left Shandong and arrived at the Korean border area in early November. Mao's last order to the 9th was to enter Korea immediately upon its arrival at the border.

On November 6, Peng provided Song with his objective in the Second Offensive Campaign. "You should lure enemy forces deep into Kujing-ri and Changjin Line and wipe out two regiments of the U.S. 1st Marine Division."[29] The X Corps advanced north rapidly toward the Yalu. On November 11, responding to MacArthur's repeated calls, Almond ordered all his divisions to speed up their movements. He visited the 7th Infantry Division's headquarters the next day and told Maj. Gen. David G. Barr, its commander, "The general (MacArthur) and I hope that your division will be the first U.S. infantry to get to the Yalu. Do you understand?"[30] Almond's intelligence officers were convinced that there were at most one to two Chinese divisions on the eastern front. At that moment, the 42nd Army was continuing its resistance against the 1st Marine's northward drive.

According to Peng's plan, the two divisions of the 42nd would continue to entice the X Corps to advance farther north while covering the 9th Army Group's secret, southeast march from the Yalu to the eastern front. On November 12, Peng was briefed on the 1st Marine's turn west toward Puseong-ri. On November 16, Peng ordered the two divisions to pull out of the Chosin area and move westward to south of the Kurchang area. Song Shilun had no way to trap or stop any of the UNF troops at Chosin since his army group had just crossed the Yalu. The X Corps' intelligence officers reported on November 18 that "the enemy's recent delaying operations are apparently concluded and he is once again withdrawing to the north. The speed of his movements has caused a loss of contact at most points."[31] On November 18, the X Corps, including the 1st Marine and 7th Army Divisions and the Capital Division of the ROK 1st Army, approached the Chosin area, where no Chinese forces were to be found. On November 21, after defeating a few weak North Korean units, the 17th Regiment of the 7th Division occupied the town of Hyesanjin and the surrounding area all the way to the Yalu. This was the first and only American unit that ever reached the Chinese-Korean border area. MacArthur immediately sent his "heartiest congratulations" to Almond.[32]

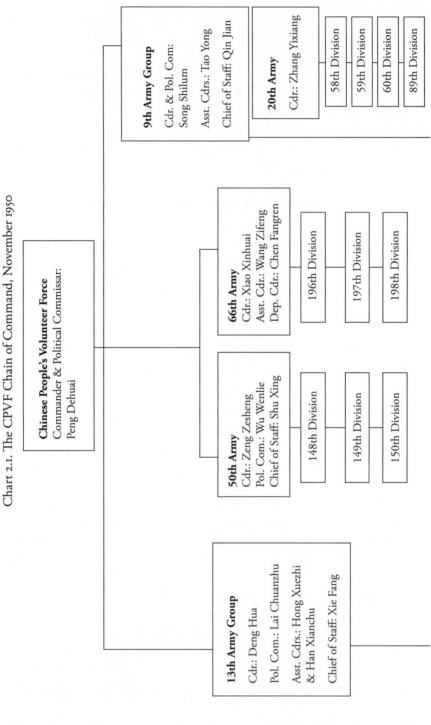

Chart 2.1. The CPVF Chain of Command, November 1950

Chinese People's Volunteer Force
Commander & Political Commissar:
Peng Dehuai

9th Army Group
Cdr. & Pol. Com:
Song Shilum

Asst. Cdrs.: Tao Yong

Chief of Staff: Qin Jian

20th Army
Cdr.: Zhang Yixiang

58th Division

59th Division

60th Division

89th Division

66th Army
Cdr.: Xiao Xinhuai
Asst. Cdr.: Wang Zifeng
Dep. Cdr.: Chen Fangren

196th Division

197th Division

198th Division

50th Army
Cdr.: Zeng Zesheng
Pol. Com.: Wu Wenlie
Chief of Staff: Shu Xing

148th Division

149th Division

150th Division

13th Army Group
Cdr.: Deng Hua

Pol. Com.: Lai Chuanzhu

Asst. Cdrs.: Hong Xuezhi
& Han Xianchu

Chief of Staff: Xie Fang

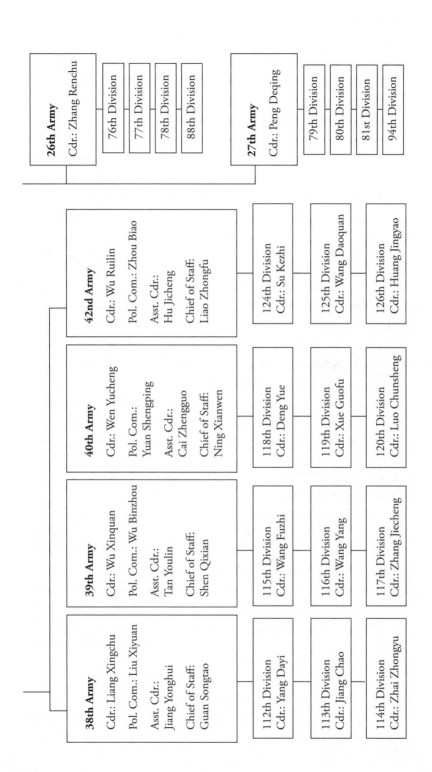

38th Army
Cdr.: Liang Xingchu
Pol. Com.: Liu Xiyuan
Asst. Cdr.: Jiang Yonghui
Chief of Staff: Guan Songtao

- 112th Division — Cdr.: Yang Dayi
- 113th Division — Cdr.: Jiang Chao
- 114th Division — Cdr.: Zhai Zhongyu

39th Army
Cdr.: Wu Xinquan
Pol. Com.: Wu Binzhou
Asst. Cdr.: Tan Youlin
Chief of Staff: Shen Qixian

- 115th Division — Cdr.: Wang Fuzhi
- 116th Division — Cdr.: Wang Yang
- 117th Division — Cdr.: Zhang Jiecheng

40th Army
Cdr.: Wen Yucheng
Pol. Com.: Yuan Shengping
Asst. Cdr.: Cai Zhengguo
Chief of Staff: Ning Xianwen

- 118th Division — Cdr.: Deng Yue
- 119th Division — Cdr.: Xue Guofu
- 120th Division — Cdr.: Luo Chunsheng

42nd Army
Cdr.: Wu Ruilin
Pol. Com.: Zhou Biao
Asst. Cdr.: Hu Jicheng
Chief of Staff: Liao Zhongfu

- 124th Division — Cdr.: Su Kezhi
- 125th Division — Cdr.: Wang Daoquan
- 126th Division — Cdr.: Huang Jingyao

26th Army
Cdr.: Zhang Renchu

- 76th Division
- 77th Division
- 78th Division
- 88th Division

27th Army
Cdr.: Peng Deqing

- 79th Division
- 80th Division
- 81st Division
- 94th Division

Encouraged by the good news from the 7th Division, other X Corps divisions also sped up their pace. By November 24, the 1st Marine and 7th Divisions had all reached the Chosin area.

Apparently, the precampaign situation in the west favored the CPVF. Peng had six armies, totaling 240,000 men, against 130,000 UNF troops.[33] More importantly, the Chinese armies had been prepared and were waiting for three weeks for the UNF to move farther north into the trap. In the east, the situation favored the UNF since the U.S. divisions had occupied Chosin in mid-November when the 9th's armies were still far away from the area. There was no Chinese trap in the east.

Mao realized the problem of Peng's "one-size-fits-all" offensive plan on the eastern front. Peng should have planned a defense for Song's armies to stop the X Corps, instead of an attack on the U.S. regiments. The CPVF 42nd Army could have slowed down the X Corps' drive, instead of luring it deep into the north, to allow more time for Song's combat readiness and more preparation to avoid heavy casualties. Later, neither Mao nor Peng accepted any responsibility for the military disaster of the 9th Army Group at Chosin. Xu Yan explains, "Although Mao Zedong was very concerned about the battle in the east, he believed that Peng and other commanders knew the situation better on the front."[34] Therefore, on the eastern front the war situation favored the UNF. Neither the UNC nor the X Corps had detected any trace of the Chinese 9th Army Group's movement to Chosin.

The 9th Marches through the Snow Mountains

To achieve the two objectives of the campaign—stopping the X Corps and annihilating two of the American regiments—Song had to launch a surprise attack at Chosin. At 1:00 P.M. on November 5, he issued an order to the 20th, 26th, and 27th Armies, that the task of the 9th Army Group was to stop the X Corps at the Chosin Reservoir.[35] Song decided to let the 20th Army enter Korea first, and rush to Chosin to stop the 1st Marine and 7th Divisions. Then, the 27th would enter Korea from Linjiang on November 12 to destroy the marine regiments. The 26th Army would temporarily stay at the Yalu as the reserve and wait for the promised Soviet weapons and equipment shipments in order to replace the army group's old Japanese-made weapons.[36]

Song followed Peng's deception strategy and made it clear to his army commanders that they should conceal their movements from the Yalu River to the Chosin Reservoir, a distance of about 120–200 miles. The army and division commands silenced radio communication and tightened up the control of troop movement information from November 10 to 25. Any use of bugles and whistles was prohibited before the attacks. Song also urged his commanders to reach the Chosin area as soon as possible since he knew that the 9th Army Group was behind Peng's offensive schedule.[37]

After crossing the Yalu, all the armies marched at full speed across North Korea toward Chosin. They had to travel the Rangrim Mountains and Kaema (Kaima) Highlands between the Yalu and Chosin. The 9th Army Group had to cross the Rangrim first, a north–south mountain range with elevations of 3,000–6,000 feet. These mountains constitute a natural watershed in North Korea. Then, the Chinese troops had to march through the Kaema Highlands, at an average altitude of 5,000 feet—a landscape with thick forests and few roads. On the highlands, it usually started snowing in October and early November, and the temperature could drop to around zero degrees Fahrenheit. Chosin Lake was a man-made reservoir surrounded by mountains as high as 4,000 feet.[38]

On November 8, the 20th Army began a forced march. To conceal the large-scale movement of these infantry divisions, Zhang Yixiang, the army commander and political commissar, led his four divisions 120 miles through the heavily forested Rangrim Mountains.[39] In the wintry conditions, it was impossible for the 20th Army to move with any kind of speed. Although the artillery battalions had some horses, the animals refused to walk on the narrow ice-covered paths along the cliffs. It was just too slippery and dangerous. The men came up with the idea of laying down their comforters on the cliffs to cover the snow and ice. The idea worked, and they led their horses safely through the pass.[40] The 20th Army crossed the mountains by marching sixty miles in four nights. The army continued its movement toward Chosin through the hills and forests of the Kaema Highlands. On November 21, Song ordered the 20th Army to rush to the Chosin area; all the troops were to reach their staging sites before the 26th as the army was scheduled to launch its attack on the next day.[41]

Peng Deqing, commander of the 27th Army, told the divisions on November 13 that all the troops should avoid any town, village, or populated area on their way to Chosin to conceal their movement through the Rangrim and Kaema. "The large troops should rest in the forest while taking cover against possible air raid and reconnaissance."[42] To conceal their southern movement, Commander Peng led his four divisions through the mountains at night and rested during the day. After seven nights of marching, his army reached the Chosin area by November 20 with the 79th Division at Liantang-ri, the 80th at Lishang-ri, the 81st at Lishuiping, and the 94th at the outlet of the Houchang River.

Chart 2-2. The Ninth Army Group Chain of Command

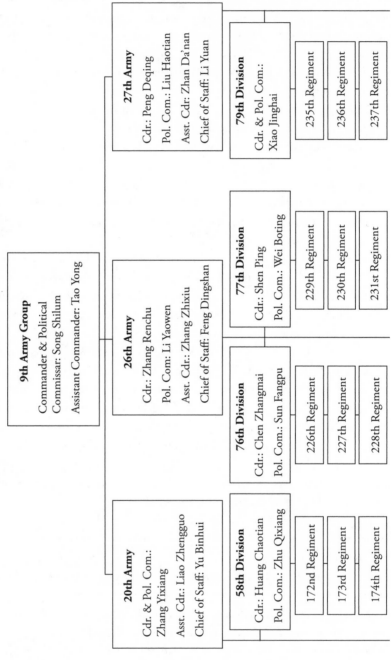

9th Army Group

Commander & Political
Commissar: Song Shilun

Assistant Commander: Tao Yong

20th Army

Cdr. & Pol. Com.:
Zhang Yixiang

Asst. Cdr.: Liao Zhengguo

Chief of Staff: Yu Binhui

26th Army

Cdr.: Zhang Renchu

Pol. Com: Li Yaowen

Asst. Cdr.: Zhang Zhixiu

Chief of Staff: Feng Dingshan

27th Army

Cdr.: Peng Deqing

Pol. Com.: Liu Haotian

Asst. Cdr.: Zhan Da'nan

Chief of Staff: Li Yuan

58th Division

Cdr.: Huang Chaotian

Pol. Com.: Zhu Qixiang

76th Division

Cdr.: Chen Zhangmai

Pol. Com.: Sun Fangpu

77th Division

Cdr.: Shen Ping

Pol. Com.: Wei Boting

79th Division

Cdr. & Pol. Com.:
Xiao Jinghai

| 172nd Regiment |
| 173rd Regiment |
| 174th Regiment |

| 226th Regiment |
| 227th Regiment |
| 228th Regiment |

| 229th Regiment |
| 230th Regiment |
| 231st Regiment |

| 235th Regiment |
| 236th Regiment |
| 237th Regiment |

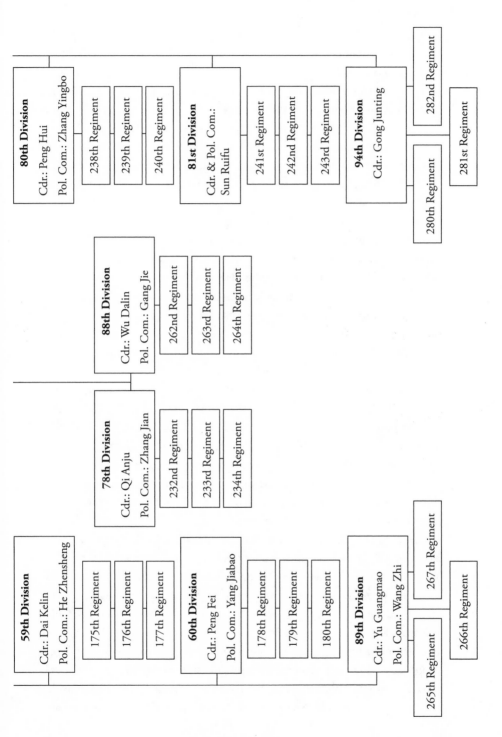

When the 9th Army Group crossed the Yalu in mid-November, the U.S. Air Force was conducting close and tight surveillance of the Chinese-Korean border area on a daily basis. American warplanes also bombed the highways, railroads, bridges, and villages in the Korean border areas. Nevertheless, the 9th had remained undetected through its march to Chosin. None of its twelve divisions, totaling 150,000 troops, were spotted by U.S. reconnaissance. Military journalist and historian Joseph C. Goulden described "the CCF [CPVF] capacity for forced march as phenomenal by any standard." "One division averaged 18 miles daily for eighteen days, over rough mountain roads . . . invisible to aerial photographs and observers."[43] Despite their successful concealment, the Chinese armies faced three serious problems during the march from the Yalu to Chosin.

The first challenge was the lack of transportation in North Korea. The armies did not have enough trucks or trains. Without air defense, most of the highways, railroads, and bridges were destroyed or damaged by the USAF. The 27th Army had neither train nor trucks available for its artillery and ammunition transportation in Korea. The army lost twelve trucks to an air raid during its first day in Korea, and lost forty-five out of fifty-two trucks, all the army had, in less than two weeks.[44] Without enough trucks, the army had to leave most of its heavy artillery pieces (75 mm or larger field guns) at the border. The troops could only carry small mortars.[45] The men carried all the ammunition. Each man carried eighty bullets for his rifle and had to carry artillery shells as well.[46] During their march, when the Chinese met some retreating North Korean officers and soldiers, the latter were surprised by the poorly equipped and supplied Chinese troops. The NKPA troops were armed with Soviet-made automatic weapons and tanks, which were much better than the Japanese-made WWII rifles the Chinese possessed. Since many of the NKPA troops were withdrawing into China, some of them gave their guns and food to the Chinese.

The second problem was the weather: the cold winter hit the 9th Army Group exceedingly hard. When the 9th's divisions were crossing the Yalu, other CPVF troops were shocked to see they were going into Korea without winter clothing. To achieve strategic superiority of troop numbers, Mao and the CMC had hastily summoned the 9th Army Group from the subtropical region of Southeast China to Korea. When the troops reached the Chosin area, the weather became even more severe and the temperature dropped below zero.[47] In most cases, the Chinese troops had only one or two cotton-padded quilts for every squad of more than ten soldiers. They rolled out the two quilts on the frozen ground and hugged together lying on it to beat the cold. No troops were allowed to use fire day or night because of the constant threat of air strikes by American planes. Moreover, a fire or smoke might reveal the army's movement or position to UNF air reconnaissance.[48]

The temperature had dropped to 20–40 degrees below zero at Chosin in late November.[49] Veterans of the campaign recalled that exposure to the winter weather of North Korea proved as hard and deadly as the American bombs. In a world of snow and ice, the Chinese faced frostbite, the consequent loss of hands or feet, and the peril of freezing to death since more than an half of the 9th's troops did not have any winter clothing. Around November 25, a heavy snow fell in the Rangrim-Chosin area. The officers of the 9th, who came from the subtropical climate of South China, had no idea of the severity of cold winter weather in North Korea. Captain Wang Xuedong, 1st Company, 172nd Regiment, 58th Division, CPVF 20th Army, recalled, "We came from Southeast China, where the average annual temperature is about 72 degrees Fahrenheit. When we left our homes in early November, the temperature was about 60 degrees. Two weeks later, when we entered Korea, the temperature there had dropped to below zero."[50] Many men of the 58th Division became ill and could not keep up with of the push to cover approximately 120 miles in seven days, through mountains and forests. The division lost 700 men to severe frostbite in the first night of the march.[51]

The divisions of the 27th Army also suffered casualties from frostbite during their secret march from Linjiang to Chosin. Although there were winter clothes and shoes available for the army, many of its troops ended up not taking them because of miscommunication and confusion. According to Li Gelin, operation chief of the 81st Division of the 27th, when the division crossed the border first, troops were ordered to travel light since they would have to keep a rapid pace. Therefore, many soldiers tried to carry enough food and ammunition rather than winter clothing. Then, when the division arrived at the border and saw the winter coats and shoes left behind by the first-wave troops, they thought their comrades had saved the coats for the second-wave troops. They decided to do the same and left the coats untouched at the border for the later troops.[52] Since more than half of the 27th Army's troops left China without winter clothing, many of its casualties were caused by the cold weather.

The veterans of the 80th Division of the 27th Army told similar stories about their rapid march toward Chosin in their interviews. Song Xiesheng, assistant captain of 7th Company, 3rd Battalion, 238th Regiment, 80th Division, recalled that when the men rested, they had to take turns sleeping for no longer than one hour at a time since they could freeze to death in their sleep. Before an hour was up, they were awakened and they moved around for twenty to thirty minutes before they could go back to sleep. When they slept, they held each other's feet to keep them warm. Song had vivid memories of these extremely cold nights. "Nobody takes off his shoes. If you did, you could never put them back again on your feet next morning due to swelling caused by overnight frostbite."[53] The 6th Company of the 2nd Battalion, 239th Regiment, learned a hard lesson when the company lost 120 out of 160 men in one day to frostbite on their feet. The 27th Army suffered more than 30 percent of its noncombat casualties due to frostbite during the Battle of Chosin.[54]

The third problem was that the logistics services failed to keep up with the 9th Army Group's movement. As a result, troops began starving during their march toward Chosin. The troops hastily thrown into combat without good preparation faced serious breakdowns in their supply systems. As noted already, without air defense, most bridges and roads had been destroyed or damaged by U.S. air strikes. Deputy Army Commander Liao Zhengguo recalled, "Our [20th] Army's food supply was transported from Northeast China by train into Kanggye [North Korea]. Our army logistics unloaded the grain to the horse wagons and handcarts, which carried the grain for 70–90 miles to the bottom of the mountain ranges. Then, the men and women of the army logistics had to carry the grain bags, between 25 and 75 lb., on their backs through the mountains about 20–30 miles to the front."[55]

The shortage of food was a serious issue across the board for the entire CPVF. During the first two campaigns from October to December 1950, the CPVF met only one-quarter of the food needs of its frontline troops. These shortfalls seriously constrained CPVF operations.[56] After arriving at Ji'an on the evening of November 7, the 58th Division of the 20th Army was ordered to cross the Yalu with light carry-on weight in two hours. All the men carried only a small ration for three days, consisting mostly of crackers. The division began to cross the river at 11:00 P.M. that evening. After the 58th Division entered the Rangrim Mountains, the men began to starve on the fourth day during their rapid march. Captain Wang Xuedong recalled that the men became very hungry when they had to walk twenty to thirty miles every night. "When our regiment ran out of food, we had to trade our blankets, towels, and even medicines with local Koreans for their rice, corn, and vegetables."[57]

Food shortages were a major ongoing logistics issue. Most of the troops had only one or two meals a day, and some troops had nothing to eat for two or three days at a time. Most of the logistics and material supplies depended on North Korean civilians who had to shoulder-carry ammunitions and food to the front.

Since the 9th Army Group entered Korea in mid-November, almost no additional supplies came until early December. Liao Zhengguo, deputy commander of the 20th Army, recalled that his army ran out of food on the fifth day in Korea. His 59th Division sent its officers to look for food in the local villages. Many of them came back emptyhanded, since these were remote, sparsely populated mountainous areas, and many local peasants had fled their homes because of the war. Some of the officers brought back some frozen potatoes. The 60th Division allowed its troops to collect dead animals, including horses, water buffalo, goats, dogs, cats, and rats.[58]

The 26th Army also faced serious food shortages, even though the divisions asked the men to carry seven days' worth of rations. After the eighth day, the entire army became hungry and faced a crisis. These troops experienced low morale, and some panicked. The soldiers began to desert from their units, and some officers left their men too. Army Commander Zhang Renchu ordered his division command to collect and discipline the deserted soldiers and officers. Before the Battle of Chosin, Zhang rounded up hundreds of deserters, including both soldiers and officers. More than twenty of these officers were punished. Army Group Commander Song Shilun shot a battalion commander of the 26th Army, who had abandoned his troops and begun walking back toward China. Song told the officers at a commanders meeting that he could not discipline the men without executing that officer.[59] Song recalled later that the hunger, hardship, and deadly environment "were even worse than these during the Red Army's Long March" in 1934–35.[60]

The troops of the 9th Army Group could not have a hot meal for eight to nine days through their rapid march from the Yalu to Chosin since no fires were allowed. At that time, there was almost no canned food industry in China. A lot of Chinese troops fought for days without any meal during the First Offensive Campaign. They either got food from captured enemy supplies or went to local North Koreans for help. After weighing several options, the Logistics Department of NEMR proposed to use cooked wheat flour as the main staple food for the hundreds of thousands of CPVF forces in Korea. After wheat flour was stir-fried with oil and salt, it was easy to carry and preserve for weeks.[61] Upon Peng's approval in early November, the NEMR and civilian governments in Northeast China began to mobilize the population to make the cooked flour for the CPVF. On November 12, for example, the Government of Northeast China issued an executive order instructing the provincial, metropolitan, and county governments to organize the cooking campaign for twenty days, producing at least 150,000 pounds of the flour mix per day. Nevertheless, the cooked flour powder did not have enough nutrition for the battle-fatigued troops. Many CPVF soldiers soon suffered health problems due to malnutrition.

The planners of the CPVF headquarters were not aware of the three problems the 9th Army Group faced during the march from the Yalu to Chosin. On November 20, Peng Dehuai and the CPVF Command ordered the 9th to launch attacks on the U.S. X Corps at night on November 25 in coordination with the Chinese attacks on the western front. Peng was afraid of an immediate withdrawal of the X Corps in the east after the CPVF attack on the 8th Army in the west. Later, the X Corps provided reinforcements to the western front after the events of the 25th proved Peng's miscalculation and unnecessary pressure on the 9th Army Group.

After receiving Peng's telegram, Song quickly found out that his two armies could not complete the battle preparations for such a large-scale attack as planned. The 27th Army could not move into staging positions before November 22, and the 26th was still far from its designated battle sites in the Chosin area. Hence, Song asked for a two-day delay in his telegram on November 21.[62] The CPVF Command had to accept the fact that the 9th Army Group must delay its attack.

On November 25, two days after Thanksgiving, the CPVF launched the Second Offensive Campaign against MacArthur's forces. In that evening, four Chinese armies conducted an all-out attack on the 8th Army's I and IX Corps over a hundred-mile-wide front on the western front. The next day, the CPVF 38th Army on the right broke through the defenses of the ROK 7th Division of the IX Corps.[63] The 38th reported that it had annihilated more than 5,000 South Korean troops and occupied Tokchon by that evening.[64] In the meantime, the CPVF 42nd Army, also on the right, attacked the positions of the ROK 8th Division of the IX Corps at Yongwon. After the 38th and 42nd breached the IX Corps' right flank, they were able to turn southwest and envelop the 8th Army at the Chongchon River on November 27.[65] During the morning of November 28, the 38th Army continued its penetration and rushed to Samso-ri, outflanking the entire IX Corps.[66] On November 29, the UNF Command began an overall retreat along the western front to allow the 8th Army to withdraw back into South Korea. On December 4, the UNF evacuated from Pyongyang, which the Chinese 39th Army occupied on December 6.[67] The Second Offensive Campaign liberated North Korea and forced the United States to change its war aims. As MacArthur put it, the Chinese had created "an entirely new war." The CPVF's Second Campaign was a strategic victory for China.

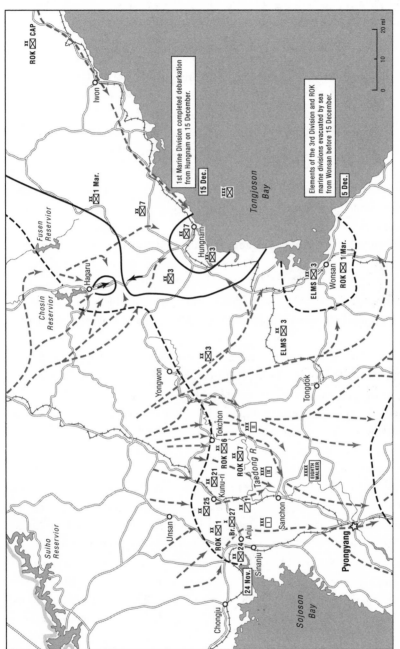

The Second CPVF Offensive Campaign, November–December 1950.

Map by Erin Greb Cartography.

Obviously, the South Korean troops had been the weakest link in the IX Corps line. Since General Walker, commander of the 8th Army, deployed the 6th, 7th, and 8th Divisions of the ROK 2nd Army next to each other at the right flank to protect the wing of his offensive, these ROK divisions had been targets of the CPVF's penetration, flanking, and encircling operations. The Chinese armies were able to exploit the IX Corps' weakness and break through the lines of the two ROK divisions on November 26. From the outset of the Chinese intervention in late October, the CPVF generals had learned that the ROK divisions were the most ill-trained, ill-equipped, and poorly prepared of the UNF units arrayed against them, as many of the soldiers were put into uniform only months, or even weeks, before. When Peng Dehuai planned his surprise attack with deception as the Second Offensive Campaign, he first set his eyes on the ROK 7th and 8th Divisions. As expected, these divisions, surprised by the night attacks, quickly lost their fighting will and spirit in great panic and ran helter-skelter.[68]

Song's Plan: Attack All the Marines

On the eastern front, when the 9th Army Group attacked the X Corps two days later, Peng Dehuai ordered Song Shilun to attack the U.S. Marine regiments rather than the 3rd or Capital Divisions of the ROK 1st Army under the command of the X Corps. In fact, Song intended as his campaign goal a larger entrapment than the CPVF Command had planned for him. On November 5, Mao put the 9th Army Group under the command of the CPVF general headquarters. Mao informed Peng, "The army group will be under the direct command of your headquarters. We will not allow command supervision from afar."[69]

On November 6, when Peng planned the CPVF Second Offensive Campaign, he provided Song with the objective of the Battle of Chosin. "You should lure enemy forces deep into Kujing-ri and Changjin line and wipe out two regiments of the U.S. 1st Marine Division. . . . With such deployment, the deeper the 1st Marine moves north into Kujing-ri, the better. Two armies [of yours] should use two divisions to hold the front while other seven divisions attack the enemy from flank and rear."[70] Meanwhile, Peng and the CPVF commanders kept close watch on developments around Chosin. Finding that the 1st Marine had moved westward and split from the U.S. Army 7th Division on November 11, Peng telegraphed Song on the next day about a possible separation of the two U.S. divisions. "The entire 27th Army and one division of your 20th, totaling four divisions, should encircle and destroy two regiments of the U.S. 7th Division; three divisions of the 20th Army and 126th Division of the 42nd Army should encircle and annihilate two regiments of the 1st Marine after they reached west of Yudam-ni."[71] At that time, Song agreed with Peng's plan to concentrate all his divisions to attack only two marine regiments.

In Beijing, Mao was concerned about the 9th Army Group's campaign goal to destroy two marine regiments. The chairman cabled Peng on November 12, "It is said that the U.S. 1st Marine Division has the best combat effectiveness in the American armed forces. It seems not enough for our four divisions to surround and annihilate its two regiments. [You] should have one to two more divisions as a reserve force." Mao warned the CPVF commanders in the same telegram, "Combat must be fully prepared for, and the campaign commands must be carefully organized. Please continuously instruct Song and Tao [Yong] to accomplish their task."[72] Mao had good reason to worry about the Battle of Chosin since the war situation on the eastern front was much different from that on the western front.

On November 19, however, Song intended to change the campaign goal from attacking two marine regiments to attacking four American regiments after his armies arrived at Chosin. His 20th Army reached the area to the west and south of Yudam-ni (Yutam-ri) that day, while the 27th Army moved in north of Yudam-ni and Sinhung-ni (Shinheung-ri), east of the Chosin Reservoir the next day.[73] (There are two Sinhung-nis around the reservoir.) Song found that the U.S. X Corps had not detected the 9th Army Group's deployment on the eastern front. Millett reaches the same conclusion that "Far East Command and X Corps had completely missed the movement of the CPVF Ninth Army Group into the mountains on either side of the Changjin Reservoir."[74]

Song discussed with Tao Yong, deputy commander of the 9th the format of their attack: should the 9th concentrate its divisions or disperse its forces?[75] They believed that their eight infantry divisions had traveled secretly some 200 miles deep into eastern North Korea and had successfully deployed at Chosin undetected by the UNC. The Chinese infantry troops employed camouflage with good skill, and MacArthur's air intelligence did not pick up their movements.[76] Both concluded that a surprise attack could bring them a bigger victory over the marines.[77] Lynn Montross and Nicholas A. Canzona agree with the Chinese generals that "in addition to the advantage of mass, the Reds held the trump cards of mobility and surprise. They enjoyed superior mobility because they were unencumbered by heavy weapons and hence could use primitive routes of approach in the darkness. They had the advantage of surprise because their practice of marching by night and hiding by day had concealed their approach to a large degree from UN air observation."[78]

On November 19, the 9th Command asked the CPVF Command for a larger offensive operation: to employ the main strength of the 20th and 27th Armies to "annihilate the two regiments of the U.S. 1st Marine and . . . the two regiments of the U.S. 7th Division."[79] According to Song's intelligence, that was the entirety of the American force at Chosin. In his reply the next day, approving Song's plan of attack, Peng still emphasized the annihilation of the two marine units as the 5th and 7th Marine Regiments. Peng instructed Song "to concentrate the main strength of your army group to encircle and destroy the U.S. troops of the two regiments (5th and 7th [Marine] Regiments) at Hagaru-ri (Hakilyo-ri or Hahwaok-ri) and Koto-ri on the eastern line in the evening of November 24 or 25."[80]

However, Song Shilun wanted to attack all the American regiments at Chosin. Because his intelligence reports were flawed, he lacked accurate information on the U.S. X Corps, which had six rather than four regiments around the Chosin Reservoir at that time. In addition, the 1st Marine was the largest (having an effective strength of 25,473 men at the time) and most lethal U.S. division in Korea. Song underestimated the firepower of the marines. Confident he would defeat the X Corps at Chosin, he told his commanders at the headquarters, "Americans troops are nothing extraordinary. They depend on two things: airplanes and artilleries. But we have two better things: attack and defense. We will defeat them as long as we are perfect at our things."[81] Song and his 9th Army Group, unlike Peng Dehuai and his 13th Army Group, had not yet faced American firepower, and they did not pay a great deal of attention to the lessons from the CPVF's First Campaign in October.

Nevertheless, Song shared a concern with Peng, who was afraid of an immediate withdrawal of the X Corps in the east after the CPVF attacked the 8th Army in the west. Peng said in his November 20 telegram, "the enemy in the east will probably pull back fast, after the first attack in the west becomes successful."[82] His concerns certainly worried Song, who might lose the opportunity to annihilate two or more of the American regiments if the X Corps were to make a rapid withdrawal. In its instructions for the Second Offensive Campaign, the Political Department of the CPVF Command also called for annihilating more enemy troops: "we must understand that the bigger the victory we can achieve, the better the situation we will face [in the Korean War]."[83] Song recalled many years later that he knew he dispersed his forces and failed to concentrate his main strength on the two marine regiments in November 1950. His strategy was to encircle all the American regiments at Chosin first, and then see which one could be annihilated first, and which one second.[84] A similar strategy had worked against the Nationalist Army in the Chinese Civil War, but it failed against the U.S. Marines in Korea.

Song Shilun also overestimated the combat effectiveness of his armies, which were not fully prepared for the tough battle at Chosin. After requesting a delayed attack on the marines to enable better combat readiness, Song was confident of his larger entrapment at Chosin. His optimistic calculation led to his battle plan to attack all the American regiments at once around Chosin. His overconfidence prevented him from concentrating his main strength on the two marine regiments.[85] His troops were hampered by the severe and extremely cold weather in late November and early December at Chosin. To march fast and secretly into attack staging positions without being detected by the UNF air force, they left their supplies behind, including winter clothes and food.

Moreover, Song Shilun believed in a quick victory over the UNF in Korea. After the 9th Army Group headquarters arrived in its frontline command post, Song gave a brief speech to his officers and staff the next morning. The army group commander asked all of them to endure the hardship, overcome current difficulties, and even be prepared to sacrifice their lives for victory. Song emphasized that it would not take long; it could be as short as three months, and no longer than six months, for the CPVF definitely to drive the American imperialist forces out of Korea.[86]

The objective of Song's offensive campaign was therefore to attack the 1st Marine and 7th Infantry Divisions at the same time and destroy the entire marine division at Chosin. This goal helps to explain why Song encircled six American regiments at once on November 27. He underestimated the battle capability of the Americans and failed to concentrate his main strength on the two marine regiments. The immediate large-scale engagement against a strong American force put overwhelming pressure on Song and his commanders, who rose to the challenges of unexpected problems.[87] They did not have any experience or even knowledge of how to fight Americans, and many of them were still influenced by the victories they had won against the GMD forces a year before in the Chinese Civil War. But the U.S. Marines were not the Chinese Nationalist Army.

Song's objective was to wipe out most, if not all, of the intruding 1st Marine Division, including the 1st, 5th, and 7th Regiments; the main strength of the 7th Division, including the 31st and 32nd Regiments, and an artillery regiment. Song's dispersion of his armies was aimed at encircling more American regiments for a bigger victory at Chosin. Apparently, Song was confident in his familiar campaign strategy during the Chinese Civil War: engaging the enemy in mobile operations (*yundong zhan*) to cut off the Nationalist forces' retreat and wipe out entire enemy units (regiments and divisions). Information missing from Song's military records had led some American military experts to conclude that the 9th Army Group had little combat experience against the Nationalists.[88] In fact, through their large-scale encirclements and annihilations, Song and his 9th Army Group had destroyed tens of thousands of Nationalist troops in the Battle of Ji'nan in 1948 and the Battle of Shanghai in 1949. His success had made him one of the twenty-four army group commanders in China and a four-star general of the PLA. But he had no idea what fighting against the Americans would entail. At the Battle of Chosin, Song's employment at Chosin of tactics from the Chinese Civil War—surprise, mobile operation, and night attack—did not work.

At 2:00 P.M. on November 26, Song ordered the 20th Army to attack the American regiments from the south to cut off their connections and retreat routes. Since the X Corps was so widely spread and was not aware of the assembly of large Chinese forces in the area, the 9th Command believed that its divisions could divide and encircle the American regiments, making it possible to eliminate them. Song ordered "the 20th Army (minus the 60th Division) and main force of the 27th Army to destroy the main strength of the U.S. 1st Marine Division in the areas of Hagaru-ri, Shinta-ri, Kujing-ri, Yudam-ni, and Sinhung-ni." In the event they succeeded, the army commanders were told to "continue your attack to annihilate the 31st Regiment of the 7th Division and reinforcements from the 1st Marine."[89] Obviously, Song overestimated the combat effectiveness of his divisions and underestimated the strength of the American regiments. His divisions were dispersed at five different places around the Chosin Reservoir. The Chinese divisions at each encirclement did not have the attacking capability to wipe out an American regiment.

Although Song failed to concentrate his forces on the 5th and 7th Marine Regiments, his army commanders had opportunities to modify the dispersal of their divisions by concentrating some of their troops. The 27th Army could have put together more troops to attack one marine regiment at the time to reach the battle objective. Peng Deqing, commander of the 27th Army, shared Song's optimism, confidence, and concerns about a quick withdrawal of the X Corps to the south. The 27th Command issued the order and launched the attack on the residing American troops, which had just finished a daylong action and were ready to retreat to their tents to rest. The Chinese tactic of dividing and encircling the American forces was successful during Song's initial attack since they achieved the element of surprise, as their movement to the eastern front had remained undetected by the X Corps.

In his instruction on how to defeat the American troops, Army Commander Peng Deqing emphasized night attacks, close-range combat, and immediate and total destruction of entire enemy units rather than simply repelling them. He followed Song's plan and divided his three divisions to attack and encircle four American regiments at Yudam-ni and Sinhung-ni (east). He even pushed Song's plan further by instructing his division and regiment commanders to develop "small tactical encirclements inside a large-scale encirclement to destroy the enemy units one by one."[90] Although one CPVF division could encircle one American regiment, his division did not have the striking force and firepower to destroy any encircled marine units, not even a battalion or a company. With the division and regiment commanders under tremendous pressure to repeatedly attack U.S. Marine regiments, the Chinese assault troops suffered very heavy casualties. The 9th Army Group lost 10,000 men during the first night of attacks on November 27.

3

Massed Attack on the Marines

November 27 saw heavy snowfall throughout the eastern front. The temperature at Chosin dropped to 20–30 degrees below zero, making it the coldest winter in the area in fifty years.[1] With snow two to three feet deep, every road, pass, and bridge was icy and slippery. The Chinese attacking force, including eight infantry divisions of two CPVF armies, totaling more than 100,000 troops, had moved to designated attack staging sites undetected by the U.S. X Corps and UNF Command.[2] The 20th Army were staged west and south of Yudam-ni, and the 27th Army had moved into the area north of Yudam-ni and Sinhung-ni (east).[3] Song Shilun, commander of the 9th Army Group, planned to surprise his enemy through a combination of rapid night marches and deep encirclements. He would launch a full-force attack on the X Corps, including the 1st Marine and U.S. Army 7th Infantry Division around the Chosin Reservoir, using his strategy of "divide, encircle, and destroy."[4] His operational concept would exploit the 1st Marine's dependence on a roadbound advance of forty miles that left their lines exposed and vulnerable to ambush. His tactics stressed close encounters of a deadly kind that would neutralize the firepower of tanks and artillery.[5]

Between 4:30 P.M. and 3:00 A.M. that night, seven Chinese divisions launched their attacks at Chosin. By the morning of November 28, four Chinese divisions, comprising 50,000 troops, had separated the 1st Marine into four pockets at Yudam-ni, Hagaru-ri, Sinhung-ni (Sinheung-ni), west of the Chosin Reservoir, and Koto-ri. Song reported to Peng Dehuai that his 79th and 59th Divisions had encircled the 7th Marine Regiment, two battalions of the 5th Marine, and two battalions of the 11th Artillery Regiment at Yudam-ni. The 58th Division encircled the 1st Marine Division headquarters, two battalions of its 1st Regiment, one battalion of its 5th Regiment, and one tank battalion at Hagaru-ri. The 60th Division cut off the marines' connection between Hagaru-ri and Koto-ri.[6] Although the Chinese attacks continued through November 28, none of the four assault divisions was able to annihilate any marine unit—not a regiment, battalion, or even a company.[7]

This chapter examines the problems of the Chinese combat preparations before the battle, including inadequate firepower, lack of training, and persistently poor attacking capabilities. It focuses on three major reasons for Song's failure in the annihilation campaign. The first was his lack of intelligence and poor communication, which led to his miscalculations. Song failed to identify the weak link of the marine defense. He aimed his knockout blow at the Yudam-ni perimeter, farther northwest at a forward marine position that could be easily cut off and isolated. Song did not know that the marines deployed two regimental combat teams there.[8] Although his two attack divisions were able to maintain the encirclements and beat back an attempted breakout by the marines, they were incapable of conducting sustained offensive operations and delivering a last crushing blow to any encircled marine unit.

The second reason for the failure of the annihilation campaign was inadequate supplies, which seriously constrained the Chinese offensive. The lack of winter clothing, limited ammunition, shortage of food, and broken supply lines seriously impeded the combat effectiveness of the Chinese attacks at both Yudam-ni and Hagaru-ri. Many men were lost to frostbite, starvation, and the lack of medics. In both the Anti-Japanese War of 1937–45 and the Chinese Civil War of 1946–49, the Communist forces as the "Chinese people's army" could fight a major campaign with support and supply from local people. Without the "people's support" in North Korea, the 9th Army Group could not sustain fighting a major battle without providing troops with steady shipments of food and ammunition. The Chinese army group paid the full price of unreadiness for a foreign war.

The third reason was the heavy casualties the Chinese troops suffered in the first two days. The 9th Army Group lost 10,000 men during the first ten hours on November 27.[9] Three out of four assault divisions had been virtually disabled after the second night of attacks.[10] They were unable to launch another major attack on the 1st Marine Division thereafter. While the 9th Army Group's weaknesses accumulated, the marines survived their trial of repeated night assaults. The Battle of Chosin between the CPVF 9th Army Group and the 1st Marine Division became a standoff after November 29.[11]

Out in the Snow: Attempted Annihilation at Yudam-ni

To annihilate all the marines assembled at Chosin, on November 25–26 Song Shilun ordered his armies to deploy two divisions to Yudam-ni, while assigning one division to each of the following areas around the reservoir, including Hagaru-ri, Sinhung-ni (west), and Sachang-ri. The commanders of the two armies faced the same problems as Song did: lack of intelligence and supplies. Assistant commander of the 20th Army Liao Zhengguo complained about the lack of detailed information on the battleground. He recalled, "We did not even have a military map. The army command had only one operation map of 1:5000 scale."[12] The maps his division commanders used were Japanese-drawn maps from WWII. The roads, elevations, and hills were not accurate at all. Therefore, they made the same mistake that Song did by dispersing their divisions to separate locations. Peng Deqing, commander of the 27th Army, divided his four divisions strategically by assigning the 79th Division, his best, to attack Yudam-ni from the northwest, while the 59th Division of the 20th Army would attack this small village from the south.[13]

At Yudam-ni, two U.S. Marine regiments were prepared for the Chinese attack. Two battalions of the 5th Marine Regiment were stationed inside the village with eight artillery companies, five from the 11th Field Artillery Regiment and three from the marines.[14] In the morning of November 27, the 7th Marine Regiment had occupied the northern high ground, or the north ridge, and deployed several rifle companies along a two-mile-long range. Companies D and E were on Hills 1282 and 1240 in the center, Company H occupied Hill 1403 to the left, and Company F (or Fox Company) was farther left to protect the marines' flank.[15] These forward positions and firepower from the hilltops effectively defended the village.

In the afternoon of November 27, Peng Deqing ordered his 79th Division to attack the marines in full force along the north ridge.[16] The 79th included the 235th, 236th, and 237th Regiments and the army's artillery battalion, totaling 12,000 troops, under the command of Xiao Jinghai.[17] He employed tactics familiar from the Chinese Civil War at Yudam-ni: tactical surprise, night attacks, infiltrations, sudden mortar and machine-gun barrages, timely counterattacks, and close combat.[18]

Understandably, Xiao Jinghai faced the same problems and made the same mistake as his superior commanders. Because of the lack of the information on the marines, Xiao dispersed his regiments all over the north ridge for simultaneous attacks over a two-mile front. He assigned his 235th Regiment to attack Hills 1240 and 1282, the 236th Regiment to attack Hill 1167, and the 237th to penetrate between Companies D and E through a five-hundred-yard gap to occupy Hill 1348. After reaching this point, the 237th Regiment, totaling 4,000 men, was to launch

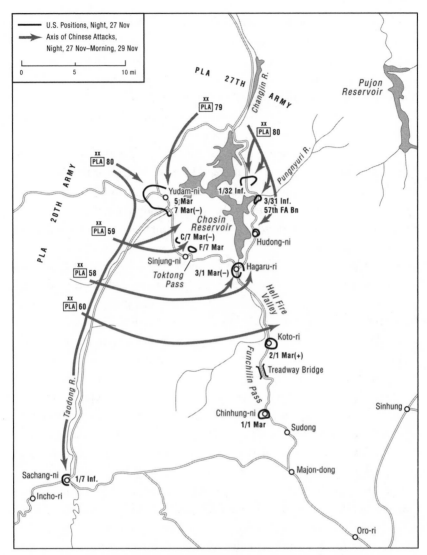

The CPVF Attacks at Chosin, November 27–December 14, 1950.
Map by Erin Greb Cartography.

an attack from behind the enemy.[19] As an experienced PLA field commander, Xiao had done such a maneuver before with good results during the civil war. He hoped these attacks would have some shock impact on the UNF defenses and force the marines to retreat down to Yudam-ni. Then his division and the 59th Division could destroy the marines in the village.

However, Xiao's regimental and battalion commanders also faced problems of information and communication. They did not have any map, Korean guide or translator, or radio. Their communication between regiments and battalions was poor as they had only bugles, whistles, flares, and foot messengers to coordinate. Since regiment commands had no effective communication with their troops, the battalions were pretty much on their own in the battle. The 1st Battalion of the 235th Regiment (1/235), for example, got lost and went to the wrong hill—1282 instead of 1240—as its assigned target. The 3rd Battalion of the 236th Regiment (3/236) followed 1/235 and also attacked Hill 1282, instead of Hill 1167 as its assignment.[20] Only one regiment, the 237th, of the 79th Division found its way to the staging site before the attack. To achieve a sudden impact, the troops of the 237th quietly moved into their assigned positions on the low ground at the center of the front under cover of dark for a surprise attack.

While the Chinese troops waited for hours through the evening, the cold weather became their worst enemy. Yang Yizhi, platoon leader of the 3rd Company, 1st Battalion, 237th Regiment (1/237), experienced the bitter cold while lying on the ground in the saddle between the two hills. He recalled, "My feet and legs gradually grew numb. The strong wind kept biting my nose and ears, and the tears from the biting pain immediately became two ice tubes on my face."[21] Yang had no coat, gloves, or winter shoes. He was still wearing the rubber sneakers he got at Shanghai in September. He and his fellow soldiers had come from Southeast China, where the temperature was about 60 degrees when they left for Korea in late October.[22] During the hours hiding, he missed his two "hugging buddies," who had always hugged together during the breaks and rests through the fifteen days of the night march from the Yalu to Chosin. The bear hug of three kept them warm enabling them to survive the cold. He also missed "jogging in place" every hour during the night. "I never like lying down in the snow. I saw many snow-covered bodies along the rough mountainous path of the 120-mile march; some mountains reaching 7,000 feet. Since the men were exhausted, some of them could not walk anymore in the heavy snow. They first knelt down and still tried to keep up with the troops. Then they crawled to the roadside, lying down and letting the others pass. They would think of just taking a short break. But they could never get up." Yang then wondered where the bugle call was for his charge. He just wanted to get up and run up the hill. He did not care what would happen then. It was the only thing he hoped throughout the three hours hiding for a close-range attack, only a few hundred yards from the marine posts.[23]

Finally, at 9:25 P.M., after a brief mortar barrage, the 237th Regiment launched the 1st Battalion for a sharp penetration through a narrow valley along the boundary between U.S. Marine Companies D and E. While the four charging companies of 1/237 blew bugles and whistles, their officers shouted commands, and eight hundred men followed. Although Yang Yizhi could not feel his feet, he somehow managed to get up and start running. He saw that some of his men could not stand up. Having broken through the line at 10:15 P.M., the 1st Battalion got behind Company E and took unoccupied Hill 1348.[24] In the meantime, the 3rd Battalion (3/237) attacked Company H and occupied Hill 1403. The Chinese commanders expected a withdrawal of the separated marines from the hilltops down to the village. However, it did not happen. From 12:00 to 2:00 A.M., the 1/237 troops repeatedly attacked Company E.[25] But the Chinese assaults could not crack the defensive positions or inflict significant casualties on the marines.

The firepower of the Chinese assault troops was no match for the defensive firepower of the marines.[26] To march fast and secretly to Chosin without being detected by UNF air reconnaissance, Song's divisions had left their heavy artillery pieces behind. Each division had only a few 75 mm field guns. Artillery heavier than mortars and pack howitzers did not come with their divisions, but stayed at the Yalu. Moreover, the lack of transportation forced each infantryman to carry mortar shells. Each regiment had only eight or nine 92 mm rocket launchers as antitank weapons. Each 82 mm mortar had forty shells, and 60 mm mortars had only ninety shells. Each infantryman was allowed to carry eighty bullets for his rifle. Each heavy machine gun had 2,000 rounds, and a light machine gun only 600 rounds.[27]

All the Chinese weapons deteriorated due to the extremely cold weather. Their water-cooled heavy machine guns froze solid and could not be used. The mortar barrels shrunk and deformed in the subzero weather. About 60–70 percent of the mortar shells failed to explode after firing due to the cold.[28] The only weapons the regiments had were rifles, hand grenades, and bayonets. The hand grenades became their most effective weapon.[29] Yang Yizhi recalled that during one charge, he could not pull open his frozen rifle bolt. Then he was unable to throw a grenade because his fingers were frozen and he could not pull out the safety pin. When he looked around for another weapon, he was shot twice. Later he awakened in a cave with 1/237 medics. Yang described feeling so bad that he did not even fire a single shot; his company lost 80 percent of its men during their first assault.[30]

Exposure to the cold weather at Chosin proved as harsh and deadly as the marines. Zou Shiyong, deputy political instructor of the 3rd Company of 1/237, never forgot that evening. "The extremely cold temperature made me feel like [I was] wearing nothing at all. I was chilled to the bone."[31] He remembered that when the captain ordered the bugles and whistles to signal the charge, some of his men could not get up; the others could not run and became easy targets of marine fire.[32] His company faced serious winter problems affecting their combat effectiveness. After each assault on the marine positions, the 1/237 soldiers busied themselves taking clothes, especially gloves and footwear, sleeping bags, and food from dead Americans, rather than press their attacks.[33]

As a light infantry regiment, the 237th could not destroy heavily armed and well-supported marine rifle companies or break their defensive lines along the north ridge without effective firepower. The assault battalions destroyed themselves pounding against the marine lines, which bent and broke in places but never collapsed. The 1/237's attacks failed to dislodge Companies D and E on the north ridge. Soon, the troops of the 1/237 on the hill were cut down by marine mortar, machine-gun, and rifle fire. Then the two marine companies organized counterattacks from two directions against the 1st Battalion. Facing superior American firepower, some Chinese officers were intimidated and hesitated taking decisive action. The 237th Regiment sent its 3rd Battalion as reinforcements. Even though the 237th defended the height through the night, two of its three battalions suffered very heavy casualties, with about 1,600 men identified as dead.[34]

In the early morning of November 28, the weather became even more severe as the temperature dropped to 30–40 degrees below zero. Because of the shortage of winter clothing, regiment and battalion commanders worried about their soldiers' vulnerability to exposure to the freezing temperature and continuing snow. Some officers and soldiers lost fingers, hands, feet, and ears to frostbite. That morning, there were men who had frozen to death in every company of both the 1/237 and 3/237.[35] That evening, the 1st Battalion of the 59th Division deployed a company to set up a roadblock south of Yudam-ni to stop a possible marine retreat to Hagaru-ri. By the next morning, all the men in that company had frozen to death at the post.[36]

On November 28, the 79th division commander, Xiao Jinghai, ordered his 235th Regiment to strike Hill 1282 again. The regiment commander sent his 4th Battalion (4/235), an entire battalion, at once to attack the marine positions on the hill and made the assault "at the height of fury."[37] During their forward movement, the charging troops of the 4/235 stepped on "lightning" mines, which lit up the ground like daytime. The marine officer did not order his men to open fire until the Chinese advanced to within ten to fifteen yards from them! The marines greeted the Chinese with an impenetrable fire. The 4th Battalion lost nearly 480 men during its twenty-minute attack.[38] The marine history notes, "When one formation was cut to pieces by machine-gun fire and grenades, another rose out of the night to take its place. By 0200, as the first attack began to taper off, the northeastern slopes of Hill 1282 lay buried under a mat of human wreckage."[39]

In the meantime, two regiments of the 59th Division of the 20th Army had encircled Yudam-ni from the south and southwest. Dai Kelin, commander of the 59th Division, occupied several hills along the road between Yudam-ni and Hagaru-ri.[40] His division included the 175th, 176th, and 177th Regiments. In the evening of November 28, Dai ordered the 177th to attack the marine defense at Yudam-ni from the south.

The 177th Regiment organized two of its battalions into several assault teams of 200–300 men each. The regiment commander led the attacks from two different directions. However, they failed to break through the marines' defense; nor did they destroy any marine unit. The officers of the 177th Regiment acknowledged, "The marines were indeed the toughest fighting unit among the UNF troops."[41] By November 29, the 177th Regiment cut off the retreat of the marines from Yudam-ni to Hagaru-ri.

The attacks by the 79th Division on November 27–28 were apparently "not synchronized."[42] One critique of the Chinese action points out that the division launched frontal attacks only through the two nights, claiming the division could have ended the marines' defense if it had organized rear and flank attacks as well. The Chinese were surprised that their superiority in numbers and quick encirclements did not bring them a quick victory. Although they were divided and surrounded, the marines immediately formed defensive perimeters and held their ground with artillery firepower and close air support. Facing superior marine firepower and air strikes, some of the regiment commanders were intimidated and hesitant to take decisive actions against the actually exhausted defending marines. Although the 79th Division had occupied several small hills north of Yudam-ni by November 28, none of its three regiments could destroy any of the marine companies.[43]

After the second night, Commander Xiao Jinghai could no longer launch another major attack due to his heavy casualties. The battle at Yudam-ni resulted in severe losses.[44] Aware of his division's limits, Peng Deqing had to order his 79th Division to halt its attack and reorganize its troops on November 29. The army command sent in its reserve force, the 94th Division, to Yudam-ni as reinforcements on December 1.

Massed Attacks and Heavy Casualties

On November 27–29, the 79th Division suffered very heavy casualties at Yudam-ni. The division lost five of its best battalions, about 6,500 men, more than two-thirds of its combat troops in two nights![45] Thereafter, the division was unable to make any major attack on the marines.[46] Since the army commanders had dispersed their troops, a massive attack on the marines and heavy Chinese casualties should have been avoided. In fact, large, usually battalion-sized, attacks were very common in the Battle of Chosin. Some Western historians describe the massed Chinese assaults as "human wave" attacks, launched "in an effort to overwhelm their better-armed opponents and capture their weapons."[47] Edward C. O'Dowd claims that "American infantrymen dubbed these massed groups of Chinese soldiers 'hordes,' and the attacks became known as 'human waves' (Ch: *renhai zhanshu*)."[48] Brian Steed states, "The Korean War is a demonstration of human wave tactics used against UN forces at the tactical level of strategy."[49] He further argues, "As the terrain became less restricted, they [Chinese forces] turned to the use of human wave assaults as the basic strategy from the operational level and below."[50]

The early Chinese offensive campaigns proved that massed attacks were effective in October 1950. Bruce A. Elleman describes the Chinese "human wave" attacks during the CPVF First Campaign: "Simultaneously, they attacked from the north, northwest, and west, utilizing frontal assaults composed of waves of infantry variously described as a 'human sea' or a 'swarm of locusts.'"[51] During that time, CPVF battalion-level attacks typically surprised UNF troops, especially the "moonlight attacks" and in close combat.[52] Some early successes of large-scale assaults were due to the "element of surprise and the Communist forces' ability to exploit the weakness of the coalition troops," especially ROK forces.[53] O'Dowd points out that, "expensive or not, the shock of a human wave attack often forced the defenders to break ranks to escape from the attacking mob, upon which the position would be lost."[54]

However, the massed attacks were not effective at Chosin in November. A battalion-sized assault often launched 600–1,000 men against one defense post at a narrow front in order to overcome marine firepower. This might allow some men to get close enough to the entrenched marines to throw their grenades, engage in close combat, and hopefully take over the post. In most cases at Yudam-ni, however, they ran head-on into strong defensive firepower and suffered heavy casualties. In fact, before the CPVF Second Offensive Campaign started, Peng

Dehuai, commander in chief of the CPVF, cautioned the Chinese generals to be "careful" in their attacks to reduce casualties. The massed attack was not among the offensive tactics in the CPVF's Operational Instruction on November 13. Mao Zedong also emphasized "self-preservation" as one of the objects of revolutionary warfare.[55]

Nevertheless, in the same article, Mao expressed the belief that "destruction of the enemy" is more important than "the preservation of oneself." "It should be pointed out," Mao says, "that destruction of the enemy is the primary object of war and self-preservation the secondary, because only by destroying the enemy in large numbers can one effectively preserve oneself." Mao continued, "China, though weak, has . . . a large population and plenty of soldiers." Thus, he suggested CCP commanders "make use of our two advantages, namely, our vast territory and large forces" by "employing several divisions against one enemy division, several tens of thousands of our men against ten thousand of his."[56]

The CPVF commanders certainly followed Mao's strategy of revolutionary war in the Second Offensive Campaign. Peng Dehuai asked all his armies to "create[e] a striking superiority" in their battle planning.[57] At the CPVF's First Expanded Party Committee meeting at Taeyu-dong on November 13, he even used the Chinese classic deception case of Sun Bin in the Warring States Period (475–221 B.C.). "We will use one regiment to pin down enemy's three regiments and concentrate our three regiments to annihilate one enemy regiment, creating a superior striking power while our forces and the enemy's force are equal."[58] Peng's November 28 instruction to the armies emphasized victory again. "This campaign is a decisive one to the Korean War. [We] hope [you] overcome all the difficulties and to be prepared to pay any price for it [victory]."[59]

The order to attack the UNF with massive troops in order to destroy more enemy units was also included in the CPVF's Political Mobilization Instruction on November 24.[60] The instruction called for the forces to "wip[e] out several more enemy divisions decisively." It called each CPVF army to draft specific annihilation plans and asked them to participate in a contest to see which army could win more battles, and which one could capture more enemy prisoners. The instruction also put forth the slogan: "Bravery Plus Tactics Means Victory!"[61]

Peng's orders and the CPVF instructions put the 9th Army Group commanders under tremendous pressure to exploit their manpower. Under these instructions, all the 9th's armies were required to use ample forces to divide UNF units into several pieces on an operational scale and annihilate each enemy piece in turn. Song Shilun and his officers agreed with Mao and Peng on "using superior striking force."[62] The field commanders believed their superior numbers would offset their inferior equipment and technology and would be a decisive factor in winning the battle. Both officers and soldiers had been told that the American army was a "paper tiger" and was suffering from "low morale," and that "American troops were not invincible but were absolutely defeatable."[63] Both officers and soldiers believed their "fighting spirit" would lead them to victory.[64] Even though the Chinese soldiers were politically motivated and able "to advance straight at the enemy," according to O'Dowd, "human wave attacks rarely are the tactical choice of a combatant" who faces an opponent with greater firepower.[65] Nevertheless, it seemed necessary for army, division, and regiment commanders to send an entire battalion to charge a hill to break through the marine lines.

Army commanders viewed such tactics as acceptable and affordable. Many even considered it necessary to sacrifice small units like an infantry battalion to help a larger force to accomplish its greater objectives. The 20th and 27th Armies had an advantage in numbers of troops since both were "oversized" armies. Other CPVF armies normally had a 3-3 formation, in which each army had three divisions, and each regiment had three battalions. However, the armies of the 9th Army Group were enlarged in China to a 4-4 formation: each army had four divisions, and each regiment four battalions.[66] Moreover, the armies of the 9th were also guaranteed reinforcements and replenishment during and after the Battle of Chosin. Therefore, at the army level, the commanders were able and willing to deploy a large-scale attack deploying and even sacrificing more assault troops if necessary. In Peng Deqing's November battle instruction, for example, the 27th Army commander demanded that his officers "make a daring attack with your troops . . . without fear of casualties, and fight the battle absolutely to the end."[67] Under the guideline, all the divisions were required to use ample troops to attack the marines in an attempt to annihilate each encircled enemy regiment. Nevertheless, the large-scale charges did not give the Chinese any overwhelming advantage in manpower to offset the marines' firepower, since the CPVF was indeed a preindustrial enlisted force, with archaic and mixed ordnance, limited mobility except by rapid marching with light loads, poor radio communications, and awful medical care. Very few wounded Chinese returned to duty.[68]

At the division level, Commander Xiao Jinghai and other officers had also deemed it necessary to sacrifice moderately sized units (like a battalion) to destroy the marines at Yudam-ni in an attempt to accomplish their mission.[69] They had not learned to flow around embattled hilltop American companies. When they launched such attacks on the night of November 27, they ran into a hail of gunfire. When the 79th Division confronted a stronger marine defense with superior firepower, the death toll among its regiments was horrendous. The division lost more than 4,500 men during the first night's attacks. Later, the division could merely reorganize the remnants of its two regiments into three companies.[70] The gap between the army commanders' optimistic plan for a big and quick overnight victory and the reality of the marines' strong firepower forced the Chinese division commanders to organize massive attacks, usually as large as a battalion, by sending more troops to charge American positions. The commanders soon found out that they were wrong about the marines, who they had believed were unprepared and afraid of night fighting, close combat, and death.

At the regiment and battalion levels, the junior officers followed the orders from the army and division to organize an entire battalion to attack. All the Chinese attacking force commanders shared the same understanding of their mission as did the commanders of the 235th and 237th Regiments, and all used similar tactics of massed formation attacks as did the commanders of the 1st and 4th Battalions. The Chinese offensives during the first night on November 27 proved that the massive attacks had lost their effectiveness, even in moonlight and at close combat. During the overnight attack, the Chinese assaults were unable to annihilate the marine units. During daytime close combat, the Chinese massed attacks were stopped by a wall of marine fire and could not even get close to marine positions. Confrontation with a modern army possessing superior firepower and air support took a horrendous toll on the lives of the Chinese soldiers.

In some cases, a battalion commander had to send all his men to attack the marines due to the serious and immediate threats of frostbite and starvation. The commander of the 2nd Battalion of the 235th Regiment (2/235), for example, had intended a small attack of fifty men against the marines first. It was a traditional PLA attacking tactic: first send a small testing team to locate the enemy's weakest link through preliminary engagement, and then commence a large-scale attack. However, none of his captains wanted to wait, and they were desperate enough to lead the charge since their men were freezing to death at the bottom of the hill. The assault would keep at least some men alive, and a successful attack over the hilltop might bring the men some winter coats, hats, and food from the Americans. Therefore, the 2/235 commander agreed and sent his entire battalion at once in a massive attack. He believed that a surprise attack with a large force of eight hundred men could overrun the marine company while they slept. He did not know that his heavy machine guns could not provide coverage due to their failures in the cold weather.[71] In addition, he did know that the marine company was prepared and waiting for their attack.

After the 2/235 commander ordered his battalion-sized attack, the four companies, more than eight hundred men, quietly approached the marine positions. In less than 20–30 feet, however, the marines opened fire, almost wiping out the two Chinese companies immediately. The 2nd Battalion continued its charge but failed to take the hill before the dawn. The massive attacks cost the battalion 650 dead overnight. Next evening, the 3rd Battalion of the 235th Regiment (3/235) came as reinforcements, replacing the 2nd and continuing the attacks. Again the massive attack on the marines lacked the element of surprise and merely exhausted the battalion. After losing two battalions, the 235th Regiment had to pull out of Hill 1282.[72]

The Chinese attacks at Yudam-ni during the first three days proved the ineffectiveness of massive attacks. The Chinese divisions continued their attacks until devastating losses were too high to launch another attack. PLA military historian Senior Colonel Shuang Shi acknowledges that the Chinese suffered such unexpected casualties because their "human wave" tactics were overcome by the marines' "fire wave" defense strategy.[73]

A Seesaw Battle over Hagaru-ri

At Hagaru-ri, the Chinese attacking force commanders shared the same concerns and had a similar understanding of their mission. On November 28, the 58th Division and one regiment of the 59th Division, some 16,000 troops total, encircled Hagaru-ri. The 12,000-man 58th Division, with Huang Chaotian as commander and Zhu Qixiang as deputy political commissar, surrounded the marines on three sides and cut off their path of retreat.[74] The division included the 172nd, 173rd, and 174th Regiments.[75] Huang deployed more troops for a tighter encirclement and the creation of roadblocks at Hagaru-ri. The hills around the village gave his troops hidden high ground, a buffer zone, unsuspected fields of fire, and valleys masked in heavy snow. Although it was the 20th Army's best division, the 58th was still not good enough to annihilate the U.S. Marines.

At Hagaru-ri, the marines included two artillery batteries, two infantry companies, an antitank platoon, and two battalion weapons companies. All the marines manning a four-mile perimeter came from engineer, headquarters, and service troops. Despite being divided and surrounded, they successfully formed defensive perimeters with their tanks and artillery firepower concentrated at three places. They also constructed a makeshift airstrip for resupply of ammunition and winter equipment, as well as for evacuating their wounded.[76] The key to the marine position was that Hagaru-ri was situated at the base of the reservoir, the site of the division headquarters and a logistical base served by the emergency airfield. Even though the Chinese trapped the 1st Marine at Hagaru-ri and cut it to five sections, they could not destroy each section completely.

About 10:30 P.M. on November 28, the 58th Division launched attacks on Hagaru-ri with its 173rd Regiment from the southwest and 172nd Regiment from the east. Huang Chaotian focused his attack on Hill 1071 in the east. He ordered thirty minutes of barrage fire of eighteen 82 mm and fifty-four 60 mm mortars. Each 82 mm fired 90 shells, and each 60 mm 120 shells, the biggest Chinese barrage during the Battle of Chosin.[77] After the barrage, the 172nd Regiment ordered its 2nd (2/172) and 3rd Battalions (3/172) to attack the marines on the hill. The massed attacks did not go very well against Hill 1071 because of the lack of coordination and communication between 2/172 and 3/172. No regiment or battalion commander had any operational map or Korean guide. The division headquarters had to send its officers to each regiment during the battle. Deputy Political Commissar Zhu Qixiang came to the 172nd and worked with the officers and staff at the command post.[78]

Political Commissar Zhu reorganized the assault of the 172nd Regiment around midnight. He sent four companies of 3/172 from two different directions against Hill 1071 around 2:00 A.M. The Chinese soldiers started by showering grenades on the marine positions, then snaked up the hilltop and opened fire, revealing their positions.[79] The Chinese troops could have attacked the marine artillery positions, which were poorly defended, to undermine the marines' defense. Eventually, by 4:00 A.M., Wu Guoxiang, deputy commander of the 3rd Battalion, led his charge and overran Hill 1071. But during the attack, Wu lost most of his men in the 4th, 5th, and 7th Companies, including the company captains. He could not continue his attack into Hagaru-ri. Zhu Qixiang ordered Wu to halt the attack but to stay at Hill 1071. Wu Guoxiang reorganized the remaining platoons and squads and dug in for the hill's defense on November 29.[80]

During the day of the 29th, Maj. Gen. Oliver P. Smith, commander of the 1st Marine Division, ordered the marines to counterattack in order to break the encirclement and to unite their scattered units. The battle turned out to be extremely fierce and difficult. Most of the Chinese soldiers killed at Hagaru-ri died not during their attacks but during their defense against the marine counterattacks.[81]

The 172nd Regiment sent more troops to the hill as reinforcements. In the morning, the deadly artillery firepower of the marines inflicted heavy casualties on the Chinese battalion, which now defended Hill 1071. The 2nd Battalion of the 172nd (2/172) ordered Captain Yang Gensi, the twenty-eight-year-old commander of the 3rd Company, to reinforce the hill with one of his platoons. The battalion command sent over a basket of yams before they moved out. Yang gave three yams to each man, who had not eaten for two days, and then led them up to the hill. The reinforcements, about fifty–sixty men, defended several positions on the hill. After they turned back the first attack of the marines, Yang had only a dozen men left. The captain reorganized his men with their weapons and ammunition. Then the marines launched the second attack with armored vehicles. Yang and his men defended their positions with one heavy machine gun and two light machine guns. However, it took four men to destroy one of the armored vehicles.[82] The marines fell back to the bottom of the hill. Before long, about fifty to sixty marines charged the height for the third time. There were only three men left in Yang's company. He asked one of them to report to the 2/172 headquarters for more reinforcements, and he stayed with the other two. When the marines broke their defense, Yang and his men ran out of ammunition. He threw himself into a group of marines while holding a twenty-pound satchel charge.[83]

Shortly after noon, the marines counterattacked Hill 1071 again. Captain Wang Xuedong, 1st Company of 2/172, recalled, "I never saw anything like the American marines' combat moves. When our defensive fire stopped their charge, the marines just dug in instead of retreating all the way back to their starting point. They stayed wherever they were stopped, waited for reinforcements, and then charged again. With each charge they came closer to our positions, until they were no more than two dozen meters away." After nearly four hours of heavy fighting and losing most of his men, Captain Wang had to pull his troops out of their defense positions on the hill. He recalled, "Our battalion ran out of ammunition, and we received no food supply at all. In addition, the temperature dropped to 30 degrees below zero. My company was nearly disabled due to combat casualties and frostbite." He had only eighteen men left in his company.[84] About 5:00 P.M., the marines began to shell the Chinese positions again, followed by a charge in the center of the 172nd Regiment by more than two hundred marines. The Chinese regiment lost several defensive positions by 7:00 P.M., when the marines stopped the counterattack and dug in their defense on Hill 1071.

Night at Chosin belonged to the Chinese. During the night of November 29, the 172nd Regiment renewed attacks on the hill. Captain Wang Xuedong recalled,

"Our regiment recovered some of the positions we had lost to the marines during the day, but we were unable to break through their lines before dawn."[85] Next morning, the marines retook the positions with well-organized counterattacks, strong firepower, and air support. The following day repeated the same story: the marines attacked and took the positions during the day, and the Chinese got them back at night. In Captain Wang's memories, his engagement with the marines at Hill 1071 was a battle that swayed back and forth, but the fighting was always intense.[86]

On November 30, the marines reattacked Hill 1071 with a dozen tanks. The 2/172 commander ordered his 6th Company to destroy the tanks. Xu Bangli, political instructor of the 6th Company, organized a few antitank teams to attack the tanks with explosives and hand grenades. Even though the company destroyed several tanks, it lost most of its men. The 2/172 battalion suffered heavy casualties during that morning. It totaled 1,200 troops before the battle, but had only about 100 men thereafter. The battalion commander, political commissar, and chief of staff were all killed in action.[87] The 172nd Regiment sent its 4th Battalion to replace the 2nd to continue the defense of Hill 1071 the next day. During the three days of fighting, the 172nd Regiment suffered very heavy losses of 3,500 men; nearly 90 percent of the regiment was gone!

The 173rd Regiment attacked Hagaru-ri from the south and west through the night of November 28. The regiment commander saw an opportunity to penetrate into the airstrip at Hagaru-ri. He sent his 5th, 6th, and 9th Companies to charge marine positions from two different directions toward the airstrip. The 6th Company, however, was slowed down by the wire entanglements, where it lost its captain and suffered heavy casualties. After the 6th Company lost its combat capacity, the 173rd Regiment sent 7th Company to continue the attack at the same point. That fresh company was able to break the marine defense and reach the airstrip with the two other companies. Without any communication and coordination, these companies engaged in house-to-house combat, and lost an opportunity to burn the supply piles and destroy the airstrip. The marines held their ground with their superior firepower and air cover. They exhausted the repeated Chinese attempts to annihilate any marine company or even smaller unit. Before the dawn, the Chinese companies had to pull out of the attack after losing so many men.

The Chinese troops also ran out of ammunition and food by the third day of their attacks. They received no food resupply, and the temperature had dropped to 30 degrees below zero.[88] Song's strategy of surprise and mobility sacrificed food supply. To march fast and secretly to Chosin, the division's daily food supply, only one-fifth that of an American division, would be cut in half. Many soldiers had not have anything to eat for three to five days by November 30.[89] Some of the companies sent officers to villages to look for potatoes, corn, yams, or anything for their starving men. Most potatoes and corn became frozen when they reached the front. Zuo Shiyong, deputy political instructor of the 3rd Company, recalled that his company had not received any food supply for four days. "Our captain asked me to look for Korean villagers around the hill with a squad. We walked for hours and could find only a couple of empty peasant houses. We were so lucky to dig out a bag of potatoes from a basement. We cooked them right there." But by the time they got back to the hill, all the potatoes were frozen. "No one complained since they were so hungry. Each man got two potatoes and began to suck on it like licking a rock."[90] The 27th Army tried to stop its troops' looting of local peasants after army headquarters received complaints that thousands of water buffalo, horses, dogs, and cats were killed and eaten by its troops.[91] The Korean peasants depended on water buffalo and horses for their farming and transportation.

Troop discipline failed and led to too much looting of the marines' clothing and food, rather than their weapons and ammunition. The desperate officers tried to save their soldiers from cold weather and starvation. Unless their troops captured American supplies, they would not survive the starvation and cold weather. Therefore, the Chinese commanders intentionally avoided shelling logistics targets at Hagaru-ri in order to capture the supplies. However, the marines destroyed all their supplies before retreating on December 3.

Commander Li Bin of the 173rd Regiment could not organize another attack in the early morning because of the heavy casualties and starvation. Addressing the surviving troops of the 7th and 9th Companies of his 2nd Battalion (2/173), he asked them to mount another attack on the airstrip. His soldiers promised to follow his order and go back to attack the marines, but, exhausted and hungry, they asked their commander to "give us one potato since we had not eaten anything for two or three days." Commander Li cried. He did not have any potatoes to give his men. He himself had not had anything to eat but some snow for two days. The 2/173 soldiers attacked the marines anyway.

Fighting for food and their own survival was common practice for the Chinese soldiers. Tang Yun, for example, a rifleman of the 9th Company of 2/173, and his squad were assigned to attack a small hill near the airstrip. All of them were starving, and they hoped to get some food from the enemy troops if they could overrun the marines on the hill. Tang had another motivation. He and four of his brothers had joined the GMD Army for food in 1948, after a famine occurred in the region and claimed the life of one of their sisters. They knew that the army would feed them. But they did not know that the GMD Army was losing the civil war to the Communists. The brothers were captured by the Communist troops in 1949, and all five reenlisted into the PLA after two months of political education.[92] Although they had no idea about Marxism and communism, they knew that they had to continue fighting in the CCP army for the same purpose: food and survival. After the PLA took over Shanghai, more than 15,000 former GMD soldiers were inducted into the 9th Army Group.[93]

There was something new for Tang Yun—political survival in the PLA. He stated, "Those who had served in the GMD Army needed to earn some new credits."[94] Fighting bravely seemed the best way to show his loyalty to the PLA, to earn himself a new identity with the CCP and gain access to political security and individual reputation. Hundreds of thousands of former GMD soldiers and officers joined the PLA and CPVF to escape criminal charges or avoid political movements, which had led to jail or execution for many of them. Of those who had already joined the PLA, a large number of so-called "liberated soldiers" were described as "new men" who wanted to stay in the PLA to establish new careers as revolutionaries. Tang Yun was eager to fight and willing to die. A heroic death would certainly earn recognition that would benefit his brothers and family within the newly founded Communist state.

After his captain signaled the charge, Tang Yun and his squad attacked the marine-held hill. After he threw the second grenade, he was knocked down by a shell and lost some teeth. "I wiped off the blood on my face, and continued to crawl into the marines' trenches." But he soon got shot in the left arm and was carried down the hill by his comrades. The 173rd Regiment recognized his bravery after the Battle of Chosin.[95]

After the 2/173 occupied several buildings around the airstrip, the men began to look for food and winter clothing instead of pressing their attack. They brought Commander Li Bin some American crackers, candies, and canned food. But two-thirds of them did not come back. The 173rd Regiment totaled almost 4,000 troops before its attacks the night of November 28. By the next morning, the regiment had fewer than 1,000 men able for combat.

Because of the heavy casualties, the 58th Division ordered the 174th Regiment to reinforce the 173rd. In the evening of November 29, the 8th Company, 3rd Battalion, 174th Regiment (3/174), was able to advance to the airstrip, but again, it had to pull out of Hagaru-ri the next morning. The 8th Company of 3/174 totaled 220 men before the night attack, but had only 100 in the morning. The 174th Regiment was then ordered to reinforce the 172nd Regiment at Hill 1071. On the night of November 30, Yao Liangen, deputy commander of the 3rd Battalion of the 172nd Regiment (3/172), led a squad to cross the front line and sneaked into several tents of the marines. They brought back three cases of American canned beans—fresh, not frozen, and delicious. In the 3rd Battalion, two men shared one can of beans that night. By November 29, the 58th Division could break only one portion of the perimeter, and the Chinese could not exploit this advantage because of marine firepower and the counterattacks by extemporized units.

After the two nights of attacks, the 58th Division suffered more than 7,000 casualties. It had only 1,500 men still capable for combat by November 30. Division Commander Huang Chaotian had 12,000 men three days prior. Because of the heavy casualties and ammunition shortages, the 20th Army Command ordered the 58th Division to halt its attack on November 30.[96] The U.S. Marines at Hagaru-ri continued their defense on December 1–6. They held the base to which the 5th and 7th Regiments could withdraw from Yudam-ni, evacuate their wounded by air, integrate infantry replacements, and load up with ammunition and fuel for "the attack in another direction" and escape to the sea. The Hagaru-ri garrison also rescued eight hundred survivors of Task Force MacLean and Task Force Faith, which had gotten strung out in a convoy of vehicles loaded with wounded.

Block the Task Force and Reinforcements

After the Chinese divisions split the X Corps at Yudam-ni, Hagaru-ri, and Koto-ri on the night of November 27, the American divisions tried to break through the Chinese encirclement and reestablish their connections and communications. The American generals did not realize that their rescue troops, convoys of reinforcements, and task forces became the easy targets of the 9th Army Group. Peng Dehuai at the CPVF Command thought of it as a new opportunity for the 9th's divisions to annihilate more UNF troops outside their pockets when they moved out from their base and tried to connect to each other. Peng cabled Song Shilun at 3:00 P.M. on November 28, asking the 9th to attack these UNF troops, which he said would "move up north to support the besieged ones"; Peng believed their exposure "would be probably most advantageous" to Song, whose aim was to annihilate them.[97]

On November 28, Peng Fei, commander of the 60th Division of the 20th Army, ordered his 179th Regiment to attack the garrison at Koto-ri.[98] His division included the 178th, 179th, and 180th Regiments. On that morning, a UNF task force was established at Koto-ri with the 41st Commando Battalion of the British Royal Marines under the command of Lt. Col. Douglas B. Drysdale. The task force was later reinforced by two companies of the 1st Marine Division and two tank platoons. Known as the Drysdale Task Force, it totaled more than 1,000 men with 141 vehicles and twenty-nine tanks.[99] Major General Smith organized it as reinforcements for Hagaru-ri from the ample forces at Koto-ri. Allan Millett points out that "General Smith ordered the move, the only error in the campaign."[100]

Later that day, the Drysdale Task Force moved out of Koto-ri with truckloads of ammunition, supplies, and communications equipment, which were needed at Hagaru-ri. The 20th Army was prepared to destroy the large convoy, which had left its defense base. Zhang Yixiang, commander and political commissar of the 20th, sent regiments from the 58th Division to reinforce the 60th Division and set up roadblocks between Koto-ri and Hagaru-ri. When the Chinese roadblocks stopped the Drysdale Task Force at Puseong-ri and Somintae-ri, the task force started attacking the Chinese defenses. The UNF troops met strong resistance from the 178th and 179th Regiments for four hours. One element of the task force broke through the Chinese position and reached Sapyeon-ri, where it was ambushed by the 58th Division on November 29.

In the afternoon of the 29th, the 60th Division's commander, Peng Fei, and chief of staff, Cai Qunfan, ordered their 179th Regiment to attack the task force. Following Peng's order, Chen Zhanshan, commander of the 179th, set up roadblocks with his three battalions to stop the convoy. At 3:00 P.M., however, the Drysdale Task Force broke a roadblock by taking over Hill 1182.1 from the 1st Battalion of the 179th (1/179) and continued its movement toward Hagaru-ri. The 1st Battalion lit up gasoline barrels in the middle of the road. Then, 1/179 Commander Zhang Baokun ordered his troops to open fire and stop the column. The tanks returned fire and continued to move forward. The 2nd Company of the 1/179 sent about twenty men with explosives and hand grenades to destroy the tanks. Led by Deputy Captain Shou Zhigao, the explosives team tried to get to the tanks and armored vehicles. Five of the twenty men eventually reached the tanks and then blew themselves up under the tanks.[101] The disabled vehicles completely blocked the road. Since the task force tended not to move off the road, it was not flexible enough to occupy the more advantageous terrain along the road before nightfall. This provided the 179th Regiment with opportunities to cut up the convoy after dark. During the fierce battle, the regiment suffered heavy casualties, and the 1st Battalion lost its deputy commander, Mao Xingbiao, who was one of a few national heroes of the PLA.

By 8:00 P.M., the Drysdale Task Force was tightly checked and held at the Keonjakea area, and it was split into three parts after several hours of fierce fighting. When darkness fell, Commander Zhang Jilun kept putting more pressure on the surrounded British and Americans by continuing attacks from the hills along the road. Lieutenant Colonel Drysdale tried to reestablish the links between his units, but the Chinese made the route impossible with ambushes and mortar fire. Around 9:30 P.M., Drysdale lost communication with and control of his team, the British and American units panicked and looked for a way out. One of the American tank units at the rear of the column was able to fight back to Koto-ri with twelve tanks in the night. The marine rifle company fought its way to Hagaru-ri the next morning with forty-eight casualties.[102]

Around 10:00 P.M., the 179th Regiment surrounded the middle section of the Drysdale Task Force. During their attack, the Chinese soldiers captured an officer who could speak Chinese since he had worked at the British Embassy in China. He was brought up to the hill to Zhang Jilun and then to Xu Fang, chief of the Political Department of the 60th Division. Xu sent him back down to the road to call the besieged troops to surrender.[103] After he got Xu's message, around midnight, Lieutenant Colonel Drysdale sent four officers to meet the Chinese commanders of the 179th Regiment and negotiate their surrender. The Chinese officers came to talk to Drysdale himself for further negotiation and reached some agreement. At 8:00 A.M. on November 30, most of the troops of the Drysdale Task Force laid down their arms and surrendered to the Chinese, including 237 British and American soldiers. However, some of the ROK soldiers, about 100 men, scattered into the woods.

Song Shilun was surprised by the successful attack on the Drysdale Task Force. He could not believe that when the 58th Division, the main strength of the 9th Army Group, failed to destroy a marine battalion in three days, the 60th Division wiped out an entire tank task force over one night. In the citation issued by the army group command, Song praised the 179th Regiment of the 60th that it "won the battle at a ratio of almost 1:1, while we usually could only defeat such American troops by employing five times more troops of ours than the Americans."[104]

Word that the 1st Marine Division was being cut off and surrounded by the Chinese forces at the Chosin Reservoir area shocked Washington. The U.S. Joint Chiefs of Staff (JCS) decided to intervene directly in command decisions by ordering General MacArthur to turn his offense into defense immediately and connect the 8th Army with X Corps to maintain an operational consistency.[105] By refusing to accept the JCS's order as usual, MacArthur ordered the X Corps to retreat to the Hamhung and Hungnam areas, breaking out of current encirclement and separations, and to be prepared for either a dig-in defense or an attack to the west to facilitate the 8th Army in its next operation.[106]

The shallow envelopment at Yudam-ni had allowed the marines to escape. The 59th Division failed to block the marines' withdrawal from Yudam-ni south to Hagaru-ri on November 30, about fifteen miles away. Division Commander Dai Kelin deployed his 177th Regiment to set up the roadblocks. The 1st and 2nd Battalions of the 177th (1/177 and 2/177) could only put together some simple roadside defense works because of the cold weather and lack of any equipment. Without effective air defense, the Chinese battalions suffered heavy casualties during the marine air attacks and artillery shelling.

The 5th Company of 2/177 lost half its men to the bombardment in the early morning of November 30. About 10:00 A.M., a marine company charged the defensive position of the 5th Company with three assaulting lines, each having thirty marines. The Chinese captain ordered his men to open fire when the first line of the marines reached a distance of 120–150 yards. After the 5th Company stopped the first attack, marine air and artillery bombed its position again for about an hour. Then, the marines charged again under cover of fire by the tanks. The 5th Company organized antitank teams to stop the tanks with explosives and hand grenades. It took a couple of teams, each with about seven to twelve men, to destroy one tank. In most cases, each team tried to cover one man to reach the tank and blow himself up with explosives. By noon, the 5th Company had lost all its officers and men. Zhou Wenjiang, political commissar of the 2/177, sent another company to defend the roadblock until that company, too, lost all of its men.[107] The marines broke the Chinese roadblocks at Yudam-ni the next day, enabling the 7th Marine Regiment to retreat south to Hagaru-ri.

The 9th Army Group's attacks on the U.S. Marines at Chosin became ineffective after November 30. Song Shilun realized manpower limits as well as the capabilities of the marines, not only to defend their positions, but also to inflict heavy casualties. Because of such huge, unexpected casualties, Song gave up his campaign goal of annihilating the 1st Marine Division. Chinese official military historians point out that after November 29, following three days of attacks at the Chosin Reservoir, Song had "an improved understanding of the American forces."[108] At 2:00 P.M. on November 29, he and Qin Jian, chief of staff of the 9th Army Group, cabled Peng that the Army Group Command decided to readjust campaign operations to concentrate its main strength to annihilate the U.S. 31st Regiment of the 7th Infantry Division at Sinhung-ni (east).[109] On November 30, with CPVF approval, Song Shilun and his commanders shifted their campaign objective from annihilating the 1st Marine Division to containing it while turning to an offensive against the 7th Division.

4

Annihilate the U.S. 31st Regiment

After three days of attacks against the U.S. X Corps on November 27–29, the CPVF 9th Army Group had a better understanding of the combat capabilities of the 1st Marine and 7th U.S. Army Infantry Divisions.[1] On November 30, the 9th's commander, Song Shilun, called a strategy conference because of the disappointing battle situation on the western side of the Chosin Reservoir. The 9th Army Group faced a standoff with the 1st Marine Division.[2] Song asked his subordinates about their thoughts on how to wipe out one or more American regiments to achieve his campaign goal. 27th Army Commander Peng Deqing's answer was to destroy the 7th Division's 31st Regiment first, since his army had isolated the infantry regiment on the eastern side of the reservoir.[3] Zhang Yixiang, commander of the 20th Army, agreed with Peng, saying that the 31st had become the weakest link of the X Corps so there was a better chance to wipe out the regiment. At the conference, Song decided to concentrate his divisions to annihilate the American infantry on the east bank of the reservoir while containing the marines on the west side.[4]

There was a gap between the high command and its field generals at Chosin. Although the 9th's commanders could hardly ignore or refuse the unattainable campaign goal set by Mao Zedong and their own chief, Peng Dehuai, they would always work out some tactical flexibility so that realistic objectives could be pursued and lower expectations met. After they found it almost impossible to destroy the 1st Marine Division, they shifted their campaign focus to the 7th Division at Chosin. While emphasizing loyalty to the high command and discouraging strategic debates, the CPVF field generals had to find their own ways to fight and win the battle. With CPVF Command approval, Song and his commanders changed the focus of their offensive campaign at Chosin. Instead of attempting to annihilate the 1st Marine, they made the 31st Infantry Regiment at Sinhung-ni on the eastern side of the Chosin Reservoir their priority target.[5]

How did the 9th Army Group Command deploy its divisions at Sinhung-ni (east)? On November 30, to reinforce its attacking force, according to the new plan, the 27th Army would combine two of its divisions, the 80th and 81st, at Sinhung-ni (east), while its 94th Division would remain in reserve. The 79th Division of the 27th Army and the 58th and 59th Divisions of the 20th Army would continue their attacks on the marines at Yudam-ni and Hagaru-ri to prevent the 1st Marine Division from any rescue attempt of the 31st Infantry Regiment. The 9th Command also ordered its 26th Army to march south day and night to participate in the Battle of Chosin.[6] Song Shilun intended to go to the front command post of the 27th Army. Tao Yong, deputy commander of the army group, refused Song's leaving from the army group command in the northern mountains, about eleven miles north of Chosin. Instead, Tao came to join Zhan Da'nan, deputy commander of the 27th Army, at the combined front command post of the 80th and 81st Divisions to execute the new annihilation plan.[7] As an experienced field commander, Zhan Da'nan had been in charge of Chinese forces at Sinhung-ni (east) since November 27.[8] At that moment, Zhan was confident in his troops' ability to annihilate the American infantry troops, since his division, more than 14,000 strong, outnumbered the estimated 1,000 American defenders.[9]

Misinformation and Delays, November 27

Zhan's intelligence was wrong. On November 27, he lacked accurate information on the U.S. forces on the eastern front. The American infantry that advanced to the eastern side of the Chosin Reservoir under the command of Colonel Allan D. MacLean were designated Task Force MacLean.[10] Colonel MacLean was the commander of the 31st Regiment, U.S. Army 7th Division. The regiment was known as the "Polar Bear Regiment" from a presidential award it had received for its tough fighting in Siberia during World War I. At Chosin, Task Force MacLean included an infantry battalion from the 31st Regiment, a battalion from the 32nd Regiment, a field artillery battalion from the 7th Division, a battery from the 15th AAA (Anti-Aircraft Artillery) Automatic Weapons Battalion, and a tank company. The task force was composed of regiment combat teams (RCTs), totaling 3,200 officers and men, three times more than the Chinese commanders expected.[11]

On the afternoon of November 27, Task Force MacLean traveled north along the eastern bank of the reservoir from Hagaru-ri and dispersed to seven different locations over eight miles along the road. The forward units of the task force, the 1st Battalion of the 32nd Regiment (1/32) and the RCT of the 31st Regiment (RCT/31), under the command of Lt. Col. Donald C. Faith Jr., advanced north about twelve miles from Hagaru-ri to Neidongjik. Then, four miles behind, the 3rd Battalion of the 31st Regiment (3/31) held its position in Sinhung-ni (east) around the inlet of the reservoir at the mouth of the Pungnyu-ri River, which some American troops just called "the Inlet." MacLean's command post and a heavy-mortar company were positioned between Neidongjik and the Inlet. The 57th Field Artillery Battalion (FAB) under the command of Lt. Col. Ray O. Embree was in positions on the western side of Hill 1656, about a mile south of the Inlet. Another four miles to the south, the tank company, a medical company, and the rear command post of the 31st Regiment stayed at Hudong-ni, a roadside village about four miles from Hagaru-ri.[12]

At 4:30 P.M. on November 27, Zhan Da'nan issued his order to the 80th Division to attack all the units of Task Force MacLean along the eastern side. The division included the 238th, 239th, and 240th Regiments. After receiving the 242nd Regiment from the 81st Division, the 80th had four regiments and totaled 14,334 officers and soldiers with Rao Huitan as commander. Among other divisional officers were Zhang Yingbo as political commissar and Peng Hui as assistant commander.[13] After the Battle of Chosin, Peng Hui became the commander of the 80th Division.[14] Zhang Yingbo was promoted to chief of staff and deputy commander of the 23rd Army. He was killed on the front in central Korea on February 21, 1953.[15]

As Song Shilun had done to the 1st Marine Division on the west bank, Zhan Da'nan decided to attack and encircle all the American infantry troops at the same time on the east bank of the Chosin Reservoir. He would then conduct a "piecemeal" annihilation, destroying the enemy groups one by one. Zhan assigned his 238th Regiment to lead the attack from the northwest with the center of Sinhung-ni as the primary target for annihilation. The 238th Regiment had four infantry battalions plus some artillery units under the command of Yan Chuanye.[16] According to Zhan's order, the 239th would attack Sinhung-ni from the east by taking over Hills 1456 and 1200 to assist the 238th Regiment. The 240th was assigned to attack Neidongjik from the north. In the meantime, the 242nd Regiment would attack from the south and encircle Task Force MacLean from behind to cut off its escape route to Hudong-ni.[17]

Lack of good intelligence seriously undermined the combat effectiveness of the Chinese regiments. The commanders of the four regiments thought that each regiment would attack one U.S. infantry company with a small artillery unit as the annihilation target.[18] They did not know that each Chinese regiment actually faced an entire American battalion with strong artillery support and tank units. Moreover, the regiments did not have any operational map or a Korean guide. After the 238th's commander, Yan Chuanye, ordered his 1st and 2nd Battalions (1/238 and 2/238) to move into their staging sites, both battalions went to the wrong locations. Following an outdated WWII Japanese map, the battalion commanders moved to a point four miles away from their attack staging site. Commander Yan had to reassign his 3rd Battalion (3/238) as the attacking force. The redeployment delayed the 80th Division's attacks for hours. Around 12:00 A.M., the division command ordered all its regiments to wait since the 238th Regiment was not ready.[19]

By 1:30 A.M. on November 28, the division had not yet ordered the attack. Its regiments could not wait any longer since the extremely cold temperature began to take its toll on troops hiding in the snow. Zhang Guijin, political commissar of the 2nd Battalion of the 239th Regiment (2/239), complained to his regiment commander. "Why don't we start our attack? We're freezing to death while waiting here!"[20] His concerns about the deadly temperature worried other officers as well that evening. The 7th Company of the 2/238 was also hiding in the snow through the night. Song Xiesheng, assistant captain of the 7th, witnessed an entire Chinese company freezing to death that night! During the hiding period, Song Xiesheng saw another company lying in the snow on the other side of a hill path. After making contact, Song knew that they were the Security Company of the 238th Regiment, and that they had to wait in the snow for their battalion's return from the wrong location. When Song Xiesheng received the order to attack, he sent his men to contact the Security Company. His men came back with the sad news that all the soldiers of that company had frozen to death in their hiding place. "Are you sure?" Song could not believe it. His men replied they had checked all the frozen corpses and there were no survivors.[21]

By 2:00 A.M., Zhang Guijin and his 2nd Battalion could not wait any longer, since they had captured a few American guards from their outpost on Hill 1200 for information.[22] The American prisoners told Zhang that the American company, having been told that the Chinese troops were about 50–60 miles away, had not built any defensive works and did not expect any attack that night.[23] Nevertheless, Zhang Guijin became worried about the American change of guards who would soon find out about the missing men. After his urgent requests, the regiment commanders asked the division command for an immediate attack. Another reason for Zhang's repeated requests was his troops' hunger. The men had not eaten anything for two days. All they wanted was the go-ahead to attack, which would give them the opportunity to get food and winter clothes from the Americans.[24]

Surprise Attack and Cutoff, November 28

Finally, about 3:00 A.M. on November 28, the division issued the order to all its regiments to attack Task Force MacLean in full force at multiple points. The 239th Regiment launched its 1st Battalion (1/239) to attack Hill 1456, while the 2nd Battalion (2/239) struck on the left to flank Hill 1200 (or 1190), and the 3rd Battalion (3/239) attacked on the right. Without detailed information on the American troops, the Chinese battalion commanders had to locate the American positions, probe their fire points, and press their attack. Both the 2nd and 3rd Battalions were able to take over the hill and fight their way into the campgrounds and command post of U.S. 3/31.[25] When the 2nd Battalion ran up to Hill 1200, there was no resistance since all the Americans were still sleeping in their tents. The battalion political commissar of the 2/239, Zhang Guijin, ordered his men to shoot into the tents before the Americans could get out.[26] After they gained control of the hill, Zhang led his battalion to attack Hill 1456.[27]

The Chinese attacks were effective through the first night since American companies of the 3/31 and the FAB batteries were caught by surprise. The Chinese battalions did not look for prisoners by checking American soldiers on the ground since they did not want to slow down their charge, nor did they have any food for POWs. (Only the command of the 3rd Battalion reported capturing eleven American POWs during the night.[28]) The Chinese believed that some American soldiers played dead during the attack. Later Zhang ordered his men to do an "additional shot" at all the dead Americans lying on the ground or under vehicles.[29] The 2nd Battalion of the 239th Regiment received the army's recognition after the Battle of Chosin.[30]

Led by Captain Li Changyan, the 4th Company of the 2/239 quickly overran Hill 1100, where the Chinese faced little organized resistance as they did at Hill 1200. Most of the Americans were killed around their tents as they rose up to return fire. The 4th occupied the hill with only a few casualties.[31] Some of his soldiers were shot when they entered American tents looking for coats, food, and ammunition. Other men were killed before they could figure out how to use American automatic weapons with which they had just replaced their WWII Japanese-made 38-model rifles.[32] The company also lost its political instructor, Zhuang Yuandong, at Hill 1100. Captain Li did not stop at Hill 1100; the 4th Company continued to advance west toward the field artillery battalion by following the communication wires on the ground.[33] One American officer later reported that the Chinese "infiltrated through the line because the men were not alert." He believed that the Chinese "caught the soldiers dozing in their foxholes and simply bypassed or overran some positions before they were discovered."[34]

When they approached several houses on the roadside, the 4th Company of the 2/239 faced a strong defense and lost a couple dozen men. Captain Li Changyan divided his company into several teams to fight a house-by-house battle. Although one of the teams broke into one big house and shot several American officers, they did know it was the 3/31 battalion command post. The assault teams inflicted some casualties, and those wounded in the close combat included the commanders of both the 3rd Infantry Battalion and the 57th Artillery Battalion.[35] The Chinese, however, did not have time to destroy the 105 mm howitzers. Therefore, the artillery battalion was able to use these guns to fire on the Chinese the next morning. Before dawn, 4th Company pulled out of the village with only sixty-seven casualties.[36] Its successful first-night attack, which quickly and deeply penetrated the UNF line, became a combat example for other CPVF companies. The 27th Army awarded the 4th Company of the 2/239 the "Combat Model Company of Sinhung-ni" after the Battle of Chosin.[37]

While the 239th almost overran the 3/31 and the two firing batteries of the 57th FAB at the Inlet of the reservoir, the 238th Regiment eventually reached Sinhung-ni from the east. However, the 238th attack was late and lacked the element of surprise. Regiment Commander Yan Chuanye and his assault troops faced a strong defense just before dawn.[38] The 7th Company under the command of Song Xiesheng met several tanks in Sinhung-ni. His men had no antitank gun and no explosives. The company had only two pieces of 92 mm infantry artillery, which had run out of shells in a brief barrage. The only weapons they had against the tanks were grenades. Since they had to get close enough to the tanks to throw their grenades, it took more than a dozen men to destroy one tank.[39]

During the early morning attack, the 8th Company of the 3/238 was stopped by a machine gun. Kong Qingsan, squad leader of the artillery regiment, brought his 92 mm to the 8th Company to provide artillery support. Kong Qingsan ordered his men to set up the artillery piece, but they could not find another supporting point for the left leg of their 92 mm gun. Kong used his body to support the gun and ordered his men to fire. While the shell destroyed the American position, the strong recoil killed Kong Qingsan instantly.[40] The 238th Regiment, however, failed to break into Sinhung-ni (east) before dawn.

Through the night, the 240th Regiment's three battalions attacked the Americans in the north. The 3rd Battalion (3/240), under the command of Political Commissar Bi Zheyang, attacked the American positions between the Inlet and Neidongjik. After the battalion rushed to a cluster of eight or nine farmhouses, Bi ordered his 3rd and 4th Companies to organize several teams to attack them. Through fierce fighting, the companies took over these houses, not knowing that two of these houses were the command post of the 31st Regiment. Zhang Jiqing, a squad leader of the 3rd Battalion, used a large banner from one of the houses to wrap up gathered food and medicine. Later he showed it to his battalion political commissar. Bi Zheyang was astonished since it was the 31st regimental flag. It was sent to the army command and from that time became a First-Class Military Relic in China's National Military Museum at Beijing.[41]

The 3rd Battalion then joined the 1st Battalion and attacked Neidongjik. Shao Mingze, commander of the 1st Battalion (1/240), thought that there was only one American company in a forward position along the northern hills, but instead he faced the entire 1st Battalion of the U.S. 32nd Regiment (1/32). His battalion suffered heavy casualties at Hills 1318 and 1216 in the first few hours.[42] The 9th Company of the 1/240 sent its 2nd and 3rd Platoons to attack Hill 1318. The 2nd Platoon lost most of its men and officers halfway to the hill. Wu Jiangwei, leader of the 4th Squad of the 2nd Platoon, led the charge and took the hill but lost all his men. Wu stayed at the hill by himself until the 3rd Platoon joined his defense. By 4:00 A.M. the next morning, the two battalions (1/240 and 3/240) occupied the two hills at Neidongjik.[43]

Through the early morning of the 28th, the 80th Division was able to break through Task Force MacLean's defense line along the road. The 238th Regiment occupied the high ground north of Sinhung-ni to separate the 1/32 battalion from the other battalions. The 239th Regiment controlled Hills 1456 and 1200 in the east, isolating the 3/31 and 57th FA Battalions. The 240th Regiment took over the hills around Neidongjik in the north. In addition, the 242nd Regiment occupied Hill 1221 and blocked the road south to Hudong-ni. By daylight of November 28, Army Assistant Commander Zhan Da'nan had forced Task Force MacLean into to a small pocket of less than one square mile on the eastern side of the Chosin Reservoir.[44]

Nevertheless, the surprise Chinese attacks, though aggressive, were limited by misinformation and poor communication. Zhan Da'nan did not have accurate information on Task Force MacLean. It became even worse when all the telephone wires between the division command and regiment commands were cut by the

American shelling merely an hour after the 80th Division launched the attacks. Commander Zhan had no direct telecommunication with any of his regiments through the entire night.[45] Companies of the 238th and 239th Regiments had broken into Sinhung-ni, but they had no coordination or cooperation at all. Each company, platoon, and squad was fighting its own battle, and all failed to destroy the artillery pieces and tanks, which the American troops then used for their counterattacks the next morning.[46] Major General Shao Mingze still complained many years later, after he became the deputy commander of the 27th Army. As a battalion commander at Neidongjik, he was misinformed and thus miscalculated. He organized a massive attack by sending his entire battalion against what he thought was an American company. After taking heavy losses, he realized that there was an entire American battalion (1/32) at the hilltop.[47]

Moreover, the weather affected their tactics. Heavy snow caused operational problems and led to higher casualties, including both combat and noncombat. During the predawn attack, all three regiments of the 80th Division suffered heavy casualties.[48] The 238th Regiment had lost 58 percent of its combat troops during the four hours of its attacks. Wang Kefu, operation chief of the 239th Regiment, recalled that the next morning he looked through the hills and saw hundreds and hundreds of dead bodies wearing yellow uniforms. He cried because he knew that many of them were not killed in their attacks, but were just wounded. Since the regiment did not have enough manpower and medical personnel to take them down the hill, most of the wounded soldiers froze to death through the night.[49] The 240th Regiment also suffered heavy casualties. The 3rd Company of the 3/240, for example, lost three of its four platoons. The captain, political instructor, and other company officers were all killed during a two-hour attack on Neidongjik. The 242nd Regiment lost seven of its ten attacking companies.[50] Through the first morning, the 80th Division lost nearly 30 percent of its troops, more than 3,200 men, the heaviest casualty rate of all the seven attacking divisions at Chosin.[51]

Maintaining the Encirclement, November 28–29

In the morning of November 28, Commander Zhan Da'nan was not excited about having successfully separated Task Force MacLean from the other UNF units. He became worried. First, battleground intelligence convinced him that the size of the American force was three times what he had expected. Second, he had lost so many men in the first night of attacks that his division could not destroy the 31st Regiment alone. Third, his offensive had not yet inflicted significant casualties on the American troops, which soon organized counterattacks on the 28th. Zhan ordered all his regiments to withdraw from their held positions to the hills and high ground outside Sinhung-ni.[52]

After receiving the withdrawal order, some battalion and company commanders did not understand why they needed to pull out since the American troops seemed to be defeated. Zhang Guijin, battalion political instructor of the 2/239, called the division headquarters and requested to continue his attack during the daytime. The division staff rejected his request by warning him of daytime heavy air attacks that could cause more casualties. The division would resume the attacks later that evening. Zhang, however, insisted: "OK, we would stop our attack, but how about staying where we are. We can build our defense here [at the hills]. Don't have to pull back." The division officer countered that all Chinese troops were to pull out of their occupied positions before daybreak on November 28.[53]

Zhan's calculation was correct this time. The RCTs of the 31st and 32nd Regiments organized counterattacks in the morning and tried to break the Chinese encirclement. The tank company from Hudong-ni, about two miles south, moved northward with air support and tried to reconnect with Task Force MacLean. Brig. Gen. Henry I. Hodes, assistant commander of the 7th Division, also rode with the convoy.[54] The 3rd Battalion of the 242nd Regiment on Hill 1221 blocked the column, including sixteen tanks under the command of Capt. Robert E. Drake.[55]

The 3rd Battalion deployed its 9th Company on the eastern side of the road and the 7th on the west.[56] Around 7:00 A.M., the tank column approached the roadblock and was stopped by the fire from both sides. Captain Drake ordered four tanks to attack the Chinese 9th Company and three tanks to target the 7th Company. Ye Yong'an led his antitank team of the 9th Company, hiding on the low ground and waiting for the tanks. When the four tanks moved close to their position within about twenty meters, Ye and two men jumped out of their hiding place, throwing their grenades and setting one tank on fire. Without riflemen's fire protection, the other tanks stopped, trying to find their way around the burning tank. Ye and his team members immediately climbed onto the other tanks, scrambling up their sides; they destroyed three more tanks.[57] Captain Drake and his tanks swept the Chinese troops with machine-gun fire. U.S. planes also struck Chinese troops on Hill 1221 with napalm, rockets, and machine guns. But the tank column failed to pass the hill. After losing four tanks, Drake returned to Hudong-ni in the late afternoon since he did not want to stay on the road without riflemen through the night.[58]

Lt. Col. Don Faith, of the 1/32 battalion, at Neidongjik also tried to reclaim the high ground lost the night before and reconnect his forward companies. He struck the Chinese troops with air attacks and artillery, but the Chinese refused to give up on these hills. Faith sent the reinforcements from Headquarters Company to his C and B Companies to retake a knoll occupied by the Chinese during the night.[59] By the afternoon, the troops of the 1/32 drove the Chinese away and cleared the knoll. General Ned Almond visited the Task Force MacLean command post by helicopter and represented Faith and two other men with the Silver Star.[60] The general told Faith, "We're still attacking and we're going all the way to the Yalu. Don't let a bunch of goddamn Chinese laundrymen stop you!"[61]

The 3/31 battalion also launched counterattacks against the Chinese-held hills in the south. The Chinese officers were surprised and not ready to defend their positions on the hills along the road. Thinking they had defeated the American troops, they were busy going through captured American weapons and supplies. The 240th Regiment suffered heavy casualties due to napalm, rockets, artillery shells, and machine-gun fire. By the afternoon, the regiment pulled out of its defensive positions from Hills 1100 and 1200.[62] U.S. planes dropped tons of supplies at Sinhung-ni and Neidongjik in the late afternoon.

Through the day, Zhang Guijin, political commissar of the 2/239, failed to defend his positions and lost the high ground to the American troops. Zhang recalled that his battalion suffered very heavy casualties. His 6th Company, for example, had only 20 men by noon after more than 150 men had been killed.[63] In the afternoon, the 239th Regiment's chief of staff came to Zhang's battalion command post and organized a counterattack that included the 5th Company of the 2/239. Zhang disagreed with his superior officer, arguing that the 5th was the 2/239's reserve and the last company left. This daytime counterattack would expose this company to American air and artillery firepower. But Chief of Staff Wang insisted and ordered Zhang to send his 5th Company to retake the high ground immediately. Zhang refused and complained to Regiment Commander Zhang Jinyi: "Chief Wang is ordering our attack with the 5th Company right now. It will sacrifice our battalion. We have no men left. We can wait for tonight. We will have a better chance to retake the hill without heavy casualties, and save our battalion." Commander Zhang agreed and talked his chief of staff into a delayed counterattack that evening.[64]

Around 6:30 P.M. on November 28, the 80th Division resumed its attack on Task Force MacLean. The battalions of the 239th Regiment organized a company-sized attack with a couple hundred men at once. They again advanced into Sinhung-ni from the south and east, inflicting some casualties on the 3/31 troops. Because of the lack of communication and cooperation, the Chinese soldiers engaged in haphazard battles, including hand-to-hand fights, inside the village. They fought in separate, different directions without any coordination. All the Chinese soldiers were eventually killed inside the 3/31 perimeter. Song Xiesheng recalled, "We were told that the enemy force was a paper tiger. Therefore, we organized massive attacks. Hundreds and hundreds of soldiers charged the enemy without artillery coverage and firepower protection. Then, we found out the enemy was not a paper tiger, but a real tiger with strong firepower and combat effectiveness." Song was still critical of the political propaganda many years after the Battle of Chosin. "Why didn't you tell us the truth about the American army? We could have been better prepared and reduced the huge casualties. Many men could have lived today."[65]

The 240th Regiment renewed its attack on Lieutenant Colonel Faith's 1/32 battalion at Neidongjik. Around midnight, the division command ordered a barrage on only two of Faith's battalion's positions. Due to lack of ammunition, the artillery shelling lasted for only five minutes. The 240th then sent its battalions to attack from the left and right. Its 2nd Battalion was able to penetrate Faith's right flank, attacking B Company and heading toward Faith's command post.[66] Since the Chinese soldiers' most effective weapons were their grenades, they had to run up to the hill and get close enough to throw their grenades toward American positions. Under machine-gun fire, the attacking troops suffered heavy casualties, and soon lost too many men before they could break Faith's battalion.[67] Around 2:00 A.M. on November 29, Faith received the order from Colonel MacLean to retreat. Faith ordered his battalion to pull out of their perimeter around 3:00 A.M., retreating south to join the 3/31 at the Inlet.[68]

Commander Zhan Da'nan again had to stop the attacks the next morning after his regiments suffered so many casualties.[69] The second-night attacks were not as successful as those on the first night since the American companies were prepared. The Chinese troops still recovered some of the high ground lost to the Americans during the daytime.[70] All four Chinese regiments, however, had very heavy casualties after two nights of attacks, losing 52–68 percent of their combat troops. The 238th Regiment reorganized its troops into a mere six infantry companies, about 50 men in each company, totaling 300 able-bodied soldiers. (The regiment had more than 3,600 men two days prior.) The 239th Regiment could form only three infantry companies and one machine gun company.[71] The 3rd Battalion of the 239th had just 120 men left.[72]

Reinforcements and Roadblocks, November 29–30

In the early morning of November 29, Faith's 1/32 began to move out of Neidongjik and retreat south to join MacLean's 3/31 at Sinhung-ni (east). Zhan ordered the 239th Regiment to stop Faith's vehicular column before it reached the Inlet. The regiment dispatched the 2nd Battalion to set up roadblocks north of the village. Zhang Guijin, political commissar of the 2/239, decided to establish a roadblock near the mouth of the Pungnyu-ri River where the road made a sharp turn. Zhang and his men waited on the high ground along the road until later that morning when Faith's motor column moved within range. Zhang opened fire and stopped the trucks on the road.[73] Faith deployed his machine guns to return fire and sent troops to attack the Chinese on the high ground.[74]

While Faith's motor column was under attack, Col. Alan MacLean was watching the fight directly across a narrow expanse of ice on the reservoir finger. Hearing a shot fired from across the reservoir finger, MacLean thought his own forces had fired on Faith's, and he tried to run across the ice to stop the shooting. He was mistaken and was shot dead by the Chinese.[75] Faith broke through the roadblock and joined the 31st Regiment around 12:30 P.M. on November 29.

After Colonel MacLean's death, the task force was redesignated as Task Force Faith. Lieutenant Colonel Faith, a thirty-two-year-old Georgetown University graduate, assumed the command of the two infantry battalions and one artillery battalion. Faith, who had served in the U.S. military mission to China after WWII, knew a great deal about the PLA's strategy and tactics from the Chinese Civil War of 1946–49. In the morning of November 30, Maj. Gen. David G. Barr, commander of the 7th Division, flew to the Inlet perimeter by helicopter. Faith reported to the 7th Infantry Division commander that he had more than 500 wounded to bring out in case of a withdrawal. It was also reported that an American soldier had frozen to death in a sitting position in his foxhole.[76] After returning to Hagaru-ri, General Barr informed General Almond of the situation on the east bank of the Chosin Reservoir at the commanders' conference. After the meeting, General Hodes was instructed to prepare an order for Faith to withdraw all his troops from the Inlet perimeter back to Hagaru-ri.[77]

South of the Inlet, the tank company under the command of Captain Drake tried again to connect to the 31st Infantry from Hudong-ni through Hill 1221 on November 29. Drake hoped that the infantry support could help his tanks to make a breakthrough, which had failed the day before. The 3rd Battalion of the 242nd Regiment continued to occupy Hill 1221 and high ground on both sides of the road. The 242nd Command reinforced the 3/242 with the 2nd Battalion. Around 7:00 A.M., the tank column approached the roadblock. The 9th Company of the 3/242 burned several vehicles on the road to stop the tanks.[78] Having learned Chinese antitank tactics from the day before, all the tanks avoided getting too close to the Chinese, instead shelling and firing on the Chinese positions from a distance and inflicting heavy casualties on the 9th Company. After a full day of attack, however, Captain Drake failed to break through the roadblock or take Hill 1221.[79]

In the afternoon on November 29, U.S. planes dropped a large quantity of ammunition and food to Task Force Faith. Some of the supplies fell on the Chinese positions, however, including food, ammunition, and medicines. Faith's only hope depended on the 2nd Battalion of the 31st Regiment (2/31). General Almond had ordered the infantry battalion to move northward to rescue Task Force Faith. Nevertheless, the 2nd Battalion was still more than thirty miles away at Majon-dong to the south.[80] Moreover, the infantry battalion did not have sufficient transportation and was afraid of the Chinese roadblocks like those that had helped destroy the Drysdale Task Force on November 29–30.

Zhan Da'nan could not launch another major attack through the night of November 29 because of his heavy casualties. After two nights of attacks on November 27–29, his division had lost about 60 percent of its combat strength, more than 6,150 casualties.[81] Hunger, fatigue, and frostbite had turned many of the rest of Chinese soldiers into victims of exhaustion. Through the day, Zhan interrogated several POWs himself and was convinced that his division faced the RCTs of the 31st and 32nd Regiments, including two infantry battalions, one artillery battalion, and logistics units. The American troops had more than four battalions rather than four companies as Zhan was told before the battle.[82]

Nevertheless, the battleground situation favored the 80th Division since the American RCTs had been weakened through the two nights of attacks. The Chinese troops had a good opportunity to achieve a battle of annihilation on the east bank of the reservoir.[83] Zhan and his officers concluded that the American infantry demanded uninterrupted supplies, and would most likely operate during daytime since they depended too much on firepower, including air, artillery, and automatic weapons on the ground, and their mechanized units traveled along roads only.[84] If they could not organize superior firepower, or receive armored support, the individual infantry soldiers were not as effective as the Japanese soldiers in WWII.[85]

Therefore, Zhan Da'nan called the army command requesting reinforcements for him to continue the attack and eventually destroy Task Force Faith. He knew that the eastern side of the reservoir was not the direction of the main attacks, which had focused on the 1st Marine on the west side of the reservoir with four divisions. The 9th Army Group and the 27th Army put only one division against Task Force MacLean on the eastern side. Zhan explained that the 80th could not succeed without reinforcements due to the heavy losses. But he was confident that reinforcements from the 27th Army would guarantee a successful annihilation of the Americans on the eastern bank.[86]

At that moment, the 9th Army Group desperately needed a victory, after losing tens of thousands of its troops in the first two nights. To destroy Task Force Faith might be the only opportunity for a victory still left to Song Shilun since the battle with the marines had become a standoff by November 29. Therefore, Song and Tao Yong agreed with Zhan Da'nan and shifted the focus of their main attack from the 1st Marine Division to the 31st Infantry Regiment.[87] Song Shilun and his army commanders adjusted their campaign operation at the commanders' conference on November 30, by sending reinforcements to annihilate the 31st Regiment at Sinhung-ni first, and then coming back for the marines at Yudam-ni and Hagaru-ri.[88]

On November 30, the 9th Command ordered the 81st Division to reinforce Zhan Da'nan at Sinhung-ni. The division included the 241st, 242nd, and 243rd Regiments under Sun Ruifu, commander and political commissar of the 81st Division.[89] After the Battle of Chosin, he was promoted to assistant commander of the 27th Army. With reinforcements, Zhan Da'nan replaced the badly damaged 238th with the 241st Regiment and deployed the 242nd south to set up more roadblocks along the only road between Sinhung-ni (east) and Hagaru-ri to stop any UNF reinforcements from south and any withdrawal from north.[90]

Final Attack and Pursuit, November 30–December 2

After night had fallen on November 30, the temperature dropped drastically. Zhan Da'nan ordered his 80th and 81st Divisions to launch the final attack on the 31st Regiment from four directions. To avoid any communication and coordination problems, he set up a joint command post including all the commanders from both divisions.[91] Zhan attacked Sinhung-ni with the 238th Regiment from the southeast, the 239th from the south, the 240th from the northeast, and the 241st from the southwest. In the meantime, the 242nd Regiment set up a roadblock in the south at Hill 1221 between the Inlet and Hudong-ni.[92]

After a rapid fifteen-minute barrage in the late evening, the four regiments flooded the village through the night.[93] The regiments repeated the similar tactics of massed attacks and close combat to overrun the American defenses.[94] Again, there was no communication and coordination among the attacking regiments, and Zhan did not have any effective way to command the attacks. Each regiment, battalion, and company fought its own battle through the night.[95] By the early morning of December 1, all the Chinese regiments had broken through American positions and pressed the American troops into small pockets inside Sinhung-ni. And again, the Chinese attacking troops suffered heavy casualties. The 3rd Company of the 240th Regiment engaged in house-by-house fighting through the night. In the early morning, only one man was left in the entire company.[96] All the men of the 5th Company, 240th Regiment, except one liaison officer and a straggler, froze to death at their roadblock as they waited through the night to face any retreating Americans.[97]

In the morning of December 1, Tao Yang, assistant commander of the 9th Army Group, decided at the eastern front command post not to pull the troops back at the daybreak, as Zhan had done the previous two mornings. Tao Yang ordered all the troops to stay in the perimeter and continue fighting until the 31st Regiment was annihilated. The close combat made any American air or artillery support very difficult, if not impossible.[98]

Around 10:00 A.M. on December 1, seeing no hope of any UNF reinforcements and with his troops continuing to take casualties, Lieutenant Colonel Faith decided at a battalion commanders' conference to stage a breakthrough of the Chinese roadblock. He planned a retreat of the task force all the way back to Hagaru-ri to join the 1st Marine Division. At 1:00 A.M. the next morning, Faith ordered all supplies to be destroyed and led the rest of his troops to force their way out under cover of air support and fire from a dozen tanks.[99] It seemed manageable for him to bring the battalion south six miles along the road. His motorized troops would certainly run faster than the marching Chinese, who had suffered heavy casualties to the UNF air support covering the retreat.

Zhan Da'nan immediately turned his regiments from encircling and attacking operations into pursuit operations. The 238th, 239th, and 240th Regiments sent their troops after the retreating Task Force Faith.[100] Without communication and coordination, the Chinese companies, platoons, and squads fought separately whenever and wherever they encountered the American troops. Sui Chunnuan, squad leader of the 2nd Platoon, 7th Company, 3/240, led his men at a run for miles to stop a group of retreating Americans and engaged in a hand-to-hand fight to wipe out the American group, taking five POWs. Sui was decorated after the battle, and his squad became the "Combat Model Squad of Sinhung-ni."[101]

The waiting 242nd Regiment gave the retreating task force a head-on attack about two miles from where Faith had left. The 3rd Battalion of the 242nd (3/242) set up the roadblock and tried to stop the movement of Faith's motor column to the south. The 3/242 battalion fired ferociously into the retreating American troops from positions on Hill 1221.[102] Faith could not overrun the roadblock because the 3/242 battalion had destroyed the only road bridge. Around 4:30 A.M. on December 2, led by the tanks, Faith attacked the 3/242's positions with close air support and artillery bombardment.

Faith bypassed the destroyed bridge, managing to break through the 3/242 roadblock and continue his southward retreat.[103] Soon the 2nd Battalion of the 242nd (2/242) arrived as reinforcements to Hill 1221.[104] The 2/242 battalion chased the Task Force Faith column and charged into American troops from both sides of the road. The task force suffered casualties, and Faith was critically wounded and later died.[105] After Faith was wounded, Maj. Robert E. Jones, intelligence officer of the 1st Battalion, 32nd Regiment, took over the command of the task force. Before dark, Jones and the vehicular column broke through the roadblock at Hill 1221 and continued retreating south.[106]

At 9:00 P.M. on December 2, Major Jones reached Hudong-ni, about two miles from Hagaru-ri. Unfortunately for Major Jones and his men, the tank company and troops of the 31st Regiment had left the village and withdrawn to Hagaru-ri a day before.[107] The Chinese division had occupied Hudong-ni. When the Chinese fired on the task force from the village, Jones had fewer than two hundred men. The officers tried to break through the Chinese defense by speeding their trucks into Hudong-ni. But after the drivers were killed, the Americans were pushed out by the Chinese. Then, around 11:00 P.M., the task force collapsed, splitting into several groups that each struggled to make its way southward. Billy Mossman describes, "By midnight only the dead and seriously wounded remained at Hudong-ni. Among them was Colonel Faith, who sat dead of his wounds in the cab of a 2 1/2-ton truck."[108] At dusk, a group of American soldiers led by several tanks tried to break through to the west on the Chosin Reservoir. The lake ice broke and some of the tanks and troops sank into the reservoir.[109] Another group of the 3/31 made a final attempt to escape. But the Chinese troops from the 1/242 overran the Americans.[110] Starving and cold, some of the pursuing Chinese soldiers stopped to go through abandoned backpacks and supplies in search of food, winter clothes, and ammunition. As a result, some of the American soldiers evaded capture.

By 4:00 A.M. on December 3, the battle against the U.S. 31st Regiment was over.[111] Stephen R. Taaffe concludes that "of the approximately 3,200 soldiers deployed to the Chosin Reservoir's eastern shore, only 385 escaped to Hagaru-ri, most by crossing the ice to safety."[112] This is the only case in the Korean War where the CPVF destroyed an entire U.S. Army regiment.[113] The Chinese attackers at Sinhung-ni (east) also suffered heavy casualties. The 239th Regiment, for example, had three battalions, totaling 3,800 men, on November 27 before their first attack. By the end of the battle on December 2, the regiment had only one battalion with fewer than 600 men. The regiment lost 3,200 men in four days.[114] On November 30, the 240th Regiment, 80th Division, 27th Army, attacked the 31st Regiment. Its 5th Company faced a strong enemy covered by suppressing artillery fire. All the men were forced to lie down in the snow under the artillery barrage. When the 240th's charging bugle was blown for the final attack, none of the 120 soldiers of the 5th Company stood up. They were all frozen to the ground and dead.[115] The other regiments also suffered heavy casualties, and none of them could engage again for six to eight months in Korea. The 27th Army suffered more than 20,000 casualties from November 27 to December 2.[116]

Song Shilun reported to the CPVF Command that morning: "The 27th Army has completely annihilated the retreating enemy from Sinhung-ni at the Hudong-ni line, capturing 150 enemy soldiers and most trucks and vehicles."[117] Peng Dehuai cabled Song right back: "Congratulations to the 9th Army Group! Congratulations to the 27th Army!" Late on December 2, Mao telegraphed the CPVF Command, "Celebrate the two big victorious annihilations by our 9th Army Group!"[118] An hour later, Mao sent another telegram to Peng and Song with more encouraging words. "Our 9th Army Group has achieved a great victory after its engagements during the past several days. The army group not only destroyed most of the 1st Marine Regiment, and several other reinforcement units in the Hagaru-ri area, but also completely wiped out more than one regiment of the American 7th Division in the Sinhung-ni area."[119] Peng later recalled the successful annihilation by the 27th Army at Chosin. "Only once [throughout the entire Korean War] during the Second Campaign, we annihilated an entire American regiment, and no single enemy soldier could escape. In most battles we usually attacked enemy units of battalion size."[120]

The battle at Sinhung-ni (east) had seriously rocked the X Corps across the eastern front. Nevertheless, the continuous fighting of Task Force MacLean and then Task Force Faith for five days had pinned down the main strength of the 27th Army, reducing the pressure on the 1st Marine Division at Hagaru-ri. The CPVF 27th Army had to concentrate three out of its four divisions to encircle and destroy the task force from November 28 to December 2. Moreover, the three Chinese divisions had suffered heavy casualties at Sinhung-ni and lost their combat effectiveness. Obviously, it became impossible for the 27th Army to return to the fight at Hagaru-ri and to destroy the 1st Marine. In other words, it became possible for the marines to break through the Chinese roadblocks and retreat from the Chosin Reservoir to the south. After the 8th Army retreated south toward Socheon and Suncheon, Gen. Ned Almond, commander of the X Corps, issued orders to this troops to immediately make full withdrawal to Hamhung and Hungnam.

Zhou Enlai signs the Sino-Soviet Treaty of Friendship, Alliance,
and Mutual Assistance, Moscow, February 1950.

Photograph from the author's collection.

Mao Zedong and Peng Dehuai
in Beijing, October 1950.
Photograph from the author's collection.

Zhu De and Song Shilun,
Shandong, October 1950.
Photograph from the author's collection.

Peng, Kim, and other commanders of the CPVF-NKPA Joint Command,
Taeyudong, North Korea, November 1950.
Photograph from the author's collection.

The troops of the 9th Army Group cross the Rangrim Mountains, November 1950.
Photograph from the author's collection.

Chinese division commanders plan an attack on the U.S. Marines
at Chosin, November 1950.

Photograph from the author's collection.

The 172nd Regiment, 58th Division, CPVF 20th Army
attacks the Marines at Chosin, December 1950.
Photograph from the author's collection.

The Chinese attack from a hill, December 1950.
Photograph from the author's collection.

CPVF logistics unit repairs a road in North Korea, April 1951.
Photograph from the author's collection.

5

Failed Roadblocks and Pursuit

The CPVF 9th Army Group continued its encirclements at Yudam-ni and Hagaru-ri and accelerated its plan for the annihilation of the 1st Marines on the western side of the Chosin Reservoir after the elimination of Task Force Faith of the 7th Division on December 1. Having suffered heavy casualties since November 27 and exhausted supplies of food and ammunition by November 30, both the 20th and 27th Armies of the 9th Army Group were to be relieved by the 26th Army, which had been in reserve. Army Group Commander Song Shilun requested the commitment of his 26th for a final battle against the 1st Marine Division. In his telegram to the CPVF Command at 9:00 A.M. on December 1, Song explained, "Since the possibility that a large number of enemy forces would move west has significantly been reduced according to the present situation, we would propose that these divisions would . . . go to the front and participate in the attacks."[1] Song wanted to strengthen his frontline forces with four fresh divisions of the 26th Army.

Peng Dehuai approved the 9th Army Group's request around 5:00 P.M. on December 1, informing Song: "At the western front, we have achieved victory. The encircled enemy force at your [eastern] front has been cut by half with heavy casualties. Hope you will go all out to wipe out the surrounded enemy troops."[2] Nevertheless, Peng and other commanders at the CPVF Command cautioned the 9th Army Group: "You should by no means relax your vigilance on deploying forces against enemy northward reinforcements before the 26th Army would arrive."[3] Mao Zedong in Beijing was eager to have the 9th annihilate the 1st Marine Division at the Chosin Lake area. In his telegram to Peng, Song, Tao Yong, and other CPVF commanders at 1:00 P.M. on December 2, Mao said he "really hope[s] Song and Tao would pay all their attention to the great advantage of wiping out the encircled U.S. 1st Marine Division through tonight and tomorrow night. Before the battle is completely finished, serious attention must be paid to strengthening the defense . . . to check the forces from breaking through."[4]

With instructions from the high command, Song ordered his 26th Army to move forward to the front line on December 1 to annihilate the 1st Marine. He also instructed his 20th and 27th Armies to continue the strategy of encirclement of all marines in the Chosin area until December 3, when the 26th would launch attacks.[5]

This chapter explains why the three armies failed in Song's last attempt to destroy the 1st Marine Division in North Korea from December 1 to 15. Among the four major reasons were weak firepower, lack of transportation, shortage of supply, and heavy casualties. First, the light infantry weapons the 20th and 27th Armies used were ineffective against American tanks and armored vehicles. Their roadblocks ultimately failed to stop the marines' withdrawal. Second, without any trucks, the 26th Army, a fresh force of 50,000 troops, did not arrive in time to engage with the 1st Marine before December 6.[6] Their pursuit thereafter could not match the speed of the motorized marines. Song's three armies applied strategies of blocking and pursuing from December 7 to 12. Exhausted and fragile, the 20th and 27th Armies were unable to stop the marines' withdrawal from Chosin to Hamhung, where the 1st Marine linked with the U.S. Army 3rd Division on December 12. The U.S. X Corps was able to completely pull out of North Korea through the Hungnam Port on December 23.[7] Song thus failed in his campaign goal of annihilating the 1st Marine Division in the Battle of Chosin because of his strategic miscalculation, inadequate transportation, and lack of supplies.

Roadblocks at Yudam-ni, December 1–5

According to the army group's order on December 1, the 26th Army was to take over the encirclement from the 20th Army and attack the 1st Marine at Hagaru-ri on December 3.[8] The 26th, however, did not launch its attack until the evening of December 6 because it had to march nearly seventy miles through the snowy mountains in order to get to Hagaru-ri. Song made a crucial miscalculation when he deployed his reserve force, the 26th Army, one-third of his army group, a hundred miles from the front line. Some Chinese historians try to explain that the army group commander might have been worried about a lack of food for his 150,000 men, or that the army waited for the arrival and replacement of Soviet-made weapons at the border.[9] One American military historian has guessed that "this error of judgement on his [Song Shilun's] part must have grown out of his belief that he would not need those troops in the destruction of the X Corps troops in the Chosin Reservoir area—and if he did need them, he could bring them up in time to finish off what he concluded would be a decimated remnant of the X Corps forces unable to escape his trap."[10]

Therefore, the 20th and 27th Armies had to remain engaged with the 1st Marine Division until the 26th Army could arrive at Chosin. According to the 9th Command's order on December 1, the 27th Army, together with the 59th Division of the 20th Army, should maintain its encirclement of the marines at Yudam-ni and attack the enemy troops if they broke out from the village. The 20th Army's 58th Division should continue its encirclement of Hagaru-ri and send some troops forward to Sangtong-ri and Hatong-ri.[11] Its 60th Division would move to Hwangchoneung to check and block the marines from running south, and the 89th Division would continue to defend Sachang-ri.[12]

Maj. Gen. Ned Almond carried out General MacArthur's order to withdraw his X Corps to the Wonsan-Hungnam area. On November 29, he ordered the 1st Marine Division to pull out and break through the passages to Sinhung-ni (west) and Koto-ri; the 7th Division to withdraw from Hyesanjin down south to Hungnam; the 3rd Infantry Division to protect Wonsan, safeguard the highway from Sudong to Hamhung, and block the road from Seochang-ri to the east; and the ROK 1st Army to withdraw to Hamhung and protect the safety of the X Corps' right flank.[13] On December 1, Maj. Gen. Oliver Smith, commander of the 1st Marine Division, ordered his 5th Marine Regiment at Yudam-ni to conduct rearguard operations, and the 7th Regiment to force through the roadblock from Yudam-ni to Hagaru-ri. Smith also ordered his troops to hold their positions at Hagaru-ri at all costs until they could be joined by the retreating regiments from Yudam-ni. They would pull back south together after they combined.[14]

From December 1 to 4, the 27th Army assigned its divisions to set up roadblocks along a twelve-mile stretch of road from Yudam-ni in the north to Hagaru-ri in the south. Its 59th Division established two roadblocks to check the marines. The first was at Saeungleung, and the second at Seoheung-ri. The 79th Division occupied Hill 1542 west of Yudam-ni to prevent any marine attempt to move westward. The 94th Division defended the high ground west of Huiso-ri, from which they could attack the encircled marines along the road.[15]

Starting on December 1, the 7th Marine Regiment from Yudam-ni began to attack the two roadblocks of the 59th Division.[16] With close air support, strong artillery firepower, and more than two dozen tanks, the marines' RCT from the northeast launched repeated ferocious attacks on the Chinese positions on Hills 1419 and 1542 at Saeungleung.[17] Peng Deqing, commander of the 27th Army, ordered Dai Kelin, commander of the 59th Division, to hold fast to Saeungleung. Dai assigned his 177th Regiment to stop the marines.[18] Hu Yi, regimental political commissar of the 177th, reported to Dai that his regiment would resolutely hold the roadblocks at Saeungleung. Hu sent its 2nd Battalion (2/177) to Hill 1419.

Zhou Wenjiang, assistant commander of the 2/177, led the 5th and Machine Gun Companies to defend one of the three positions atop Hill 1419. Around 9:00 A.M. on December 1, the marines began air attacks and shelling of the hill. The 7th Marine Regiment then launched its 3rd Battalion (3/7) to attack Zhou's positions throughout the entire morning. At 3:00 P.M., the 1st Battalion of the 7th Regiment (1/7) also joined the attacks. Zhou Wenjiang continued his defense while losing many men to marine firepower. Although the 2/177 command sent the 6th Company as reinforcements to Zhou in the afternoon, he had to pull off the hill after almost losing three companies around 7:30 P.M. Major Zhou Wenjiang later recalled, "There were only twenty men left when we walked down the hill."[19] In the night, the 177th Regiment counterattacked the marines and retook Hill 1419 at 3:00 A.M. the next morning. However, the 7th Marine broke the Chinese roadblock again the following day.[20]

The cold weather at Chosin continued to deteriorate; daytime temperatures plunged to close to 40 degrees below zero. For more than a week, the troops of the 27th Army fought against the superior logistics, equipment, and technology of the U.S. Marines at Yudam-ni with shoulderloads of ammunition and frozen potatoes. Perhaps the worst thing was that most of the 50,000 men lacked winter clothing.[21] They tried to find anything they could to wrap themselves up against the deadly nighttime cold. By December 2, the 59th Division had lost more than 65 percent of its platoon, company, and battalion commanders to frostbite. The 79th Division lost 2,157 officers and soldiers to frostbite while suffering 2,297 combat casualties. The division had to reduce its combat units from fifty-three infantry companies to five and was rendered incapable of engaging the marines effectively.[22]

Severe cold weather had significantly undermined the effectiveness of their weapons. About 60 percent of fired mortar shells failed to explode because of the cold. Thousands of rifles were reported to have broken like a frozen ice stick during the battle.[23] In spite of all the unimaginable difficulties the 27th Army faced, the commanders of the 9th Army Group were determined to continue their attacks on the marines. Senior Colonel Shuang Shi explains how Song Shilun evaluated the battleground situation and accepted the heavy casualties of his troops. The PLA historian believes that Song had the choice either to attack or not attack at that moment: "Song Shilun was firmly resolved to continue attacks and was willing to sacrifice his army and himself for the strategic task, to sacrifice a small 'us' [the army] for the larger 'us' [the country]."[24] Moreover, Song and his commanders were confident in their reinforcement of the 26th Army, which was not yet arrived at Chosin by December 2.

In the morning of December 3, General Oliver Smith sent a task force with several tanks from Hagaru-ri to attack the 59th Division from the south. The Chinese division, under attack from two directions, finally lost its defense of Saeungleung. After two days of continuous fighting, the Chinese withdrew from Hill 1419 at 7:30 P.M. because of a lack of supplies, hunger, serious frostbite, and heavy casualties.[25]

In the late evening of December 3, after the marines from Yudam-ni broke through the 59th roadblock at Saeungleung, the 27th Army ordered its 89th Division to reinforce the 59th at Seoheung-ri, the second roadblock, to stop the marines' retreat. The 243rd Regiment of the 89th rushed to Seoheung-ri and confronted the RCT of the 5th and 7th Marine Regiments with a head-on attack. After a few seesaw battles, the marines backed off to Saeungleung that night.[26]

The next morning, the marines resumed attacks on the blocking 243rd Regiment and broke through its defense. The other regiments of the 81st Division were late in plugging the hole of the roadblock. Finally, around 5:50 P.M. on December 4, the 1/7 Marines broke through the second roadblock and reached Hagaru-ri. Unable to stop them, the 27th Army received orders to pursue and slow the marines' retreat until the 26th Army, which was still more than fifty miles away, could join the battle.[27]

The next day, the 59th Division evacuated its positions at Saeungleung and Seoheung-ri and advanced to Hagaru-ri. Division Commander Dai Kelin, however, discovered that the 1st Battalion of the 177th Regiment (1/177) did not evacuate the hill. He called Hu Yi, regimental political commissar of the 177th. Hu told Dai that all the men either had frostbite or were wounded, and they could not move down the hill themselves. Dai Kelin had to send his officers, staff, guards, and cooks from the division headquarters to the hill to carry the soldiers who could not walk down the hill.[28]

The 27th Army could not destroy the marines or stop their retreat by itself because of the heavy casualties it suffered during the weeklong attack. In his report to Peng Dehuai and Mao Zedong at 10:05 P.M. on December 4, Song Shilun requested, "The 27th Army should rest for two days after having concluded battle at Yudam-ni and Huiso-ri."[29] In the meantime, the 20th Army also suffered heavy casualties and could not launch another major attack on the marines. Its 59th Division, which had maintained the encirclement of the 1st Marine Division at Hagaru-ri for a week, had only eight hundred able men because of the combat casualties, frostbite, and trench foot.[30]

On December 5, Division Commander Smith decided to undertake a general withdrawal of the 1st Marine Division from Hagaru-ri to Koto-ri on the 6th. Smith's well-known explanation of the retreat, in response to a reporter's question—"Retreat, hell—we're attacking in another direction"—made headlines in the United States and has been forever associated with the marines at the Chosin Reservoir.[31] Mao was extremely attentive to the battle situation at Chosin and asked the 9th Army Group Command several times on December 4 for its plans to thwart and annihilate the 1st Marine.[32] The 9th's only hope was the timely arrival of the 26th Army, but that army was still away from the front line. On December 4, Song was so upset about the delayed arrival of the 26th that he yelled at his command staff, "Where is the second echelon? Where is the 26th Army?" Angry and frustrated, he threw his teacup to the ground after his staff told him the main strength of the 26th had not yet reached Chosin.[33]

The 26th Army had time to better prepare for its engagement at the Battle of Chosin. To deal with the firepower of the marines, the army command brought heavy guns of three artillery battalions on the march through the snowy mountains. The 26th Army, under the command of Zhang Renchu, had four infantry divisions, including the 76th, 77th, 78th, and 88th, with fresh troops of 48,894 men.[34] However, the march of the 26th Army toward Hagaru-ri fell behind schedule, and thus could not launch attacks before the marines' retreat to the south.

Delayed 26th Attack at Hagaru-ri, December 6

Zhang Zhixiu, chief of staff and assistant commander of the 26th Army, believed the major factors that delayed the army's arrival were misinformation and miscommunication.[35] Major General Zhang Zhixiu recalled that, at 7:00 P.M. on December 2, five days after the Battle of Chosin started, the 9th Army Group ordered the 26th Army to move forward to the front line. According to Song Shilun's order, the 26th should replace the 20th Army on December 3, taking over its task and attacking the marines at Hagaru-ri that evening.[36] Mao Zedong in Beijing also worried about the delayed reinforcement of the 9th Army Group. Mao telegraphed Peng, Song, Tao, Qin, and other CPVF commanders at 1:00 A.M. on December 3: "First of all, it is hoped that Song and Qin will consider promptly moving the 26th Army southward to strike at the reinforcements. . . . It is expected that Song and Qin will consider whether the above plan is workable. Please take the entire situation into account and make your decision accordingly."[37] Following Mao's instruction, the 9th Army Group Command ordered the 26th to launch its attacks on the marines at Hagaru-ri at 7:00 P.M. on December 3.[38] Although the army commanders were confident they could accomplish the task, most of the army was still about sixty miles away from Hagaru-ri. The 26th had to call the 9th Command and request postponement of its attack one day to the evening of December 4.[39]

The first combat unit of the 26th to arrive at Hagaru-ri on December 4 was the 228th Regiment of the 76th Division under the command of Chen Zhongmei.[40] His division had to wait for two days until the 26th Army began its attacks at Hagaru-ri in the evening of December 6.[41]

With the arrival of a fresh force, Song, Tao, and Qin reported to the CPVF Command and the CMC at 10:05 P.M. on December 4 with a new operational plan: the 26th Army was to replace the 20th Army to lead the attacks on Hagaru-ri, which would commence the next evening. If successful, the 26th would continue south toward Hamhung. After the 20th Army completed the transfer of its Hagaru-ri mission to the 26th Army, the 58th and 60th Divisions as its main strength would move to the south of the Huangtuling area, setting up roadblocks against the enemy reinforcements to the north. Its 59th Division continued its pursuit of the fleeing enemy southward from Yudam-ni. The 20th should also prepare to annihilate the enemy forces at Koto-ri after the 26th Army turned to the south and continued its attacks. The 89th Division of the 20th should move to Sangtong-ri and Hatong-ri to intercept the marines and seal off their retreat from the Chosin area. In addition, the 27th Army was fighting the fleeing enemy that evening.[42] One regiment of the 27th should facilitate the main attack by cutting off the marines at Orlo-ri.

Peng immediately approved the 9th Army Group's new plan the same night.[43] Mao was pleased by the updated attack plan of the 9th Army Group. He cabled Peng and Song at 7:00 A.M. on December 5, "Song-Tao-Qin's plan in their telegram of 22:05 of December 4 is perfect. Please start the campaign immediately." Mao even added more tasks by instructing the 9th Command: "It will be extremely significant if you, besides annihilating the surrounded enemy forces and being prepared to attack the enemy's reinforcements, can possibly destroy two more regiments of the American 3rd Division in the Sachang-ri area by employing the main force of one of our armies."[44]

Mao was so excited about the early success of the Second Offensive Campaign in Korea that he drafted a news release himself on the CPVF's operations on both the western and eastern fronts for Xinhua News Agency at 1:00 A.M. on December 5. Mao wrote about the Battle of Chosin: "Our People's Volunteers have cut off and encircled the main forces of the American invading army's 1st Marine Division and 7th Infantry Division in the Changjin Lake area, north of Hamhung. Most of those enemy forces have been destroyed. The remnants are under continuous attack. . . . The enemy forces on both the eastern and western fronts are running for their life with extreme anxiety and in great panic." Mao also instructed his aide to "put this article on the air *immediately*, and have it appear in the newspapers on the fifth."[45]

However, there was no effective encirclement, no new major attack, and no possibility of destruction of the 1st Marine Division since the main strength of the 26th Army would not arrive at Hagaru-ri until the evening of December 5. According to Army Assistant Commander Zhang Zhixiu, by 7:00 P.M. on the 4th only one division, the 76th, had reached Hagaru-ri, and three other divisions were still marching through the mountains and forest in the snow. The army command had to ask for yet another day, delaying its attack on the marines until December 5.[46]

As noted earlier, among the major reasons for the late arrival and excessive fatigue of the 26th Army was misinformation. One of the delayed divisions was the 77th, the main strength of the 26th Army. Lacking information on the mountain paths, the division command had to send several reconnaissance companies to look for passable ways, while waiting in the mountains for another day.[47] Ma Rixiang, assistant political instructor of the Machine Gun Company, 1st Battalion, 231st Regiment, 77th Division, recalled that his men had run out of food days before. They received rations for three days before the forced march. The food was dried steamed buns cut into small, thin pieces like crackers. They did not know that the forced march would take six days and nights. During the march through the snowy mountains, the regiment commanders decided not to allow the men to eat their food without permission since they would not receive any food resupply anytime soon. Ma said, "Somehow, before we reached Hagaru-ri six days later, our food had long gone since the men were very hungry through the forced march for six days."[48] Major Ma Rixiang complained that the weather again provided more help to the U.S. Marines than to the 77th Division.[49]

In the meantime, without any current operational maps, the 88th Division got lost and went to a wrong location. The troops stayed on the road overnight

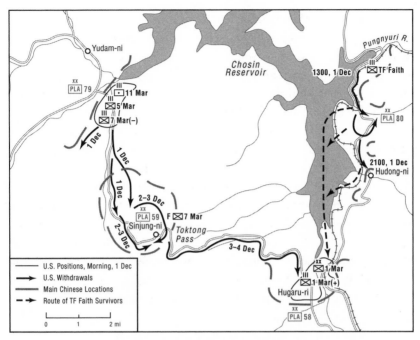

Roadblocks and Pursuit, December 1–4, 1950.
Map by Erin Greb Cartography.

before they could get back on the correct path. Wu Dawei, staff member of the Operation Office of the 88th Division, refused to accept the blame put on the 26th Army for its "slowness and inflexibility," which resulted in the lost opportunity to destroy the 1st Marine Division. He recalled that his division waited for a week as part of a reserve force near the Yalu River, more than a hundred miles from the Chosin Reservoir. On December 2, almost a week later, they received the order from the high command to rush to Chosin. The division was too far away from the front line and had no chance to attack the marines on December 3.[50]

The 88th Division Command carried out the army's order and tried to get to Hagaru-ri as soon as possible; the division was composed of the 262nd, 263rd, and 264th Regiments under the command of Wu Dalin.[51] Wu's officers and soldiers marched day and night through the high mountains and thick forest. Exhausted and hungry, some of the men fell into the snow and could not get back up. The division received no winter clothing or food supplies during the march. Moreover, constant air raids and extreme cold weather slowed down the march and inflicted many casualties.[52]

General Zhang Zhixiu recalled, "After [we] received the divisions' reports, [we] had to call the group army command again and requested to postpone our attacks to the 6th."[53] The 26th Army Group had to put off its attacks on Hagaru-ri since only two divisions had arrived by the 5th. Song was very disappointed by the delayed arrival of the 26th since the 1st Marine began withdrawing from Hagaru-ri in the early morning of December 6.[54]

Around 4:30 A.M. on December 6, the 1st Marine began retreating from Hagaru-ri to Koto-ri, about eleven miles south.[55] There were about 10,000 marine and army troops and more than 1,000 vehicles at Hagaru-ri for evacuation.[56] Around 7:00 A.M., the 5th Marine Regiment began its attack on the Chinese-held eastern hill to break through the roadblock. At 7:30 A.M., U.S. airplanes bombed the Chinese positions south of Hagaru-ri. After 9:30 A.M., the 5th Marine Division launched its 2nd Battalion (2/5) to attack the positions of the 88th Division on the eastern hill.[57] The 58th Division of the 20th Army, which had encircled the 1st Marine Division at Hagaru-ri for more than a week, was unable to defend its roadblock.[58] By 2:30 P.M., the 2/5 Marines took the eastern hill and opened the road for a southward retreat.[59]

On December 6, the 9th Command had to make an adjustment to its December 4 plan. According to the new plan, the 26th Army should launch the attacks immediately upon its arrival at Hagaru-ri. The 20th Army would move southward and set up roadblocks between Hagaru-ri and Koto-ri. The 27th would engage in a pursuit operation after the retreating marines from the Chosin Reservoir.[60] By the time the 26th Army started attacks in the night of December 6, most of the marines had already pulled out of Hagaru-ri.[61]

In the evening of December 6, the 26th Army finally launched attacks on the U.S. Marines left at Hagaru-ri. Army Commander Zhang Renchu did not have his full force since two of his divisions, the 78th and 88th, were still on the march.[62] Zhang Renchu ordered his 76th Division to attack the eastern hill around midnight, where the Chinese could cut the connection between the 5th and 7th Marine Regiments. On the eastern hill, the 2/5 Marines organized a strong defense with the firepower of artillery pieces and tanks. The 76th Division failed to break the 2/5's defense on the eastern hill.[63] Then, Commander Zhang organized the second attack on the eastern hill around 2:00 A.M., while also ordering his 76th to attack the 7th Marine on the road between Hagaru-ri and Koto-ri.[64]

The troops of the 76th Division, however, were exhausted from their march, and many of them had been wounded due to heavy air raids and bombing on the way to Hagaru-ri. Then they were thrown into a fierce battle upon their arrival.

Wu Dawei believed that the hasty night battle was not well prepared. He recalled that the march through the snowy mountains had undermined the combat effectiveness of the divisions of the 26th Army. Many men were lost to frostbite and starvation, and the division still received no supply of food or ammunition.[65]

The 76th Division failed either to retake the eastern hill or to stop the marines' retreat from Hagaru-ri. Before their second attack, the regrouping Chinese troops were caught in the middle of U.S. air bombing and artillery shelling at the bottom of the hill. The 5th Marine Regiment attacked the Chinese at their staging area and captured 220 Chinese soldiers. It was the largest number of Chinese POWs captured in one engagement at Chosin.[66] In the early morning of December 7, one company of the 76th Division broke into the column of the 7th Marine Regiment on the road and engaged in hand-to-hand fighting until the Chinese company lost most of its men and withdrew. Around noon, the last marines of the 2/5 withdrew from Hagaru-ri after they blew up piles and piles of supplies and ammunition in the village.[67] The soldiers of the 26th Army rushed into the flames of burning supplies, searching desperately for food and winter clothing.[68]

Again, the 26th Army, just like the 20th and 27th Armies, failed to destroy the marines or stop their retreat. However, Zhi Futian, staff member of the Political Tasks Office of the 76th Division, rejected the criticism against the 26th Army for allowing the marines' escape. Lieutenant Colonel Zhi Futian recalled that the troops of the 76th Division, as the main strength of the 26th Army, had fought bravely at Hagaru-ri.[69] All the division's units suffered heavy casualties. On December 6, the division had the 226th, 227th, and 228th Regiments, totaling fifty-four infantry companies with 14,000 troops. By December 10, after only three days of fighting, the division had only nine infantry companies left. Among other regiments, the 227th Regiment had only two companies with able men. The commander of the 3rd Battalion of the 227th Regiment (3/227) became lost in the mountains, and his troops could not find their way back on time. The majority of the 3/227's 1,000 men froze to death overnight. After the Battle of Chosin, both the battalion commander and political commissar of the 3/227 were removed from their positions and punished by court-martial.[70]

Failed Blocking between Koto-ri and Hamhung, December 7–11

Around 5:45 A.M. on December 7, the retreating marines arrived at Koto-ri. At that moment, more than 14,229 USMC–U.S. Army troops, 1,200 vehicles, and fifty tanks regrouped at Koto-ri.[71] At 6:50 P.M. that evening, General Smith ordered a new withdrawal from Koto-ri to the eastern coast for a general evacuation of

X Corps from North Korea to South Korea.[72] In its telegram of 11:00 P.M. on December 8, the 9th Army Group Command ordered its three armies to continue their engagements by blocking, checking, and attacking the marines between Koto-ri and Hamhung, a distance of about forty miles. The 9th Command aimed to stop the marines' retreat at Hamhung.[73]

After the 1st Marine Division broke out of Koto-ri, it was firmly pinned down at the narrow pass three and a half miles south of the village. To stop the marines' southward retreat, the 20th Army received orders to pursue them and slow their retreat by destroying all the bridges along the road until the 26th Army could join the battle.[74] Zhang Xiangyi, commander of the 20th Army, order its 60th Division to blow up the bridge of Funchilin (Fuchilin) Pass. It was a concrete bridge over a hydroelectric plant and spillway of four penstocks, or large steel pipes, which ran down the mountainside sharply to the power plant in the valley below. Division Commander Peng Fei sent his troops to Funchilin and destroyed part of the bridge at the power plant for the first time on December 1.[75] The marine engineers then fixed the bridge the next day by covering the holes with some wooden materials. On December 4, Commander Peng ordered his troops to destroy the entire bridge for the second time.[76]

However, the marines were able to put the Funchilin Bridge back in service by using metal piles to reconnect both sides of the bridge. In response, the 80th Division ordered its 240th Regiment to destroy the temporary bridge. The regiment commander assigned his 7th Company of the 3rd Battalion (3/240) to carry out the task. On the night of December 6, Jiang Qingyun, captain of the 7th Company, organized a "dare-to-die" team with two platoons to attack the marines who guarded the bridge. Jiang and his team approached to the bridge, each of them carrying twenty pounds of explosives. When the marine guards saw the Chinese on the bridge less than a hundred yards away, they opened fire. Although Captain Jiang lost most of his men on the bridge, he managed to destroy it, creating a gap of more than twenty feet between both ends.[77] Marine historians state, "Between the cliff and the sheer drop down the mountainside there was no possibility of a bypass."[78]

The 1st Marine Division and its supporting units in and out of the Chosin area put their technological superiority to full effect as they tried to break through the Chinese roadblocks one after another. After the 240th Regiment had blasted the only bridge over the deep valley at the narrow Funchilin Pass south of Koto-ri, the U.S. forces managed to airlift eight sections of a huge M-2 steel treadway bridge, weighing 2,500 pounds apiece, all the way from Japan and dropped by parachute from C-119 transports to the ice and snow of Koto-ri on December 7.[79] A steel bridge that could support over fifty tons of vehicles was constructed in less than two days.[80]

Song Shilun and his army commanders were surprised to see the American forces rebuild the bridge with an airlifted bridge in such a short period of time. They could not even imagine such a technological miracle on the battleground.[81] The commanders of the 20th Army regretted that they did not deploy enough troops at this key, narrow pass since they believed that the marines could never cross after they had totally destroyed the original bridge. Failing to stop the marines at Funchilin Pass, the 20th Army had to order its 58th Division on December 7 to stop the marines' retreat with roadblocks at Hills 1304 and 1350.[82]

The division command sent Hu Qianxiu, chief of staff of the 58th, to the front command post.[83] After the 58th Division transferred its positions and assignment at Hagaru-ri to the 26th Army, the division rushed to Hwangchoneung below Koto-ri to set up roadblocks. Hu Qianxiu reorganized the 173rd and 174th Regiments into four companies to defend Hills 1304 and 1350 at Hwangchoneung.[84]

On December 8, the 174th Regiment sent its 3rd Battalion (3/174) to defend the roadblock at Hwangchoneung. Yao Genlian, assistant battalion commander of the 3/174, led the 8th Company, the only company that the 3/174 had, to occupy the position. Exhausted and short of ammunition, the men of the 8th Company could not stop the tanks, which inflicted heavy casualties on the troops. By the afternoon, the 8th Company had only twelve men left.[85] Around 5:00 P.M., the marines shelled the Chinese positions again when Yao Genlian finally received the order to pull the few survivors out of Hwangchoneung. Yao was wounded and could not walk. He asked the deputy political instructor of the 8th Company to take the twelve men down the hill immediately, and he began to crawl out of the position in the dark.[86] One of the division messengers saw him in the snow and brought him back to the division headquarters. There, he had a meal of two frozen potatoes from Huang Chaotian, commander of the 58th Division.[87] The division command sent the 3rd Battalion of the 173rd Regiment to continue the defense of the hills at Hwangchoneung through the evening.[88]

The next morning, U.S. airplanes dropped napalm and bombs on the Chinese positions around Hills 1304 and 1350. The 58th Division command post was hit by napalm, and Hu Qianxiu, chief of staff of the 58th Division, was killed in the air raid. He was the highest-ranking Chinese officer killed in the Battle of Chosin.[89] All the division and regiment staff at the front command post were killed during the air raid. Among other officers killed were Hao Liang, political commissar of the 174th Regiment.[90] After two days' defense, the 58th Division lost its positions at Hwangchoneung to the marines.[91]

The night of December 8 was probably the coldest of the winter of 1950 when the temperature dropped to an unbelievable low of 45 degrees below zero at the Koto-ri area.[92] The 1st Battalion of the 1st Marine Regiment (1/1) attacked Hill 1081 during the day. The 180th Regiment, 60th Division, 20th Army, was assigned to the defense of the hill.[93] The 2nd Company of its 1st Battalion (1/180) defended the main position throughout the day. The next morning, the 1/1 Marines resumed the attack and charged the hill without any resistance. When the marines reached the hilltop, they found all the Chinese soldiers, more than one hundred men of the 1/180, frozen to death.[94]

On December 10, the marines passed Hwangchoneung. Zhang Yixiang, commander of the 20th Army, made his final effort at 5:00 P.M. He organized a pursuit force of two hundred men, the only able men available from his two divisions, the 58th and 60th. Under command of Cai Qunfan, chief of staff of the 60th Division, this force followed the marines for another ten to twelve miles on December 10–12.[95] At the Funchilin Bridge, Cai and his men engaged the marines' rear guard with its dozen tanks. Cai ordered his troops to attack the tanks in the afternoon of the 10th and continued his attack through the evening. The marines continued their retreat and passed over the bridge. Around 2:00 A.M., the marine engineers blew up the treadway bridge at Funchilin.

While the 20th Army failed to stop the marines' retreat, the 27th Army could not do it either since the entire army had only 2,000 men available, out of 50,000 troops it had two weeks before. Its 79th Division, for example, had thirty-eight infantry companies and fourteen special companies, more than 12,000 troops, on November 27. It had been reduced to merely five infantry companies and two special companies, about 300 men, by December 10.[96]

The 26th Army also participated in the pursuit operation under tremendous pressure because of its delayed arrival and failure to annihilate the marines at Hagaru-ri. The 26th Army Command ordered its 77th Division to use all means to chase and capture the retreating marines. The division and its regiments sent most of their staff members to the companies to assist the pursuit operations. Ma Rixiang and his Machine Gun Company of the 1/231 had one staff member from the 77th Division and one intelligence officer from the 231st Regiment command, who led the pursuit and maintained communications with the command post.[97] According to Ma, his company was still in good shape with three infantry platoons and two mortar platoons, totaling 204 men, at the beginning of the pursuit on

December 8. For three days, Ma recalled, they raced over the hills and did not sleep at all. Finally, they got ahead of the 1st and 5th Marine Regiments, and the regiment command ordered his company to set up a roadblock and attack the marines.[98]

On the morning of December 10, Ma ordered his men to let the tanks pass their positions. They then opened fire on the marines' column from behind the tanks. However, since their hilltop positions were too far away from the road, their grenades did not reach the marines and their rifles could not stop the motorized column. While sending a small group of riflemen under cover of machine-gun fire to charge the hill, the marines continued their southward retreat along the road.[99] Ma Rixiang asked the officers' permission to lead a team to attack the marine vehicles on the road to stop the traffic. The officers agreed and provided some covering for his attack. Ma ordered his men to shoot the drivers to stop the convoy during their attack. He also told his men not to throw grenades in the trucks so they could get some food and winter clothes from any disabled vehicle. When they got close enough to the road, they threw the grenades and actually stopped the marines' retreat.[100]

Before long, however, the marines took the hill positions supporting Ma and cut off his attacking force from behind.[101] He had to pull his men off the road, but he was able to grab four cans of food from a truck. His company suffered heavy casualties. During the night of December 11, Ma received the order to pull his company off the hill. He had only 12 out of 204 men fit for duty.[102] He later learned that the 76th and 77th Divisions of the 26th Army suffered very heavy casualties during their pursuit operations. The 76th Division had more than 14,000 troops before the attacks, and had fewer than 5,000 men by December 12, having lost nine infantry battalions. Among its three regiments was the 237th, which had merely two infantry companies left, out of twenty companies it had before the battle.[103]

Exhausted and fragile, the three armies of the 9th Army Group failed to stop the marines' withdrawal from Koto-ri to Hamhung. On December 12, having broken the Chinese roadblocks and staving off attacks on the way south, the 1st Marine linked up with the U.S. Army 3rd Division at Hamhung.[104]

Hopeless Pursuit, December 12–15

The 9th Army Group continued pursuit and attack operations against the marines retreating from Hamhung to Hungnam. According to the 9th Command's order, the 26th Army attacked Hamhung with the support of some troops of the 20th Army. The main forces of the 20th began to rest and wait for supplies at Koto-ri. The 27th Army moved toward Hamhung via Sachang-ri. Its 94th Division attacked Hamhung from the direction of Puchimneung in cooperation with North Korean troops.[105] The NKPA forces seized Wonsan on December 9 and cut off the X Corps' retreat route.[106]

For the next week, the 20th Army harassed the marines with small-scale attacks. Captain Wang Xuedong recalled, "We would ambush them, hit them hard, and then run. During the nights, we set up roadblocks in order to stop or delay their southward withdrawal. During the daytime, however, the marines broke through our roadblocks and moved farther south about a few miles every day. They traveled on the road while we stalked them on the hills and high grounds along both sides of the road."[107] Captain Wang had only eighteen men left in his company. He shared some food left behind by the marines with his men. Wang Xuedong also cut his blanket into pieces and gave them to those who suffered from frostbite. The men wrapped their cold, injured hands and feet with the pieces of cloth.[108] The 20th Army lost many men to both combat and noncombat casualties. Zhu Wenbin, staff member of the 173rd Regiment, 58th Division, 20th Army, recalled that his regiment had been reduced from more than 4,500 troops on November 27 to about 320 fit men in mid-December.[109]

On December 12, the 58th Division Command ordered the 173rd Regiment to continue its pursuit of the marines. All the staff members, security guards, medics, and cooks at the 173rd command post were organized into companies to participate in the operation.[110] Zhu Wenbin walked through the hills with an infantry company for days. He saw the marines at the bottom of the hills, traveling along the road with many trucks, tanks, artillery pieces, and Korean refugees. His company had only two engagements during the week.[111]

One morning, the battalion commander saw a sharp curve in the road as a good site to set up a roadblock. He ordered Zhu to instruct the company, only about fifty men, to build up some defensive works on the hill. Zhu Wenbin recalled, "We couldn't dig holes because the frozen ground was like concrete. I just asked the men to get some rocks and dead tree chunks to put up some simple defense positions."[112] Through the morning, the commander waited for the tanks and armored vehicles to pass by. Before noon, when he saw a column of the marines walking into the curve, the commander ordered his men to fire. Zhu threw all of his three grenades first, and then fired his rifle into the marines. After about ten minutes, the tanks turned around and came back, firing at the Chinese positions. As the 173rd troops pulled out of their roadblock, U.S. airplanes began to bomb the hilltop. Zhu was surprised that the U.S. air raid came so fast and could get so close since there were only about fifty to eighty meters between the marines and Chinese troops. Zhu's force lost half of its men during the battle.[113]

The last attack by the 173rd was a hit-and-run raid one night when the marines were resting along the road and setting up their tents. Zhu Wenbin recalled, "It was so cold that we had to hug together with two or three men to keep warm. We waited for the commander's order. We were excited about the night attack since we may be able to get into Americans' tents and find some food."[114] They talked about their favorite American food from canned meat to Tootsie Roll candy. But the most popular American things among the men were Marlboro cigarettes. Zhu Wenbin regretted that he could not get into one of the marine tents to get some American winter clothes and food. They had not eaten for three days. None of the men could get into the tents as the marines soon pushed the attacking troops back up the hill. When they received the order to cease their pursuit and return to Koto-ri, there were only eight men left in the company.[115]

By 1:00 P.M. on December 15, the pursuit operations ended since the Chinese could not organize even a company-sized attack. The 9th Army Group failed to eliminate the 1st Marine Division. The CPVF Command ordered the 9th Army Group to conclude its actions on the eastern front. The order brought the Battle of Chosin to an end.[116] The Chinese divisions occupied the airport at Yongpu on December 19.[117] This and other operations forced the X Corps to retreat to the south by sea.

For the massive sealift actions, the U.S. Navy had assembled more than 300 ships with extensive fire support. The Chinese artillery fired a few shells at Hamhung to disrupt the X Corps' operation. The sealift shipped 105,000 marine and army troops, 17,500 operable vehicles, and 350,000 tons of supplies out of the Hungnam Port.[118] On December 23, U.S. X Corps had completely pulled out from North Korea. Some 100,000 Korean refugees were also transported. On December 24, the marines boarded ships at Hungnam Harbor and withdrew to Pusan, South Korea. Afterward, the U.S. Navy bombarded the abandoned port into a heap of wreckage.[119] The Chinese Second Offensive Campaign was over by December 25 when the 27th Army occupied the evacuated city of Hamhung.[120]

The marines had fought their way through the Chinese roadblocks while being pounded by Chinese shellfire from the surrounding hills. Those engaged in this retreat, "The Chosin Few," as they now call themselves with pride, endured tough fighting. The 1st Marine Division's retreat has become a part of marine lore. David Halberstam concludes that "of all the battles in the Korean War, it is probably the most celebrated, deservedly so, and the most frequently written about. As the news reached Washington and then the country about the dilemma of the First Marines, seemingly cut off and surrounded by a giant force of Chinese, there was widespread fear that the division might be lost."[121] Two weeks later, however, the 1st Marine had fought its way back to Hungnam. But it was still a retreat, not a victory. As Stanley Sandler quoted Churchill's famous dictum after Dunkirk, "Wars are not won by evacuations."[122] The fierce fighting, combined with the bitter cold, made Chosin one of the worst battles of the Korean War for both the Chinese and the Americans.[123] During the Battle of Chosin, marine casualties totaled 10,600 men, including "more than 700 dead, nearly 200 missing, 3,500 wounded, and more than 6,200 non-battle casualties—mostly frostbite victims."[124]

The 9th Army Group had hastily raced from subtropical East China to the icy and snowy North Korean front without adequate preparations. It was rushed into attacks against the American armed forces' most elite troops, the 1st Marine Division, at the Chosin Reservoir. The Chinese armies on the eastern front fought without supplies of ammunition and food almost twice as long as the CPVF armies did on the western front. Despite taking huge casualties, they successfully accomplished the task of turning the tide of the war on the eastern front in favor of the CPVF and of protecting the CPVF flank and rear, even though they did not achieve the goal of destroying the 1st Marine at Chosin.

Mao and Peng were pleased with the outcome of the Battle of Chosin. On December 15, the CPVF Command praised the 9th's operational efforts in the battle. "You have fought a tough battle in a frozen and snow-covered battleground for almost a month and defeated the American invading forces of the 1st Marine Division and the [U.S. Army] 7th Division. Your troops have overcome many difficulties and extreme hardship, retaken many important towns, cities, and strategic key points, and achieved a great victory of the campaign. The entire army [of the CPVF] should learn strong fighting spirit and dauntless heroism from you!"[125] On the 17th, Mao cabled Peng Dehuai and Song Shilun: "Under extremely difficult conditions, the 9th Army Group has accomplished its gigantic strategic task in the campaign on the eastern front. It lost as many as 40,000 men due to the cold weather, a lack of supplies, and the fierce fighting. The [CCP] Central Committee cherishes the memory of those lost."[126]

Overall, the Second Offensive Campaign from November 25 to December 24, 1950, was a major victory for the CPVF. According to Chinese statistics, the CPVF inflicted 36,000 UNF casualties, with American troops accounting for two-thirds of the total.[127] American air power forced the Chinese to operate in the countryside and at night, and most of the Chinese supplies were carried on foot.

The Chinese attacked from the surrounding hills and often established roadblocks, which not only forced American troops back, but also threatened to cut them off. Most PLA soldiers demonstrated tremendous physical endurance, but the Chinese suffered more than 80,000 casualties during the Second Campaign.[128] Among the Chinese casualties were 30,700 combat and 50,000 noncombat casualties. Mao's son, Mao Anying, was killed on November 25 in a U.S. air raid against CPVF general headquarters.[129] In less than a month, the CPVF pushed the battle line back to the 38th parallel and recaptured Pyongyang, the capital of North Korea. The Second Offensive Campaign "represented the peak of CPVF performance in the Korean War."[130]

6

Recovery and Reengagement

It was in the Second Offensive Campaign that the CPVF reversed the tide of the Korean War since the UNF Inchon landing in mid-September. General MacArthur's goal of occupying North Korea and concluding the war before Christmas of 1950 was crushed. By mid-December 1950, the CPVF had not only taken over Pyongyang, but also pushed the UNF back to the 38th parallel. Suddenly, the seemingly invincible American military power now appeared weak, arrogant, demoralized, and vulnerable. Almost every Communist leader, including Mao Zedong in Beijing, Kim Il-sung in North Korea, and, to some extent, Joseph Stalin in Moscow, expressed that it was only a matter of time before the UN/U.S. forces were driven out to sea. Nevertheless, Peng Dehuai had not scheduled a new offensive because CPVF armies were exhausted after four weeks of constant movement and fighting during the Second Campaign. The CPVF also faced mounting problems, including food and ammunition shortages. On December 8, before the end of the Second Offensive Campaign, Peng requested a pause until the following spring to confine the forthcoming campaign to areas north of the 38th parallel. The chief commander requested that Mao "let [the troops] stop in areas several miles north of the 38th parallel, allowing the enemy to control the parallel, so that we will be able to destroy the enemy's main force the next year."[1]

This chapter reveals that Mao did not share the same feelings and views of his field commanders. The Second Offensive Campaign had greatly strengthened the confidence and morale of the Chinese leaders in Beijing, especially Mao. After receiving the campaign report from the CPVF Command, Mao immediately instructed his aide to forward the report to all the CCP's regional bureaus, provincial committees, and metropolitan committees, and to all the PLA's regional commands, army groups, and army commands. The chairman pointed out in his instruction, "This is an extremely important experience and [I] hope much attention will be paid to the study of this report. The fighting experience of the CPVF forces have proved that our military forces can very well win over the superior and highly equipped American forces who also possess air supremacy."[2] Encouraged by the CPVF's initial gains, Mao rejected Peng's request. Instead, he changed the CPVF's strategic goal from defending North Korea, to going on the offensive to drive the UNF out of the South.

This new goal for the next offensive campaign was far beyond the Chinese force's capabilities. Mao told Kim Il-sung about his new plan during Kim's visit to Beijing on December 3. "It is better for us to take over not only Pyongyang, but also Seoul. [Our] main goal is to eliminate more enemy troops, first of all, to eliminate all of the ROK troops. This will force the U.S. withdrawal [from Korea] effectively."[3] Mao seemed confident of the CPVF's final victory that would not only save North Korea, but also solve the problem of the entire Korean Peninsula. The Soviets, too, believed that China had an opportunity to resolve the Korean problem through a total victory of the CPVF. On December 4, Andrei Gromyko, the Soviet foreign minister, told Wang Jiaxiang, the PRC's ambassador to Moscow, that "according to the current situation in Korea, it is perfectly proper [for us] to call for 'striking the iron when it is hot,' as the old Chinese saying goes."[4]

The 9th Army did not participate in the Third Offensive Campaign because it had been extremely exhausted, battle-fatigued, and seriously damaged at Chosin. The 9th Army Group did not recover and reengage in the war until January–March 1951, participating in the CPVF Spring Offensive Campaign in April–May. Below we will examine the learning curve faced by the 9th's generals in Korea. After the Chinese forces lost their Spring Offensive, on June 1, the CMC notified Peng that Song Shilun, commander of the 9th Army Group, would serve as third assistant commander of the CPVF.[5]

Recovery, Replenishment, and Assessment

Peng reluctantly agreed with Mao's plan after the Second Offensive Campaign of November–December 1950. To plan how to carry out Mao's new offensive, Peng held a CPVF Command meeting on December 15. The aim was to shape the Third Offensive Campaign against UNF defenses in South Korea. From December 31, 1950, to January 8, 1951, the CPVF launched its Third Offensive Campaign against a strong UNF defense along the 38th parallel. In the afternoon of January 4, the CPVF 39th Army and NKPA I Corps entered Seoul. The next day, the 50th Army and two divisions of the NKPA I Corps crossed the Han River.[6] On January 7, the 50th Army took over Kimpo (Keumpo), and the NKPA I Corps occupied Inchon. In the meantime, the 42nd and 66th Armies continued their drives, targeting their thrust toward central South Korea.[7] Since the mechanized UNF withdrew faster than the Chinese could advance, Peng ended the CPVF Third Offensive Campaign on January 8.

The 9th Army Group did not participate in the Third Offensive Campaign because it had been seriously damaged at Chosin. All three of its armies had suffered heavy casualties, and the main strength could not engage again until the spring of 1951. From December 22 to February 13, the 9th Army Group began its rest and reorganization in Korea. In mid-February, the 9th Command was deployed to the defense of the eastern coast of North Korea. In March, its 26th Army was ordered to take a part in the CPVF Fourth Offensive Campaign (from January 25 to April 21). Instead of a mass offensive, it became a series of back-and-forth mobile battles. From April 23 to June 3, the partially recovered 9th Army Group returned to the front and participated in the CPVF Fifth Offensive Campaign, also called the Spring Offensive.

In mid-December 1950, Song and his commanders knew that their soldiers had exhausted all their energies and were at their physical condition's end. Having been cut off from supplies, the 9th's troops had lived in an extremely treacherous environment, and had fought for weeks while cold and hungry. During the Battle of Chosin, the 9th Army Group lost 48,156 men in three weeks of fighting, about 32.1 percent of the group's total forces.[8] Its combat casualties totaled 19,202 men, while 28,954 officers and men were disabled by severe frostbite, and more than 4,000 died due to the cold weather.[9] The 9th liquidated three divisions after the battle. The entire army group became a giant field hospital for three months as men recovered from frostbite. Its poor preparation and heavy casualties became a lesson of what to avoid that Mao, Peng, and the CPVF Command drummed into their other army group commanders.

Song's troops badly needed rest, food, and shelter for the winter. After his disengagement with the marines on December 15, Song requested an immediate rest and reorganization of the 9th Army Group in his telegram to Mao and Peng at 5:00 A.M. on December 17. Mao replied the same day by recalling the badly depleted army group back to China:

> It [the 9th] lost as many as 40,000 men due to the cold weather, a lack of supplies, and the fierce fighting. The Central Committee cherishes the memory of those lost. To regain its full strength, recuperate, and

replenish its energies, and be ready for new battles, [I] suggest that the army group should, in its entirety, be transferred back to the Northeast [of China] after it completely finishes its current campaign. It needs to be replenished with new recruits, rested, and reorganized for two or three months, and then it can enter Korea again for new operations.[10]

After receiving Mao's telegram, Song called his army commanders to ask their opinion on what was best for the 9th: to return to China or to rest and reorganize in Korea? He also held a staff and officers conference at the headquarters to discuss how and where the 9th could better and more quickly recover from the depletion and damages of battle. Unhappy with the results of the battle and having pent-up grievances, all the army commanders wanted to stay at their current locations for their troops' rest and reorganization. Some of the officers worried that, if they returned to China, they would never be able to come to Korea again.[11]

Therefore, Song declined Mao's offer to bring the army group back to China. Song explained to Peng in his telegram of December 19 that it would be very difficult to transport more than 20,000 wounded soldiers back to China in the middle of the cold winter, and that it would be better for the 9th Army Group to rest and recover in the Hamhung area of North Korea.[12] Peng supported Song and cabled Mao at 12:00 A.M. on December 20: "I agree with Song that it is better for his army group to spend the winter in the Hamhung area, resting and reorganizing for two months. [They will] try their best to transport the seriously wounded and sick soldiers back to the Northeast [of China], and ship the winter clothing to the front. Then, [they will] send officers to Shenyang to receive and train the new recruits."[13] Mao accepted Song's request and Peng's explanation by replying to Peng on December 21: "Under the circumstances you explained, the 9th Army Group had better rest and reorganize in the Hamhung area. It will only transport its severely sick and wounded back to the Northeast, and will transfer some cadres back to the Northeast to train new recruits." Mao also emphasized, "It is obviously necessary to increase the number of vehicles, and to transport immediately the cotton-padded shoes, heavy coats, winter jackets, and blankets. [I] hope that Comrade Gao Gang will take care of these issues."[14] (Gao was vice president of the PRC, chairman of the CCP Northeast Bureau, and the commander and political commissar of the PLA Northeast Military Region.)

From December 22 to February 13, the 9th Army Group began its period of rest and reorganization. Mao continued to show his concern and care for the army group's recovery, emphasizing an immediate need of replenishment to the army groups in Korea. He cabled Peng on December 13: "It is extremely important to replenish with large numbers of new recruits by mid-January next year. It is expected that Gao [Gang] will speed up the preparation for this task. . . . Song Shilun's army group needs to be replenished to full strength immediately by replacing its losses."[15] On December 30, the chairman telegraphed Song Shilun asking, "How is the 9th Army Group doing these days? Does everyone have a hot meal? Has the issue of clothes, shoes, and blankets been solved? How about taking care of the wounded? What is the total number of the wounded and sick men? What are the total casualties of this campaign on the eastern front?"[16]

On January 4, 1951, Mao drafted an order for the CMC to collect and transfer seasoned PLA veterans into the CPVF in Korea: "It is extremely important to make the call for a nationwide draft (except the armies in Tibet and Xinjiang) of the experienced veterans to replenish the Volunteer Force. It is also greatly significant to the entire People's Liberation Army. By doing so, all the combat units of the PLA will have volunteer troops to participate in the War to Resist the United States and Aid Korea."[17] It seemed to Mao that the Korean War had become a combat laboratory that offered the PLA forces essential fighting experience. Later, the PLA high command began to rotate Chinese troops into Korea to give them modern warfare experience fighting against American forces as well as to reinforce the CPVF troops in Korea.

In January, the CMC transferred 20,000 seasoned veterans from the 20th Army Group in China to the 9th Army Group in Korea. In February, the East China Regional Command sent 30,000 new recruits to the 9th's armies. In the meantime, the regional command also transferred five regiments and five battalions from East China to the 9th Command. Among these troops were 48,000 men who received newly arrived Soviet-made weapons in Shenyang before leaving China for Korea.[18] China funneled as many troops into Korea as its transportation and supply system could handle. Mao's conviction that any battle could be conducted upon the principles of mobile warfare dominated Chinese military doctrine during the early offensive campaigns from the fall of 1950 to the early spring of 1951.[19] These large-scale mobile tactics like encirclement and annihilation proved effective in the first two offensive campaigns. By mid-April, the Chinese had 950,000 troops in Korea, including forty-seven infantry divisions, eight artillery divisions, and four antiaircraft artillery divisions.[20]

Song Shilun believed that his attacks on the 1st Marine at Chosin failed because of the lack of necessary firepower. When the 9th Army Group was confronted with the defenses of the American troops, the weak firepower of the former became obvious and was an immediate disadvantage to the 9th's armies. With very little artillery support, the 9th's troops mostly depended on their light weapons, such as rifles, hand grenades, and bayonets, to fight against marine firewalls established by tanks, heavy artillery, and automatic weapons. The CPVF forces sorely lacked adequate automatic weapons and munitions in this modern war. Mao telegraphed Stalin on November 8, 1950, asking the Soviets to provide 140,000 automatic rifles with 58 million rounds of ammunition, 26,000 submachine guns with 80 million rounds, 7,000 light machine guns with 37 million rounds, 2,000 heavy machine guns with 20 million rounds, plus other weapons and munitions.[21] After its second echelon entered Korea, the CPVF demanded more Soviet military aid to support its offensive campaign against the UNF. Such aid proved indispensable for the CPVF's large-scale operations on the Korean front. During the first quarter of 1951, for example, the CPVF needed 14,100 tons of ammunition for the Korean battleground. While China's own defense industry produced a mere 1,500 tons, the Soviet Union supplied the remaining 12,000 tons between January and March.[22] Stalin also increased the number of Soviet military advisers in China. Among the 80,000 Soviets sent to China in the early 1950s, most were military advisers.[23]

Nevertheless, very few divisions of the 9th received Soviet weapons before the Fifth Offensive Campaign. In March, Hong Xuezhi, deputy commander of the CPVF in charge of weaponry and logistics, provided the 9th Army Group with additional artillery, transportation, and medical troops.[24] Its 20th Army was reinforced with two artillery regiments; the 26th Army with one field artillery regiment and three antitank companies;[25] and the 27th Army with two field artillery regiments and three antitank companies.[26] Hong Xuezhi complained that since the Soviet Union did not have sufficient transportation to deliver the arms immediately, the CPVF received Soviet arms for only sixteen out of sixty infantry divisions in 1951.[27]

During its recovery period, Song Shilun and other commanders in the 9th Army Group held a series of evaluation meetings to assess the Battle of Chosin in January–February. Song blamed himself for the army group's failure to achieve the battle goal of annihilating the 1st Marine Division. Moreover, the 9th Army Group's Party Committee also decided to punish some of the commanders and officers, who had not followed their orders, left their command positions in the middle of an operation, hesitated at crucial moments, or failed to accomplish their duties or tasks. Some of them were demoted, some lost their jobs, and the others faced court-martial.[28]

The 9th Army Group held an extended conference of its Party Committee on March 8. Song made his final report on the Battle of Chosin with an emphasis on his responsibility as the commander for the failed battle. First, he admitted his strategic mistake of not deploying the 26th Army to the front line on time, such that the army missed the opportunity to destroy the marines. He recalled with regret, "It proves that the campaign result could be totally different, if the 26th had followed the 27th Army to move into the front; then the 20th Army had concentrated its attacks on the enemy at Yudam-ni and the 26th and 27th Armies had concentrated their attacks on the enemy at Hagaru-ri."[29] Second, he also admitted making "serious" tactical mistakes during the attacks. Without these mistakes, the troops of the 9th "could have annihilated the isolated enemy. They could have destroyed the enemy a few days sooner and reduced the large number of our combat and noncombat casualties."[30] Song pointed out, "Therefore, although this campaign may have achieved a significant victory, we performed poorly on commanding the battle and executing the operations that had seriously minimized the outcome of the campaign."[31] Third, Song again blamed the logistics, including the lack of supply and transportation. At the CPVF commanders' conference on April 6, when Peng was planning the Fifth Offensive Campaign, Song still emphasized that his failure at the Chosin Reservoir resulted from lack of food, winter clothing, and ammunition.[32]

Following Song's self-criticism, the army commanders also explored their own miscalculations to share the responsibility for the failed annihilating operation. The 27th Army Command, for example, submitted their campaign report, which examined their mistakes in operations at Chosin. First, the army command did not have accurate information on the enemy forces at Sinhung-ni (west) and Hagaru-ri, where one marine battalion had been expected, but where, in fact, four battalions were encountered. Second, the army failed to concentrate its forces, and instead equally deployed its divisions at Sinhung-ni (west) and Hagaru-ri. None of its four divisions could destroy any of the marine units at either location. Third, the army command underestimated the enemy's firepower and did not comprehend the marines' combat tactics, leading to heavy casualties and several major miscalculations, such as the lost opportunity to destroy the marines at the Inlet on November 27–28 and the failure to organize a counterattack on Sihungung to stop the marine retreat on December 3. Fourth, the army did not establish a front command post; instead, its headquarters was located at Suchung, far away from its divisions. When HQ telephone lines were cut off by UNF air raids and artillery bombardment, the army command lost efficient communication with its divisions. Last but not least, the army also recognized its ignorance and incompetence in logistics, which had also led to many casualties during the battle.[33]

Following the army's self-criticism, each division command explored its own miscalculations and mistakes at Yudam-ni. The 79th Division pointed out that its commanders did not plan a good annihilating attack by flanking and penetrating the marines' positions. Instead, the division command launched a parallel attack to flush out the enemy troops. The division lost five out of its nine battalions in one night of attacks on November 27. Thereafter, the division was unable to accomplish any of its assignments, especially the roadblock to stop the marine retreat from Yudam-ni to Hagaru-ri. The 79th also reported that the division command had punished several regiment and battalion commanders who failed to follow orders during the battle. The commander of the 235th Regiment, for example, did not carry out the division orders after November 27 saying, "We lost in the first attack, and we can't attack again." His regiment lost two of its three battalions in the first night's attacks.[34] The 94th Division commanders made serious planning mistakes by exposing its troops to the air raid and cold weather, such that the division lost the combat capacity of two of its three regiments before the major engagements against the marines. The division did not accomplish any of its tasks during the battle. Moreover, some commanders and officers of the companies and platoons deserted from their command posts and ran away from the front line.[35]

No high-ranking officer was punished, however, since Mao and the CMC did not consider the Battle of Chosin a failure. As the Second Offensive Campaign in November–December 1950 became viewed as a major victory of the CPVF, the battle experience of the 9th Army Group was praised as heroic, significant, and successful by the PLA high command and Chinese media. Then, in January 1951, Beijing was overwhelmed by the victory of the CPVF's Third Offensive Campaign of December 31–January 8. After taking over Seoul, the Chinese government organized parades and parties, complete with fireworks. To many Chinese, the CPVF seemed to be winning the war in Korea.

New Offensive Plan and Logistics

After the Third Offensive Campaign ended on January 8, 1951, the CPVF Command required a more cautious strategy. By this time, the U.S. and UN forces had brought to bear superior firepower on the ground and in the air, inflicting heavy casualties and serious damage on CPVF troop movements and lines of supply and communication. However, Soviet advisers in Beijing questioned why the CPVF Command did not follow up its victory and pursue the UNF further into South Korea. Pressure was mounting to launch another attack.

Stalin and Kim urged the CPVF to launch a new offensive immediately and to drive the UNF out of Korea. Mao also cabled Peng at the end of January and urged organization of the CPVF's Fourth Offensive Campaign to drive the UNF farther south. Under tremendous pressure from the political leaders of all three Communist countries (China, the Soviet Union, and North Korea) for a quick victory, the CPVF Command recognized the growing gap between political goals and strategic realities.[36] As the CPVF struck farther south, its tactics, such as surprise attack, flanking operations, and encirclement and annihilation, began losing effectiveness. In the meantime, the UNF had recovered from its early surprise of the first three CPVF offensive campaigns and launched a counterattack on January 25. General Hong Xuezhi later recalled, "We were compelled to fight the Fourth Campaign."[37] From January 25 until April 21, the CPVF engaged in its Fourth Campaign, but instead of a mass offensive, it became a series of back-and-forth mobile battles. The 26th Army of the 9th Army Group participated in the Fourth Offensive Campaign from March 28 to April 21.

After February 1951, China's strategic goal had shifted from driving the UN Forces from the peninsula for a quick victory to that of a protracted war that the CPVF would win by inflicting heavy casualties and eliminating several U.S. and ROK divisions. Mao explained to Joseph Stalin on March 1 that, if the Chinese forces could inflict hundreds of thousands of casualties on American troops in the next few years, it would force a U.S. withdrawal,[38] and therefore the CPVF would have to deliver a heavier blow in the next offensive. Mao's goal for the Chinese forces was to eliminate four UNF divisions and two brigades, or about 50,000 enemy troops, in the next offensive.[39] After Stalin agreed with this plan on March 5, Mao issued orders to Peng Dehuai on March 7 to employ all troops along the front line, and to counterattack the UNF before it could get a firm foothold north of the 38th parallel.[40] Out of these discussions, Mao and Peng began planning the Fifth Phase Offensive Campaign in the spring of 1951.

In March, the Chinese high command was convinced that General Ridgway planned to conduct an amphibious landing in the Chinese–North Korean rear areas to cut off the CPVF and NKPA's transportation and communication lines, forcing them to fight on two fronts at once. The lack of reliable intelligence sources and limited foreign war experience seriously impaired the Chinese leaders' ability to have an accurate picture of UNF intentions. Chinese intelligence failures led Peng to miscalculate the situation and rush into a new offensive campaign before his forces were fully ready. In early March, Peng considered an immediate southward strike before the expected U.S. amphibious landing. At a CPVF Command meeting on March 11, Peng proposed having the CPVF forces strike the advancing U.S. I and IX Corps, push them back south of the 38th parallel, and retake Seoul if possible. He set mid-April as the starting time for the Fifth Offensive Campaign, when the main strength of the second echelon would reach the front.[41] On March 14, Peng stressed to his generals that "the next campaign will be the decisive battle" of the Korean War.[42] The Chinese high command seemed triumphally confident of their ability to both eliminate a large number of UNF troops and move south of the 38th parallel.

On April 6, Peng chaired a Fifth Campaign conference at Kumhwa (Keumhwa), including all the commanders and political commissars at the army, army group, and HQ levels. The chief told his generals that "the best time for our counterattacks is now. The enemy troops are exhausted and not at full strength. They have not supplied their ranks to compensate for their casualties, and have no reinforcements in sight." He added, "according to the information, MacArthur and Ridgway visited the eastern front in the past few days. The enemy seems to be planning a new offensive in the east, and a landing along the eastern coast at the Tongcheon (Tongchon)-Wonsan areas. They wanted to push all the way to the north of the 39th parallel."[43] Peng then outlined the objectives for the CPVF Spring Offensive. First, this campaign would prevent the enemy force from landing in North Korea. The chief pointed out that "this campaign is extremely important . . . [because] we must smash the enemy's plan."[44] Peng's first campaign objective was a practical one that was strategically important for Mao to accept, but not too hard for the CPVF to achieve. The second objective was to exceed Mao's expectations by destroying three U.S. divisions, three ROK divisions (Mao only asked for one), and three British and Turkish brigades (Mao asked for two). Peng asserted, "We must eliminate several enemy divisions and smash the enemy's war plans."[45] The main targets were the U.S. Army 3rd, 24th, and 25th Divisions; the ROK 1st, 2nd, and 6th Divisions; the British 27th and 29th Brigades; and the Turkish Brigade under the I and IX Corps. Simply put, Peng's overall campaign objective was to "regain the initiative."[46]

All of the commanders at the April 6 conference reflected Peng's enthusiasm and optimism. Sharing the optimism and confidence of the newly arrived commanders, Song Shilun believed that the 9th Army Group would definitely achieve a victory in the Fifth Offensive Campaign.[47] Although he did not mention it, the commanders knew that Song desperately wanted to take revenge against the Americans and regain his reputation. To strengthen the 9th, Peng and the CPVF transferred the 39th and 40th Armies from the 13th Army Group to the command of the 9th Army Group. This gave the 9th five armies total, including fifteen infantry divisions comprising 250,000 men.[48]

Thus, all three army groups, encouraged by Peng and supported by the CPVF Command, seemed ready to fight the CPVF Fifth Campaign. Peng telegraphed Mao on April 10 that the 3rd, 9th, and 19th Army Groups were to concentrate on the western front, attacking the I and IX Corps. The 9th and 19th Army Groups would flank the U.S. forces from both sides, while the 3rd Army Group would launch the frontal attack to cut the enemy forces into several pieces. Then the three army groups would conduct their all-out attacks to win a complete victory and annihilate several enemy divisions along the 38th parallel. After their success, the army groups would move farther south, deep into enemy territory.[49] Mao approved Peng's plan on April 13.[50]

On April 18, Peng ordered all three army groups to be prepared and combat-ready by the 20th and to start the attacks on either April 21 or 22. According to his plan, Peng ordered Song's 9th Army Group to engage in flanking attacks and operational encirclements on the UNF's right. The 9th would move out from Kumhwa, penetrate south, and then cut off the U.S. 24th and 25th Divisions from other UNF units.[51] Its 20th Army was to move west to cut off the rear of the British 27th Brigade and then to eradicate the British brigade. After that, the 20th Army would move into Paecheon (Paechon) to separate the U.S. 24th Division.[52] The 26th Army's mission was to hold back, by any means, the UNF's northern advance toward the CPVF's positions. After the attacks had begun, the 26th Army would move out to stop the 24th and 25th Divisions' further movement to the north or northeast to protect the 27th Army's right flank. Eventually, the 26th Army would help the 20th and 27th Armies wipe out the U.S. 24th Division.[53] In addition, the 39th and 40th Armies, both of which had transferred to the command of the 9th Army Group, would move into areas west and southwest of Sanyang-ri after the attacks began and drive through the UNF line in the middle, cutting off the UNF troops on the eastern front from those on the western front.[54]

The UNF Command's strategies became clear by the spring of 1951. After seizing and consolidating its new positions, it launched quick attacks so that the Chinese troops did not have enough time to resupply or reinforce their weary troops. The UNF used this strategy with the specific goal of exhausting the CPVF's soldiers and supplies. It worked. Although the CPVF campaign planners based their operations on receiving significant reinforcements in Korea, the issue of maintaining combat effectiveness and adequate supplies became their top priorities.

Peng and the CPVF commanders knew that they could not sustain the engagement for long if the logistics and supply lines were not immediately improved. The high command continued to improve the CPVF's logistics and transportation by establishing its own logistics department in Korea during the Fifth Offensive Campaign. Before April 1951, the PLA had delivered all food and munitions from China by the PLA Northeast Regional Command's Logistics Department to each CPVF army in Korea. Food and ammunition shipments always lagged behind the operations.[55] During the first two campaigns, the CPVF met only one-quarter of the food needs of its frontline troops. In the Third Offensive Campaign, frontline troops received 30–40 percent of their minimum needs. These shortfalls seriously constrained CPVF operations. On April 16, the CMC decided to "organize the Logistics Department of the CPVF General Headquarters between Andong [in China] and the site of the CPVF Headquarters [in North Korea]."[56] On May 19, the CMC issued its "Decision on Strengthening the Volunteer Forces' Logistics Tasks" and ordered that "the Logistics Department of the CPVF should be established immediately. It will command and manage all the Chinese logistics units and facilities within Korea. The CPVF Logistics Department is under the direct command of the CPVF leading commanders."[57] Hong Xuezhi became the head of the new department.

Under Hong, the CPVF Logistics Department set up a new system that better fit the CPVF's needs during the Fifth Offensive Campaign. The new system improved CPVF logistics capacity at the regiment and battalion levels and increased frontline troops' combat effectiveness. Logistics branches, moving closely behind the front, would provide an additional five days' food. All the logistics forces were assigned a "transportation responsibility by section," which significantly increased efficiency of transportation and the distribution of material supplies. By early May, the CPVF had stockpiled 15,000 tons of food and three to five base units of ammunition in stocks. Despite all these changes, the CPVF's logistics efforts did not fundamentally improve, and they were only capable of providing supplies to meet the soldiers' minimum requirements for a short period. There was still no guarantee that they could meet operational demands.[58] Chinese solutions to battlefield problems were neither elegant nor effective. The Chinese military's performance in Korea fit this characterization, and they faced a steep learning curve before they could achieve their battlefield objectives.[59]

The First Phase: A New Offensive but the Same Old Problem

Of all these campaigns, the Chinese Fifth Offensive proved the most decisive. Lasting from April 22 through June 2, 1951, it was the largest and longest Communist military operation of the war, as well as the largest battle since WWII. The CPVF-NKPA Joint Command deployed more than 700,000 men, including 600,000 CPVF troops, against 340,000 UNF troops. As Peng Dehuai anticipated, "This is the battle [that] will determine the fate of the Korean War."[60] However, he did not expect that the CPVF Spring Offensive would fail. Peng's sudden change, moving up the offensive starting date by almost an entire month, threw the entire second-echelon forces, including the 3rd and 19th Army Groups, into action without necessary preparations. Most of the divisions were not combat-ready, and some had not received much-needed food and ammunition. The UNF put up a strong defense, drove the Chinese forces back north of the 38th parallel, and inflicted 105,000 casualties. After the Chinese failure in this million-man battle, the war settled into a stalemate and a more conventional pattern of trench warfare emerged along the 38th parallel.

Of the three groups, the 9th Command was better prepared. At 5:00 P.M. on April 22, when the 9th Army Group, totaling 250,000 men, attacked the IX Corps in the center, the Fifth Offensive Campaign began. According to Peng's plan, Song ordered his armies to engage in flanking attacks and operational encirclements on the UNF right. His five armies struck a sixteen-mile UNF defense line held by the ROK 6th, and the U.S. 24th, 25th, and 1st Marine Divisions. The 39th and 40th Armies of the 9th broke through the line held by the ROK 6th Division and penetrated into the central mountainous area, splintering the ROK 6th from the 1st Marine and dividing the western UNF divisions from those on the eastern front.[61] The 39th Army's main force, under the command of Wu Xinquan, occupied Hwacheon and linked up with the 40th Army.[62] Wen Yucheng, commander of the 40th, sent his 118th Division to break through the UNF line at the ROK 6th Division's positions. The 118th broke the ROK 6th's defense at Hakshina-ri (Hakashinari), and then the Chinese division quickly cut deep (sixteen to eighteen miles) into UNF territory, reaching Hwaeumdong the next day.[63]

On April 23, the 3rd Battalion, 354th Regiment (3/354) of the 118th Division reached its designated target—Mukdong-ri (Mukdongri), northeast of Kapyeong—by marching five miles per hour, climbing the three-thousand-foot heights at Hyounhyeon (Hyounhyon), and crushing the UNF defense lines.[64] To guard the left flanks of the 9th Army Group, Wen Yucheng dispatched his 119th Division to Sachang-ri to protect the highway between Jichon-ri (Jichonri) and Sachang-ri from the 1st Marine at Hwacheon. Wen also ordered his 120th Division to occupy Turyusan and Jangkunsan.[65] On April 24, the 120th Division reached Mapyeong-ri, the designated operational target, and joined forces with the 39th Army to prevent the 1st Marine east of the Pukhan-gang River from moving west.[66] The 120th intercepted one battalion from the 1st Marine Division. However, it was unable to destroy the marine battalion even after an all-night attack, because it lacked artillery and antitank guns. The 120th Division then marched twelve miles deeper into the ROK 6th Division's rear, disrupting the South Koreans' force deployment. The 39th and 40th Armies had managed to split the UN forces down the middle within the first two days of the campaign, facilitating the encirclement of the ROK 6th Division.[67] Although the army commanders hoped they could capture some UNF supplies after destroying the enemy units, as they often managed to do during the Chinese Civil War, it did not happen.

In the meantime, the 20th, 26th, and 27th Armies of the 9th flanked the western UNF from the right. Zhang Yixiang, commander of the 20th Army, ordered his 60th Division to attack the ROK 6th Division. On April 24, the 60th Division sent its 179th Regiment to break through the ROK 6th lines and the ROK defense collapsed.[68] When the 6th Division fled south under the heavy Chinese attacks, it abandoned twenty-nine American howitzers, forty-one mortars, and 160 vehicles.[69] However, the Chinese could not remove the vehicles or artillery pieces since none of the soldiers knew how to drive. They secured twenty-seven trucks and destroyed all the remaining vehicles and equipment at the site.[70]

By April 24, the 9th Army Group had accomplished its first-stage task of splitting the UNF in the center and flanking the IX Corps on the right.[71] Its armies moved forward ten to eighteen miles, occupying the area of Yonghwadong. The 26th Army, under the command of Zhang Renchu, occupied positions northwest of Jipo-ri (Jipori) and began a strike toward Yeongpyeon (Yeongpyon). The 27th Army sent its 80th and 81st Divisions to break through the middle of the U.S. 24th Division's defense lines, and they occupied Yonghwadong by April 24.[72] Song Shilun, adjusting his force deployments, ordered all five armies to "seize the opportunity to cut off the enemy's southern retreat, advancing with courage and a strong will to split them into groups for annihilation." He also instructed all armies to make "bold decisions in accordance with the enemy's situation" and to act "rapidly and decisively to make sure no opportunities are lost."[73]

On April 25, the 9th Army Group began its attempts to annihilate the U.S. 24th Division, which had been cut off and encircled by the 20th and 27th Armies in five places southeast of Paecheon and south of Seopo.[74] The Chinese armies, however, were unable to destroy any of the regiments, not even a battalion of the U.S. 24th Division. There were several reasons for this: first, UNF forces, under the pressure of CPVF massive attacks, had already made a general withdrawal, allowing the 24th Division an advantage in saving its forces from the Chinese onslaught.[75] Second, Lt. General James A. Van Fleet, new commander of the U.S. Eighth Army, had studied and understood the CPVF's attack pattern and ordered his divisions to withdraw approximately twelve to twenty miles per night, which was the expected distance to keep them out of striking range of the 9th's armies, but close enough to maintain contact with the Chinese attacking forces. With an accurate view of the Chinese troops' position and movement, the 24th Division was able to call air, artillery, and tank strikes against the 9th's armies during the daytime, inflicting huge casualties on the helpless Chinese ground forces.[76] This weakened the attacking 9th armies significantly enough to reduce the threat to UNF troops of their previously terrifying night assaults.

The superior UNF ground firepower and air cover rendered the 9th's armies' chance of blocking the withdrawal of the 24th Division almost zero. The commander of the 20th Army, Zhang Yixiang, sent his 59th Division to Jangmyeong-ri (Jangmyongri) to cut off the 24th's retreat. However, because of the heavy air raids and artillery bombardment, the 59th could not reach the point and complete the encirclement before the U.S. division withdrew to the south.[77] On April 27, the 27th Army began its attacks on the 24th Division.[78] The 9th Army Group Command also ordered the 40th Army to extend its forces south of Kapyeong to block reinforcements heading toward the 24th's flank.[79] Intensified UNF air raids targeted CPVF logistics depots and transportation lines. The Chinese logistics could not keep up with the armies' movements and operations due to fierce UNF air raids and artillery bombardment. By this point, the 9th's attacking armies were running short of supplies.

On April 27, the fifth day of the CPVF Spring Offensive Campaign, the 20th and 27th Armies ran out of food and ammunition. Without ammunition and artillery shells, the two armies were unable to destroy one American battalion or even a company of the 24th Division over the next two days.[80] Marshal Nie Rongzhen, acting chief of the PLA General Staff and vice chairman of the CMC, pointed out that the troops of the 27th Army "broke through the UNF defensive line in the Hyon-ri area" and cut off the U.S. 24th Division's retreat. But "they had to call a halt to their attacks for three days to wait for supplies of munitions and food, consequently losing a good battle opportunity." The PLA marshal recalled that the UNF had "found out the pattern of the CPVF operations."[81] The chief believed that the Americans "knew that our forward offensive depended entirely on the food and munitions carried by the attacking troops themselves. Usually, the troops' food and munitions could support only a one-week-long operation; indeed, the American army called our charges 'one-week attacks.'"[82] The 9th's armies, still waiting for food and ammunition, were unable to prevent the 24th Division from breaking through roadblocks and retreating south. On April 29, after the 24th's withdrawal, the Chinese armies occupied Jinpeol-ri, Kapyeong, and Chuncheon, without having annihilated a single American unit.[83]

The failure to annihilate the U.S. 24th Division resulted from lack of supplies for the attacking forces of the 9th Army Group. Its supplies were stretched far too thin to guarantee that the 9th Army Group's armies could receive even a basic daily minimum of food and ammunition. By April 27–28, the attacking forces were running out of food and ammunition.[84] The 9th was better prepared among the three army groups, but its five armies had run out of food and ammunition by the fifth day of the Spring Campaign. Song Shilun was aware of the transportation problems that were handicapping his supply lines, and so the 9th Command required all attacking army personnel to carry enough food and ammunition for themselves for a five-day period.[85] The infantry also transported artillery shells. Soldiers carried an average of sixty to seventy pounds of supplies apiece when they launched their attacks.[86] On April 29, the 9th Army Group pulled back its 26th Army from north of Pyeongkang (Pyeongchang), and resupplied the army.[87] The 39th Army was deployed at Chuncheon and Hwacheon for resupply while it remained prepared to protect the CPVF main positions. Two days later, the 40th Army moved back to Sawon-ri (Sawonri) for resupply.[88]

After one week of offensive moves, Peng Dehuai called off all attacks along the western front due to the lack of supplies and heavy casualties. So far, the CPVF had not been able to annihilate any UNF division, or even a regiment, during their first stage of the Fifth Offensive Campaign, while suffering 35,000–60,000 casualties in less than one week.[89] Peng explained the heavy losses to Mao on April 26 saying, "We were not adequately prepared, especially on food and ammunitions, and our transportation has not been improved." Peng suggested in the same telegram: "We must build up highways from Seocheon to Yangteok as soon as possible and make it our future primary transportation and supply line in the front center without any delays caused by two-way traffic. This had caught our attention when we first entered Korea but it has not been completed today due to the lack of efforts."[90] Mao Zedong and the CMC approved Peng's request on April 28 that the CPVF end its southward offensive on the western front.[91] On April 29, the first stage of the CPVF Spring Offensive ended with minimal positive results, but with heavy Chinese casualties.

The Second Phase: Attack on the ROK Divisions

Peng Dehuai was disappointed by the negligible gains on the western front in the Fifth Offensive Campaign in late April.[92] Given the huge CPVF casualties on April 22–29, Peng was forced to balance the Chinese losses by continuing the offensive campaign. The Joint CPVF-NKPA Command looked for a new opportunity to strike the UNF south of the 38th parallel. Peng faced a dilemma. Although he sought revenge and hoped to regain the initiative, his lack of firepower and supplies made any attempt to annihilate any U.S. division or British brigade a near impossibility. Any further offensive in the west or an attack on Seoul would certainly bring more Chinese casualties and could lead to total disaster.

Thus, in early May, he decided to shift the offensive's focus from the west to the east. Rather than attacking the Americans on the western front, he would attack the weaker South Korean divisions on the eastern front, and have a better chance to win the next phase of the Spring Offensive Campaign and to balance the casualty sheet of the Korean War. Peng issued operational orders to all CPVF armies in early May: "The second phase of the Fifth Campaign must concentrate [our] forces to annihilate the ROK 3rd, 5th, and 9th Divisions at the Hyeon-ri area first, and then to annihilate the ROK Capital and 11th Divisions later depending on the campaign development on the battleground."[93]

On May 6, Peng called an operation-planning meeting at the CPVF headquarters. According to his plan, the 20th Army of the 9th Army Group would break through the defense line of the ROK 7th Division and then penetrate to the rear of the ROK 3rd and 9th Divisions at Hyeon-ri. Here the 20th Army would meet the NKPA V Corps, including the 6th, 12th, and 32nd Divisions, to complete the first, or "inner" layer of the encirclement. The 27th Army would advance along the axis of Sangnam-ri (Sangnamri) west of Inje and meet the North Korean II Corps at Maesan-ri to close the second, "middle" layer of the envelopment. Peng and the CPVF Command transferred the 12th Army to the command of the 9th Army Group. The 12th would break through the ROK 5th Division and move toward Changchou-ri (Changchouri), creating the third, "outer" layer with one division of the NKPA II Corps.[94]

On May 9, after ten days' rest, the main forces of the 9th Army Group began moving eastward. The Joint Command required all attacking forces to be supplied with adequate ammunition and food prior to May 10.[95] This would allow the attacking force to begin its eastern movement during the nights of May 9 or 10, reach the staging areas before dawn on May 14, and be ready to launch the surprise assaults by dusk of May 16. By the 15th, all the assault forces had reached the staging areas, the banks of both the Pukhan-gang and Soyang Rivers, without UNF detection. The NKPA II, III, and V Corps had also reached Inje and the areas east of the town. The CPVF Command ordered its 39th Army to cross the Soyang River and move to areas between Chuncheon and Hongcheon (Hongchon), where they could cover the wing of the 9th Army Group as it covertly advanced east.[96]

On the eastern front, after an abrupt artillery barrage at 6:00 P.M. on May 16, the CPVF and NKPA assault forces began all-out attacks on the ROK III Corps, including its 3rd, 5th, 7th, and 9th Divisions.[97] The CPVF 9th Army Group, which was the main attacking force, included the 20th, 27th, and 12th Armies, reinforced by the 11th, 25th, 26th, and 28th Artillery Regiments; all forces were ordered to attack the ROK defense lines that evening. The ROK official war history describes, "Contrary to the expectation of the UN forces, the CCF [Chinese Communist Forces] opened the May offensive with preparatory fire on May 16." The report continues: "This type of artillery fire was atypical and appeared to be fire for registration."[98] The shock of the Chinese attack caused panic in the ROK divisions, many of which abandoned their defensive positions and fell back. A huge gap was thus opened by the 9th Army Group on the U.S. X Corps' left flank.[99]

To ensure victory in the second phase of the Spring Offensive Campaign, Peng, at 1:00 A.M. on May 17, ordered Commander Song Shilun to take immediate and forceful actions:

> After inflicting substantial losses and costs on the enemy during the first stage of the campaign, we have been able to lure the U.S. forces to Chuncheon, all west of the town, all the way to Seoul. This has created the current excellent opportunity for us to concentrate our forces on wiping out multiple ROK units. Therefore, you must overcome all difficulties to meet your operational objectives, wiping out as many ROK forces as possible in order to isolate the U.S. forces for future annihilation. You must conduct bold flanking, penetration,

and encirclement maneuvers against the enemy forces with the aim of obliterating them completely. You must seize all opportunities, attacking during the day, taking advantage of the current changes to the climate, and capitalizing on the enemy's current confused state. You must use solid planning to direct units attached at the corps, division, and regiment level, to search for fleeing enemy troops, abandoned weapons, and equipment. We wish you total victory.[100]

The 20th Army, the 9th Army Group's main assault force, crossed the Soyang-gang River, with a width of approximately 50–100 meters and a depth of 2–5 meters, at 12:00 A.M. on May 17.[101] By 7:00 A.M., the 60th Division of the 20th had rapidly penetrated sixteen miles into ROK defensive areas, occupying Heong-pyeong-ri (Hongpyongri) and Omach'i on the main supply route of the ROK III Corps.[102] That evening, the 178th Regiment of the 60th Division attacked the ROK 29th Regiment of the 9th Division with concentrated mortar fire along the road, killing more than five hundred ROK soldiers and capturing seventy vehicles.[103] Jongnam Na describes that the action: "When ROK soldiers discovered the enemy in the rear, the entire force began to retreat in fear, even before the enemy's frontal attack had started. In less than two days, the ROK corps disappeared, opening a serious gap in UN defense lines."[104] The same day, the NKPA 6th Division of the V Corps occupied Kyetun-ri (Kyetunri) and advanced south during the day to reach the southern mountains of Cheorntong-ri, where the North Korean division met the Chinese 20th Army. By May 17, the CPVF-NKPA forces had completed the inner layer of their encirclement of the ROK forces at Hyeon-ri, blocking retreat routes to the south, southeast, and southwest.

The 20th Army's 58th Division sent its 173rd Regiment to attack the heights west of the Yongpu Highway at 1:00 A.M. on May 18, and the 173rd Regiment seized the key height defended by the ROK 8th Regiment of the 7th Division. In this battle, as well as in many other cases, the ROK regiment lost two companies and "could not even resist the CPVF's penetration and encirclement."[105] When the 58th Division opened an eight-mile-wide sector east of Kuman-ri, the 20th Army and NKPA V Corps used the gap occupied by the 58th as a breakthrough point to advance into the ROK rear for seventeen miles and rapidly sever connections between the ROK 7th and 9th Divisions.[106] The 20th Army cut off the ROK 3rd and 9th Divisions' retreat route. On May 19, its 60th Division occupied Maesan-ri and Mangseongkok, the meeting point of the second layer of the envelopment, even though the NKPA II Corps had not arrived.

In the meantime, the 27th Army of the 9th Army Group penetrated deep into the rear of the ROK III Corps as well.[107] At 11:00 P.M. on May 16, the 27th broke through the ROK defenses at Kuman-ri and Changmodong.[108] Its 79th Division crossed the Soyang River and occupied Oksandong. The division attacked several defense positions of the ROK 8th Regiment of the 7th Division. The army's reserve, the 80th Division, moved to the Eonon-ri (Eononri) area, preparing to launch attacks in the area.

To flank the ROK forces, the 27th Army sent its 81st Division to cross the Soyang near Kanmubong and penetrate into the ROK rear. The 81st in tandem with the NKPA II Corps attacked the ROK troops from behind at Hajinpu-ri (Hajinpuri). The division, under the command of Sun Ruifu, sent the 2nd Battalion of its 242nd Regiment (2/242) to spearhead the penetration maneuvers by attacking the sector boundary between the ROK 5th and 7th Divisions.[109] Ridgway recalled, "Later on the second day of the drive, the ROK 5th and 7th Divisions, which held high ground to the right of Chuncheon, crumpled under heavy Chinese pressure and retreated in disorder."[110] The 2/242 Battalion quickly cut into the ROK defense line by avoiding engagement and continuing its southward advance. The Chinese battalion broke through the ROK 7th Division and infiltrated the rear on the left of the ROK 9th Division. Brigade General Choi Suk, commander of the ROK 9th Division, "hurriedly ordered a withdrawal at 04:00, wary of encirclement as the battle turned fiercer with time."[111] By 5:00 A.M. on May 17, the 2/242 had marched thirty-eight miles in nine hours, reaching and occupying the heights on both sides of Amtal-dong as well as key points at Jaecheon. The 2/242 Battalion had cut off the ROK's southwest retreat route forty minutes ahead of schedule on May 17, in time to catch the ROK 9th Division as it began withdrawing from its positions.[112]

At 3:00 A.M. on May 18, Brigade General Kim, commander of the ROK 3rd Division, ordered all his forces at Hyeon-ri to withdraw via Pangdaesan to Changchon.[113] That afternoon, the 242nd Regiment of the Chinese 81st Division attacked the ROK 30th Regiment of the 9th Division as it attempted to withdraw from its positions and move southwest toward the U.S. 2nd Infantry Division. The 242nd Regiment pelted the unprepared ROK troops with a hail of fire at the roadblock, inflicting heavy casualties and forcing the ROK regiment to pull back to Hyeon-ri.[114] The CPVF 60th and 81st Divisions annihilated five ROK battalions, nearly 3,000 South Korean soldiers.[115]

By May 19, under fierce, continuous onslaught from the 20th and 27th Armies of the 9th Army Group, the ROK 3rd and 9th Divisions at Hyeon-ri were shredded, as troops fled in all directions in total defeat. By May 20, the CPVF-NKPA forces had eliminated approximately 12,000 South Korean troops, which had been the main strength of the ROK 3rd and 9th Divisions at Hyeon-ri and the areas south of the town. The 9th Army Group also captured all of the two ROK divisions' heavy equipment and weapons, while the remaining ROK soldiers fled into the mountains.[116] Ridgway was upset by the serious losses of the ROK and recalled, "The equipment abandoned by the retreating ROK forces was nothing to be shrugged off, however. It was enough to have equipped several complete divisions."[117] However, the 9th Army Group and NKPA V Corps did not expect that most of the ROK forces' command posts and senior officers would flee by American airlift and swift ground transport.[118]

Learning Curves

The CPVF-NKPA Joint Command did not reach its goal of annihilating three to five ROK divisions in the second phase of the Spring Offensive Campaign on May 16–21. The 9th Army Group's attacking forces were only able to destroy the main strength of the ROK 3rd and 9th Divisions, again due to their strategic and tactical miscalculations, unfamiliar terrain, unexpected bad weather, and both old and new challenges. Among the new challenges for the Chinese commanders was the attempt to coordinate with the North Korean army corps to complete three layers of encirclement. By May 19, the 20th Army of the 9th and the NKPA V Corps had only completed the inner layer of encirclement as planned. The joint forces failed to complete the middle and outer encirclements. The 9th Command blamed the North Koreans for the failure.[119] On May 19, the 60th Division of the 20th Army occupied Maesan-ri and Mangseongkok, the meeting point of the second layer of the joint envelopment, but General Choi's NKPA II Corps had not arrived. The main forces of the North Korean corps were hampered by steep mountains and deep snow in the Seorak-san area and could not advance south in time to trap the ROK troops at Hajinpu-ri.[120] Having realized the NKPA II Corps' failure to complete their part of the encirclement, Song Shilun gave new orders to the NKPA III Corps to resolutely block the ROK forces fleeing toward Yangyang. Song also modified his orders to the NKPA V Corps, directing it to assist the Chinese 20th Army to annihilate the ROK 3rd and 9th Divisions at and around Hyeon-ri.

The geography in the middle and eastern parts of the Korean Peninsula also restricted the joint CPVF-NKPA forces from expanding large-scale actions. Most of the mountain ridges in the area run north–south, which was advantageous for penetrating longitudinally, but which made any latitudinal movement difficult. The hills are as high as 600–1,500 meters with steep inclines, up to 60 degrees, covered with a dense growth of pine trees and thick underbrush. For all these reasons, cutting off the retreat of the fleeing ROK divisions was made a great deal more difficult than the CPVF-NKPA command expected.[121] Thus, the CPVF-NKPA forces on the eastern front had formed a mere one and a half layers of encirclement around the two ROK divisions at Hyeon-ri, and the joint forces failed to wipe out a significant number of ROK troops.

Another ongoing problem for Chinese commanders was learning how to fight U.S. forces without suffering heavy casualties. While the 20th and 27th Armies were attacking the two ROK divisions at Hyeon-ri in the east, the 12th Army of the 9th Army Group went on the offensive, attacking the ROK divisions in its center. On May 16, the 12th Army moved out of the Chuncheon and Jichon-ri areas, to press the ROK defensive line at Jangsuwon.[122] After breaking through the ROK defense, the 12th Army assailed the ROK 5th Division in an attempt to destroy Jaeum-ri, which was reportedly defended by ROK troops. However, the 12th's troops found their attack halted by the U.S. Army 2nd Division and a French battalion.[123] Zeng Shaoshan, commander of the 12th Army, requested permission to concentrate his 31st and 34th Divisions in an attack on the U.S. and French forces. Song Shilun denied his request.[124] No one had expected to encounter American forces. None of the precampaign intelligence or reconnaissance reports had indicated that possibility, and Song had learned a hard lesson at the Battle of Chosin.

The CPVF Command, however, ordered the 9th Army Group to attack the U.S. 2nd Division and French battalion, and it reinforced the 12th Army with the 181st Division of the 60th Army to strengthen the attacking forces.[125] Zeng Shaoshan had four divisions on hand to attack the American division. While he launched the 31st Division for a frontal attack, he employed the other three divisions to strike the U.S. 2nd Division to the left of the salient. The 34th Division staged attacks on the U.S. 23rd Regiment and the French battalion at Jaeum-ri, while the 35th Division established the roadblock and defensive positions on the Heongyang Highway, waiting to block the retreating U.S. and French troops and to intercept the ROK 5th Division as it attempted to reinforce them.[126] However, the U.S. 2nd Division held on to Hill 800, also known as "Bunker Hill." After four waves of attacks on the Americans and French, the 12th Army managed to break through UNF positions at Kali-san, while each of the four Chinese divisions suffered heavy casualties.[127] The 12th Army of the 9th Army Group totaled more than 12,000 casualties, a loss of three regiments.

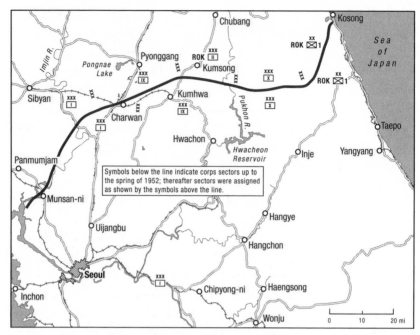

The Stabilized Front, July 1951–July 1953.
Map by Erin Greb Cartography.

The last, but not least, ongoing problem was the shortage of supplies for the Chinese forces. Although the Joint Command attempted to continue supplying its forces after May 16, it could not follow the rapid movements of those forces south of the 38th parallel. Supplies, therefore, always lagged behind operations. By May 20, the Chinese attacking forces had again run out of ammunition across the line.[128] After fighting two almost nonstop major offensive operations within one month, all frontline forces were exceedingly battle-fatigued. Some of the frontline armies had completely run out of food, and the situation for many others was nearly as dire. The HQ of the 20th Army had run out of food and for two days could only cook rice powder for its army radio section, about forty staff and technicians, who provided communication between the army group, the army, and its divisions. The other sections of army HQ resorted to sending out staff as well as officers to gather wild herbs.[129] Many CPVF troops were too hungry and exhausted to continue the fight. Some of the Chinese soldiers left their companies in small groups of five to ten men, looking for food on their own. Many were captured by UNF units.[130]

On May 20, the situation turned against the Chinese. Under these circumstances, Song Shilun concluded that the offensive would only become more difficult to maintain were it to go forward, and unless they succeeded in defeating more enemy units it would not be cost-effective. Furthermore, the U.S. 8th Army counterattacks seemed to have the potential for beating back the CPVF. Under such conditions, the CPVF and NKPA forces would become further dispersed and disconnected at the front. Song and other commanders believed the time had come for their main forces to fall back, rest, resupply, and wait for opportunities to fight again in the future. Fearful of heavy losses, Peng halted the offensive and ordered the withdrawal on May 21. On that date, the Sino-Korean Joint Command issued the order to halt attacks and to conclude the second stage of the Spring Offensive Campaign.

After the loss of their Spring Offensive, the Chinese Communist forces never again came so close to Seoul, nor did they mount another major southward incursion of such magnitude. Their defeat forced Mao to reconsider his aims both politically and militarily. Realizing the huge gap between Chinese capabilities and the ambitious aim of driving the UNF from the peninsula, the Chinese leadership became willing to accept a settlement without total victory. The Chinese Spring Offensive Campaign was the turning point that not only shaped the rest of the war, but also led to the beginning of truce negotiations in July 1951. On June 1, the CMC notified Peng that Song Shilun, commander of the 9th Army Group, would serve as third deputy commander of the CPVF.[131]

Conclusion

Lessons Learned and the Legacy of Chosin

From October 19, 1950, to July 27, 1953, confronted by U.S. air and naval superiority, the Chinese volunteer forces in Korea suffered heavy casualties. According to Chinese military records, Chinese casualties in the Korean War are as follows: 183,108 dead, 383,218 wounded, 455,199 hospitalized, 21,400 prisoners of war, and 4,221 missing in action, totaling 1,047,146 casualties.[1] The dead included Mao Zedong's son, who was serving as a Russian translator at the CPVF HQ and was killed in an air raid. The Chinese soldiers who served in the Korean War faced a greater chance of being killed or wounded than those who served in either WWII or the Chinese Civil War. Among the 21,400 Chinese POWs, 7,110 were repatriated back to China in three different groups in September–October 1953, after the armistice was signed in July.[2] Other Chinese prisoners, about 14,200, went to the Republic of China on Taiwan.[3] China did not fully withdraw its forces from North Korea until 1958. The CPVF had been on the peninsula for eight years since its first entry in October 1950—two years and nine months of actual combat and five years and three months after the Korean Armistice Agreement was signed on July 27, 1953. The PRC spent a total of about 10 billion yuan *Renminbi* (RMB, Chinese currency) during the war, equal to about US$3.3 billion, according to the exchange rate at that time. In terms of war materials and supplies, the Chinese government transported into Korea a total of 5.6 million tons of goods and equipment during the intervention. Between 1950 and 1953, China's military spending represented 41, 43, 33, and 34 percent of its total governmental annual budget.[4]

Mao judged China's intervention a victory because it saved North Korea's Communist regime, promoted China's relations with the Soviet Union, and secured China's northeastern border by preventing North Korea from being conquered or controlled by a Western power like the United States. The military intervention in Korea had maintained China's strong influence in East Asia permanently. Chinese military involvement in Korea had promoted the CCP's international status and projected an image of a powerful China as the vanguard of communism in opposition to the United States.[5] China's increasing political ambition and rising geopolitical importance demanded a strong, modern military to enhance its "prestige and influence in the international arena."[6] Chinese history books portray China as a "beneficent victor" of the Korean War. Peter Hays Gries observes, "To many Chinese, Korea marks the end of the 'Century of Humiliation' and the birth of 'New China.'"[7]

The Korean War marked the first time modern Chinese armed forces engaged in large-scale military operations outside of China. Except for the thinly disguised "volunteer" title, the Chinese military went all-out in engaging one of the best militaries in the world. The Korean War remains the only meaningful reference point for sustained PLA contingency operations beyond China's border. The Chinese generals recalled their fighting in the Korean War as a heroic rescue and an extension of their own struggle against imperialism. By the end of the war, the Chinese generals were convinced that Chinese armed forces were only a regional—not a global—force, and that it was capable of fighting only limited wars in terms of geographic scope and geopolitical objectives. This fact forced the PLA to confront the continued relevance of China's traditional approach, even though China had moved onto center stage in the international Cold War.

Marshal Peng Dehuai stated that the Korean War began the transformation of the Chinese military into a modern force.[8] Peng made important strategic and tactical changes during the war as the CPVF adjusted to changing conditions and continually reassessed its own performance. From the conclusion of the Fifth Offensive Campaign until the end of the war, the CPVF adopted a more cautious and realistic strategy, including maintaining a relatively stable front line, increasing CPVF air force, artillery, and tank units, and beefing up logistical support. Indeed, the CPVF increasingly mirrored its American counterpart in its prosecution of the war. In this respect, the United States turned out to be a "useful adversary" in the Korean War.[9]

The lessons learned from the such battles as the one at Chosin had an impact on subsequent development of the Chinese military, including war strategy and tactics, technology, organization, training, and education. By the end of the war, the CPVF emphasized the role of technology and firepower. The PLA respected its more technologically superior opponents. In order to narrow the technology gap, China purchased weapons and equipment from the Soviet Union to arm sixty infantry divisions in 1951–53.[10] Thereafter, China began a push to standardize its weaponry. The Soviets also transferred technology for production of rifles, machine guns, and artillery pieces. In 1952, the CMC made its first "Five-Year Plan for National Defense," emphasizing air force, artillery, and tank force development.[11] By the end of 1955, the PLA armed a total of 106 infantry divisions, nine cavalry and security divisions, seventeen artillery divisions, seventeen antiaircraft artillery divisions, and four tank and armor divisions with Soviet weapons. These included 800,000 automatic rifles, 11,000 artillery pieces, and 3,000 tanks and armored vehicles. By 1957, the Chinese army had completed its standardization program. Throughout the 1950s, China spent about $2 billion on arms purchases. For Peng Dehuai, who became China's first defense minister in 1954, there was no other option to supply his navy and air force.[12]

Starting in 1952, the PLA began to rotate Chinese troops into Korea to give them modern warfare experience fighting American forces as well as to relieve the CPVF troops already in theater. The PLA had previously fought in wars against Japanese and Chinese Nationalist armies, but it knew little about the American, British, Canadian, and other technologically equipped Western forces. Korea became a combat laboratory that offered Chinese officers and soldiers essential combat training. The Chinese troops sent to Korea included five Chinese air force divisions operating under the CPVF command. In all, about 73 percent of the Chinese infantry troops were rotated into Korea (twenty-five out of thirty-four armies, or 79 of 109 infantry divisions). More than 52 percent of Chinese air force divisions, 55 percent of the tank units, 67 percent of the artillery divisions, and 100 percent of the railroad engineering divisions were sent to Korea.[13] In May 1952, the PLA Department of the General Staff made a rotation plan for the 9th Army Group, including the 20th, 26th, and 27th Armies. In September, the 9th Army Group returned to China.[14]

As part of the officer training effort in the early 1950s, the CMC began an education program to eliminate illiteracy among the officer corps. It created 262 literature schools at the division and army levels to provide elementary and secondary education for the officers. Illiteracy among the PLA officer corps was reduced from 67.4 percent in 1951 to 30.2 percent in 1955. Among the rank and file, the percentage who passed the third-grade literature test increased from 16.4 percent in 1951 to 42.1 percent in 1955.[15] The PLA also opened up new military academies and colleges across the country. It established a complete officer training system from primary to advanced level. This curriculum and training trend moved away from traditional peasant army and guerrilla warfare tactics toward large-scale joint operations.[16] On July 11, 1952, the CMC issued the order to appoint Song Shilun as the superintendent of the General Advanced Army Academy (GAAA) of the PLA and dismissed him from his CPVF deputy commander position in Korea. In August, Song left Korea to take the new position in Nanjing.

From 1953 to 1959, the PLA launched a reform movement to continue its modernization that began during the Korean War. The 1950s reforms aimed to transform the PLA from a peasant army to a modern professional force with new capabilities. The reform programs, following the Soviet model, included major institutional changes, a centralized command system, technological improvement, advanced training and educational programs, reorganization of defense industries, establishment of a strategic missile force, and a nuclear weapons research and development program. At all PLA academies, Soviet advisers worked in the academy at every administrative level and made many executive decisions, hired the instructors, supervised academic affairs, and managed facilities, labs, classrooms, and equipment. It was not until 1957 that Chinese administrators, instructors, and technicians began to manage the academies and carry on the curriculum.[17] There was often a gap between the Soviet and Chinese officers in conception and in their experience of fighting wars. General Song Shilun had some reservations about the "Russianization" of the PLA when he served as GAAA superintendent in 1952–57. He questioned the Soviet advisers' attempt to install a copy of the Soviet infantry system at the GAAA. Song put a great deal of thought into how best to modify the system to fit the condition of the PLA.[18]

In March 1958, when the Academy of Military Science (AMS) of the PLA was founded in Beijing, Marshal Ye Jianying was its president and General Song Shilun became the first vice president. The following March, when the Department of Foreign Military Studies was created at AMS, Song was put in charge of foreign military studies. Ironically, the reforms caused the PLA to become more institutionalized and professionalized as the CCP and the society were becoming more radicalized and ideological. The gap between the army and the party caused a series of political problems, which eventually led to the termination of the reform programs in the early 1960s. Chinese military reform took place only within the greater context of a newly founded republic, constrained by how far the Communist Party was willing to go and what Chinese society at large could support. Marshals Peng Dehuai and Liu Bocheng, like other Chinese military leaders, fought political battles to keep top CCP and government leaders on their side to help implement their reform plans.

Like the social reforms of the period, the 1950s military reforms ended when Peng failed to realize that his relationship with Mao had weakened. Unhappy with the gap between the party and the military, Mao demanded a supportive relationship between the Party Center and the PLA high command like the one that existed during its previous military struggles. While emphasizing professionalism and institutional control, Peng had opposed Mao's personality cult within the army. In 1954, he forbade the construction of statues of Mao at military bases. In 1955, when he read the line "The victory of the CPVF won the war under the correct leadership of the CCP and of Comrade Mao Zedong" in a manuscript, he crossed out "and of Comrade Mao Zedong."[19] When Peng questioned Mao's Great Leap Forward movement, the marshal was purged at the Party's Lushan Conference in the summer of 1959.[20] That fall, 1,848 generals and officers were dismissed or jailed as members either of Peng's "antiparty clique" or the "rightists."[21]

Song Shilun survived the purge of 1959 and continued to institutionalize the PLA by working on organizational standards, military regulations, combat guidelines, and training manuals at the Academy of Military Science (PLA). After the fall of Peng, however, the military leaders split between the so-called "rightist," or pragmatic, group and the "leftist," or radical, group according to their degree of loyalty to Mao. After Peng's fall, Marshal Lin Biao became the defense minister from September 1959 to September 1972. He demanded the politics in command and promoted Mao's ideology of the "people's war." He became the second most powerful party leader next to Mao, who made Lin his successor in 1969 during the Chinese Cultural Revolution (1966–76).

The 1960s remain the most controversial as well as crucial decade in Chinese military history. The PLA made an important change in its strategy in the late 1960s, when the PLA engaged the two superpowers: U.S. forces in the Vietnam conflict and Soviet forces along the Sino-Soviet border.

As a Communist state bordering Vietnam, China actively supported the Vietnamese Communists' war against France during the First Indochina War in 1946–54 and then the war against America. Beginning in 1965, China sent as many as 430,000 troops to North Vietnam to help defend against U.S. forces in the Vietnam War.[22] Through its war efforts in Vietnam and Laos, Beijing tried to break a perceived U.S. encirclement of China. The PLA's military assistance to Vietnam maintained Beijing's influence in Southeast Asia throughout the Cold War. The PLA's deployment successfully deterred any U.S. invasion of

North Vietnam due to U.S. administrations' fear of provoking China. In 1969, however, Chinese influence over North Vietnam decreased as Soviet influence grew.[23] The PLA withdrew its antiaircraft artillery units in March 1969 and all of its support troops by July 1973.

By 1969, the Soviet Union replaced the United States as Beijing's leading security concern, prompting changes in China's strategic thought. Thereafter, the high command prepared for an expected war against the Soviet Union and to repel a Soviet invasion. In 1969–71, the PLA clashed with Soviet forces along the Sino-Soviet border in both Manchuria and Xinjiang. And the border clashes continued until the late 1970s.[24] Reportedly, Moscow's leaders considered using a "preemptive nuclear strike" against China.[25] As a result of its frequent engagements, the PLA increased to more than 6 million men, the highest point in its history. The Soviet threat and conflicts pushed the Chinese leadership to improve relations with the United States. The PRC's strategic needs eventually led to the normalization of the Sino-American relationship when President Nixon visited Chairman Mao in Beijing in 1972.[26]

Domestically, Chinese military historians consider the Cultural Revolution destructive to the PLA. In 1966, all the PLA's general departments were attacked by the Red Guards and became paralyzed in Beijing. Commanders and officers were expelled from their positions. In the course of the cruel questioning sessions, many were tormented or beaten to death. For instance, Lin's followers and leftists called for "destroying the DGPT [Department of the General Political Tasks] hell" and overthrowing General Xiao Hua, director of the DGPT, on July 25. Thereafter, forty top officers in the DGPT were purged, and most of them died in prison.[27] In the PLA Navy, there was an orchestrated "struggle between the two headquarters": the "Leftist Headquarters" and "Rightist Headquarters." In July 1967, the PLAN headquarters printed and issued the "little white book," *Chronicle of the Struggles between the Two Headquarters in the PLAN.* On October 28, the PLAN Party Committee circulated a confession by Yuan Yifen, commander of the South Sea Fleet, and concluded that Yuan "had made serious mistakes and took the wrong side."[28] Yuan was soon dismissed and jailed. From 1967 to 1969, more than 80,000 officers were accused and purged. Among them, 1,169 officers died of torture, starvation, or by execution.

General Song Shilun was also criticized and dismissed from his job at PLA-AMS in the fall of 1966. In January 1967, General Tao Yang, commander of the PLAN East Sea Fleet and the former deputy commander of the 9th Army Group in the Korean War, committed suicide by jumping into a water well to protest mistreatment and unfair investigation by the Red Guards in Shanghai. His wife was tortured to death nine months later.[29] Song's wife also lost her job and was detained by the Red Guards. Song Shilun was not allowed to visit her when she died in December 1967. Many military institutes were shut down and research programs cancelled. The number of military academies was reduced from 125 to 43. Many defense works were destroyed, and regular training actually ceased. The PLA suffered the "most serious damage since the founding of the PRC."[30] Marshal Peng Dehuai died in jail in 1974.

At local levels, the regional and provincial commands were either paralyzed or divided into two or more factions because of their involvement in local factional activities—some siding with one faction, and some with another. For example, the Wuhan Regional Command had an armed clash with the Hubei Provincial Command because of their different opinions over the local, factional mass organizations in July 1967. Their armed conflict, known as the "July 20 Incident," brought the entire province into a civil war. During and after the incident, more than 180,000 officers, soldiers, and civilians were killed or wounded in the city streets of Wuhan.[31]

In 1970, the Cultural Revolution took a sudden unexpected turn. A new political struggle between Chairman Mao and Marshal Lin erupted, a struggle that left a political arena already gasping for breath on life support. Lin and Mao differed over strategy, foreign policy, and domestic politics.[32] Lin and his family realized that Mao was directing the spearhead of his political struggle against them. Just like Peng and Liu, Lin would be the next victim of Mao's brutal political movement. Lin's son, Lin Liguo, planned to assassinate Mao on his way back from Shanghai. Mao realized the danger and returned to Beijing early from Hangzhou on September 12. Lin Liguo's plot failed. The elder Lin, who was implicated in the plot, had taken a fatal step from which there was no return. On September 13, 1971, at the urging of his wife and his son, Lin fled. He commandeered a plane at the Shanhaiguan Airport. He flew north, heading for the Soviet Union. For some unknown reason, the plane crashed in Mongolia.[33] Lin, his family, crew members, and others on board all were killed in the crash.

After Lin's death, Mao launched a nationwide movement to criticize Lin, followed by another top-down purge and shakeup in the military. Thereafter, Marshal Ye Jianying took charge of the PLA's daily affairs and became the defense minister. Song Shilun returned to his position as vice president in 1971 and then became the president of PLA-AMS in 1972. On September 9, 1976, Mao died. The power struggle in the party between the old guard and the Maoists, or the

Gang of Four, which included Jiang Qing, Mao's wifesurfaced. Real control, however, remained in the hands of Ye Jianying, who was vice chairman of the CCP Central Committee and the CMC, a member of the Standing Committee of the Politburo, and minister of defense. On October 6, Ye ordered security troops to arrest the Gang of Four and Mao Yuanxin, Mao's cousin.[34]

After the demise of the Gang of Four, Deng Xiaoping staged a comeback (his third) in 1977. He won the intense struggle of the post-Mao succession by removing the Maoists and gaining firm control of Beijing. He then brought the Cultural Revolution to an end and led China from political turmoil to a period of economic development by denying the need for a continuous domestic class struggle, which was the underlying impulse of Mao's Cultural Revolution. In 1978, Deng emerged as the new paramount leader and launched new reform policies that opened China up increasingly to the outside world.[35] The reforms Deng declared, known as the Four Modernizations—industry, agriculture, science and technology, and national defense—were unprecedented.[36] The official normalization of Sino-U.S. relations on January 1, 1979, led to the rapid creation of an institutional and legal framework for expanded economic cooperation. These efforts paid off; the United States granted Most Favored Nation trading status to China in July 1979 and gradually loosened trade restrictions, shifting the PRC to the category of friendly country in May 1983. The improved relationship was seen in the Sino-U.S. Communiqué of August 17, 1982, signed by President Ronald Reagan during his visit to China.[37]

Deng continued the efforts to modernize and professionalize the PLA in the wake of the 1979 Vietnam incursion. During the 1980–88 reforms, the PLA viewed Deng's economic reforms as favorable and necessary for military restructuring. In 1985, Deng explained his new strategic thoughts to a group of high-ranking commanders. First, the Chinese armed forces should expect a "local war" or a "limited war" rather than a "total war" or a "nuclear war" in the future. Second, to fight the next "local war" or "limited war" a professional army with modern technology was needed. This was another strategic transition from Mao's "people's war" doctrine to a new "people's war under modern conditions" doctrine.[38]

The 1980s reforms followed Deng's new doctrine of fighting a "limited, local war" and emphasized the development and employment of new technology and improvements in PLA weaponry. As the president of PLA-AMS, Song published a few books on active defense as the PLA's principal strategy before he retired in 1985. Deng made some comments on these publications and wrote that he agreed with the concept.[39] Song summarized the warfighting experiences of the PLA against the United States in Korea and Vietnam and developed a China-centered defense that would overcome the "technology gap" between the Chinese and the Western militaries like the U.S. armed forces. Song's proactive form of defense would stop the enemy outside China's borders and avoid a major confrontation on the mainland. From this time forward, China adopted an outward-looking policy, or active defensive military measures, to consolidate and protect its territory by expanding its defense parameter into surrounding areas such as the East China Sea and South China Sea.

Into the twenty-first century, China maintains its dominant power status in East Asia, and it has created favorable international conditions in which it can survive with its huge population and limited resources. Throughout the Cold War and beyond, international relations in East Asia began with China. Russia, the United States, the European Union, and everyone else must cope with China. This is the legacy of China's war for Korea. China's participation in the war contributed significantly to shaping the specific course of post–Cold War international relations. After the Chinese-American confrontation, Northeast Asia became a focal point of the Cold War. China's geopolitical position changed from peripheral to central, and this is still true today. Xi Jinping emphasized this in his speech at the "Sixtieth Anniversary Celebration of the CPVF's Participation in the War to Resist the United States and Aid Korea" in 2010. Xi stated that the tremendous impact and historical significance of the war "will never fade away with time."[40] The war led to a reshaping of China's defense strategy and the creation of a modern army with new technology and tactics. In 2017–18, Xi was reelected as CCP chairman, PRC president, and commander in chief of the PLA up to 2022. Even if largely forgotten in America, the Korean War is by no means forgotten in China.

Notes

Introduction

1. Harold L. Mulhausen met Wu Donglai at a local Chinese restaurant in Oklahoma City, Oklahoma, in July 2015. Wu paid a short visit to his son, Dr. Peng Wu, and his grandchildren, who live in Oklahoma City. The author interviewed both veterans in Oklahoma City before their dinner.

2. Peng Dehuai's telegram to the CPVF armies at 1:00 P.M. on November 28, 1950, in Marshal Peng Dehuai, *Peng Dehuai junshi wenxuan* [Selected Military Papers of Peng Dehuai] (Beijing: Zhongyang wenxian chubanshe [CCP Central Archival and Manuscript Press], 1988) (hereafter cited as *Selected Military Papers of Peng*), 348.

3. Gen. Douglas MacArthur, *Reminiscences* (New York: McGraw-Hill, 1964), 375.

4. Major General Smith also said, "There can be no retreat when there's no rear. You can't retreat, or even withdraw, when you're surrounded. The only thing you can do is break out, and in order to do that you have to attack, and that is what we're about to do." Quoted in Martin Russ, *Breakout: The Chosin Reservoir Campaign, Korea, 1950* (New York: Penguin Books, 1999), 355.

5. Gen. Matthew B. Ridgway, *The Korean War* (Garden City, N.Y.: Doubleday, 1967), 73.

6. Mao Anying was Peng's Russian interpreter and secretary at the CPVF General HQ. For more information on his death, see General Hong Xuezhi, "The CPVF's Combat and Logistics," in Xiaobing Li, Allan R. Millett, and Bin Yu, trans. and eds., *Mao's Generals Remember Korea* (Lawrence: University Press of Kansas, 2001), 118–21; Lieutenant General Du Ping, *Zai zhiyuanjun zongbu: Du Ping huiyilu* [At the CPVF General HQ: Memoirs of Du Ping] (Beijing: Jiefangjun chubanshe [PLA Press], 1989), 94–98; and Senior Colonel Yang Di, *Zai zhiyuanjun silingbu de suiyueli: Xianwei renzhi de zhenshi qingkuang* [My Years at the CPVF General HQ: Untold True Stories] (Beijing: Jiefangjun chubanshe, 1998), 292–95.

7. Stanley Sandler, *The Korean War: No Victors, No Vanquished* (Lexington: University Press of Kentucky, 1999), 127.

8. S. P. MacKenzie, "Period of Mobile Warfare," in James I Matray and Donald W. Boose Jr., eds., *Ashgate Research Companion to the Korean War* (London: Ashgate, 2014), 375.

9. Stephen Taaffe, *MacArthur's Korean Generals* (Lawrence: University Press of Kansas, 2016); Stanley Weintraub, *A Christmas Far from Home: An Epic Tale of Courage and Survival during the Korean War* (New York: Da Capo Press, 2014); David Halberstam, *The Coldest Winter: America and the Korean War* (New York: Hyperion, 2007); Brig. Gen. Edwin H. Simmons, *Frozen Chosin: U.S. Marines at the Changjin Reservoir* (Washington, D.C.: History and Museums Division, U.S. Marine Corps, 2002); Patrick C. Roe, *The Dragon Strikes: China and the Korean War, June–December, 1950* (Novato, Calif.: Presidio Press, 2000); Roy E. Appleman, *East of Chosin: Entrapment and Breakout in Korea, 1950* (College Station: Texas A&M University Press, 1990); Billy C. Mossman, *U.S. Army in the Korean War: Ebb and Flow, November 1950–July 1951* (Washington, D.C.: U.S. Army Center of Military History and U.S. Government Printing Office, 1990); Russell A. Gugeler, *Combat Actions in Korea* (Washington, D.C.: Center of Military History, U.S. Army, 1987); Russ, *Breakout*; Max Hastings, *The Korean War* (New York: Simon & Schuster, 1987).

10. MacKenzie points out, "The single most authoritative work on most of the period, however, is undoubtedly the second half of the second volume in Allan R. Millett's projected trilogy on the Korean War." MacKenzie, "Period of Mobile Warfare," 375.

11. Allan R. Millett, *The War for Korea, 1950–1951: They Came from the North* (Lawrence: University Press of Kansas, 2010), 300–301.

12. Ibid., 356.

13. Russell Spurr, *Enter the Dragon: China's Undeclared War against the U.S. in Korea, 1950–1951* (New York: Newmarket Publishing, 1988), xxi.

14. Shu Guang Zhang covers the CPVF's Second Offensive Campaign from November 25 to December 7, 1950, in seven pages in *Mao's Military Romanticism: China and the Korean War, 1950–1953* (Lawrence: University Press of Kansas, 1995), 113–19. Both of Chen Jian's books—*Mao's China and the Cold War* (Chapel Hill: University of North Carolina Press, 2001) and *China's Road to the Korean War: The Making of the Sino-American Confrontation* (New York: Columbia University Press, 1994)—provide an excellent study of China's Cold War diplomacy from 1949 to 1972 rather than a military history of China.

15. Mao Zedong's telegram to Peng, passed on to Gao Gang, Song Shilun, and Tao Yong, on December 17, 1950, in *Jianguo yilai Mao Zedong junshi wengao* [Mao Zedong's Military Manuscripts since the Founding of the PRC] (Beijing: Junshi kexue chubanshe [Military Science Press] and Zhongyang wenxian chubanshe, 2010) (hereafter cited as *Mao's Military Manuscripts since 1949*), 1:410–11.

16. Marshal Peng Dehuai, "My Story of the Korean War," in Li, Millett, and Yu, *Mao's Generals Remember Korea*, 33.

17. General Hong Xuezhi, *Hong Xuezhi Huiyilu* [Memoirs of Hong Xuezhi] (Beijing: Jiefangjun chubanshe, 2007), 429.

18. Bin Yu, "What China Learned from Its 'Foreign War' in Korea," in Li, Millett, and Yu, *Mao's Generals Remember Korea*, 17.

19. The CPVF claimed that the UNF had total casualties of 36,000 men, including 24,000 American troops. See Hong, *Hong Xuezhi Huiyilu*, 429; Du, *Zai zhiyuanjun zongbu* [At the CPVF General HQ], 125; and National Defense University's War History Series Compilation Team, *Zhongguo renmin zhiyuanjun zhanshi jianbian* [A Concise History of the CPVF War-Fighting] (Beijing: Jiefangjun chubanshe, 1992), 43. The Chinese figures, however, do not coincide with the UNF Command's own casualty accounting. The U.S. 8th Army exceeded 10,000 casualties by December 3, 1950; see Millett, *War for Korea*, 347. X Corps had 8,735 battle casualties between November 27 and December 10; see Mossman, *U.S. Army in the Korean War*, 147. In addition, the Marines had suffered 4,418 battle and 7,313 nonbattle casualties; see Hastings, *Korean War*, 164.

20. Peng, "My Story," 33–34.

21. Sunzi, *The Art of War*, in *The Seven Military Classics of Ancient China*, trans. and ed. Ralph D. Sawyer (New York: Basic Books, 2007), 156.

22. Zhang, *Mao's Military Romanticism*, 119.

23. Mao, "On Protracted War," in *Selected Works of Mao Tse-tung* (Beijing: Foreign Languages Press, 1977) (hereafter cited as *Selected Works of Mao*), 2:143–44.

24. Mao's quote from Military History Research Division, PLA Academy of Military Science, *Zhongguo renmin zhiyuanjun kangmei yuanchao zhanshi* [Combat History of the CPVF in the War to Resist the U.S. and Aid Korea (WRUSAK)] (Beijing: Junshi kexue chubanshe, 1990), 60. Mao also made the same point in his directive to the East Military Region Command on August 11, 1950, in *Mao's Military Manuscripts since 1949*, 1:181–82.

25. Mao's telegram to Zhou on October 14, 1950 in *Mao Zedong junshi wenji* [Collected Military Works of Mao Zedong] (Beijing: Junshi kexue chubanshe, 1993) (hereafter cited as *Collected Military Works of Mao*), 6:122–23. The omitted sentences were published for the first time in CCP Central Archival and Manuscript Research Division, *Dang de wenxian* [Party Archives and Documents] 5 (2000): 8.

26. See, for example, Sawyer, *Seven Military Classics of Ancient China*; Jeremy Black, *Rethinking Military History* (London: Routledge, 2004); and John Keegan, *A History of Warfare* (New York: Knopf, 1993).

27. John K. Fairbank, introduction to John Fairbank, Rosemary Foot, and Frank Kierman, eds., *Chinese Ways in Warfare* (Cambridge, Mass.: Harvard University Press, 1974), 6–7.

28. Ibid.; Keegan, *History of Warfare*, 214, 221, 332–33.

29. For the major works, see Geoffrey Parker, ed., *The Cambridge History of Warfare* (New York: Cambridge University Press, 2008); John A. Lynn, *Battle: A History of Combat and Culture* (New York: Basic Books, 2008); Victor Davis Hanson, *Carnage and Culture: Landmark Battles in the Rise of Western Power* (New York: Anchor Books, 2002); and Fairbank, Foot, and Kierman, *Chinese Ways in Warfare*.

30. For more details on the Western way of war, see Hanson, *Carnage and Culture*; Parker, *Cambridge History of Warfare*; and Keegan, *History of Warfare*.

31. For more details, see William R. Thompson, "The Military Superiority Thesis and the Ascendancy of Western Eurasia," in *Journal of World History* 10, no. 1 (Spring 1999): 143–78; and Hans van de Ven, introduction to *Warfare in Chinese History*, ed. Hans van de Ven (Boston: Brill Academic, 2000), 1–22.

32. Robin Higham and David Graff, introduction to David A. Graff and Robin Higham, eds., *A Military History of China*, extended ed. (Lexington: University Press of Kentucky, 2012), 14.

33. Major General Xu Yan, *Junshijia Mao Zedong* [Mao Zedong as a Military Leader] (Beijing: Zhongyang wenxian chubanshe, 1995), 177.

34. Mao highly praised *The Art of War* and considered it a scientific truth by citing Sunzi in his military writing: "Know the enemy and know yourself, and you can fight a hundred battles with no danger of defeat." Mao, "Problems of Strategy in China's Revolutionary War," in *Selected Works of Mao*, 1:190.

35. Peter Hays Gries, *China's New Nationalism: Pride, Politics, and Diplomacy* (Berkeley: University of California Press, 2004), 56.

36. Mao, "Problems of Strategy in China's Revolutionary War," 1:190.

37. The Soviet Union delivered its weapons to China for sixteen infantry divisions in 1951 and for forty-four divisions in 1952–1954. Marshal Xu Xiangqian, "The Purchase of Arms from Moscow," in Li, Millett, and Yu, *Mao's Generals Remember Korea*, 53.

38. Military History Research Division, *Zhongguo renmin zhiyuanjun kangmei yuanchao zhanshi*, 67.

39. For the discussions, see paper presentations at the Sino-Korean Symposium on the Korean War at Dandong in October 2000; International Cold War History Study Conference at the Wilson Center, Washington, D.C., in March 2001; and International Conference on the Korean War at Beijing in November 2002.

40. He Chuwu, Feng Ming, and Lu Hongyu, *Xuezhan Changjin hu* [The Bloody Battle at the Chosin Lake] (Chongqing, Sichuan: Chongqing chubanshe [Chongqing Publishing House], 2014), 292.

41. Yu, "What China Learned," 9.

42. Major General Qi Dexue, *Kangmei yuanchao gaoceng juece* [The Top Decisions on Resisting the U.S. and Aiding Korea] (Shenyang: Liaoning renmin chubanshe [Liaoning People's Press], 2017); Hu Zhaocai, *Chaoxian zhanzheng, 1950–1953* [The Korean

War, 1950–1953] (Beijing: Taihai chubanshe [Taihai Publishing House], 2017); Li Feng, *Juezhan chaoxian* [The Showdown in Korea] (Beijing: Zhongguo chuban jituan [China Publishing Group], 2017); Senior Colonel Hu Ruiping and Senior Colonel Li Tao, *Zhongguo renmin zhiyuanjun zhengzhan chuanqi* [Important Battles of the CPVF] (Beijing: Changzheng chubanshe [Long March Press], 2016); Shen Zhihua, *Lengzhan zai yazhou: Chaoxian zhanzheng yu zhongguo chubing chaoxian* [The Cold War in Asia: The Korean War and Chinese Intervention in Korea] (Beijing: Jiuzhou chubanshe [Jiuzhou Press], 2013); Major General Qi Dexue, *Ni buliaojie de chaoxian zhanzheng* [The Korean War You Don't Know] (Shenyang: Liaoning renmin chubanshe [Liaoning People's Press], 2011); Jiang Tingyu, *Jiedu kangmei yuanchao zhanzheng* [Understanding WRUSAK] (Beijing: Jiefangjun chubanshe, 2011); Zhang Xingxing, ed., *Kangmei yuanchao: 60 nianhou de huimou* [Resist the U.S. and Aid Korea: Retrospective after 60 Years] (Beijing: Dangdai zhongguo chubanshe [Contemporary China Press], 2011); Deng Feng, "Kangmei yuanchao yanjiu zongshu, 1996–2006" [Korean War History Research in China, 1996–2006], paper presented at the International Cold War Conference, Changchun, Jilin, China, on July 14–17, 2006; Chen Zhonglong, ed., *Kangmei yuanchao zhanzheng lun* [On the WRUSAK] (Beijing: Junshi wenyi chubanshe [Military Literature Press], 2001).

43. Among other historians and archivists are Chu Feng of the PLA Archives, Colonel Sun Lizhou of the GSD, Major General Wang Baocun of PLA-AMS, Senior Colonel Yang Shaojun of the Logistics College of the PLA, and Lieutenant Colonel Guan Zhichao of the Nanjing Political Academy of the PLA. For understandable reasons, other officers and scholars asked the author that their names not be mentioned in the book.

44. The Chinese party documents include CCP Central Archives, comp., *Zhonggong zhongyang wenjian xuanji, 1921–1949* [Selected Documents of the CCP Central Committee, 1921–1949] (Beijing: Zhonggong zhongyang dangxiao chubanshe [CCP Central Party Academy Press], 1989–92); CCP Central Archives, Central Archival and Manuscript Research Division, and CCP Organization Department, comps., *Zhongguo gongchandang zuzhishi ziliao, 1921–1997* [Documents of the CCP Organization's History, 1921–1997] (Beijing: Zhonggong dangshi chubanshe [CCP Central Committee's Party History Press], 2000); and Xinhuashe [New China News Agency], *Xinhuashe wenjian ziliao huibian* [A Collection of Documentary Materials of the New China News Agency] (Beijing: Xinhua chubanshe [New China Publishing House], n.d.).

45. Chinese leaders' papers and manuscripts include *Mao Zedong junshi wenji* [Collected Military Works of Mao Zedong] as *Collected Military Works of Mao*; *Mao Zedong junshi wenxun: Neibuben* [Selected Military Papers of Mao Zedong: Internal Edition] (Beijing: Jiefangjun zhanshi chubanshe [PLA Soldiers Press], 1981); *Jianguo yilai Mao Zedong wengao, 1949–1976* [Mao Zedong's Manuscripts since the Founding of the State, 1949–1976] (Beijing: Zhongyang wenxian chubanshe, 1989–93); *Jianguo yilai*

Mao Zedong junshi wengao [Mao Zedong's Military Manuscripts since the Founding of the PRC]; Liu Shaoqi, *Jianguo yilai Liu Shaoqi wengao, 1949–1955* [Liu Shaoqi's Manuscripts since the Founding of the State, 1949–1955] (Beijing: Zhongyang wenxian chubanshe, 2008); Deng Xiaoping, *Selected Works of Deng Xiaoping* (Beijing: Foreign Languages Press, 1994); Marshal Zhu De, *Zhu De junshi wenxuan* [Selected Military Papers of Zhu De] (Beijing: Jiefangjun chubanshe, 1986); Marshal Peng Dehuai, *Selected Military Papers of Peng*; Marshal Liu Bocheng, *Liu Bocheng junshi wenxuan* [Selected Military Papers of Liu Bocheng] (Beijing: Jiefangjun chubanshe, 1992); Marshal Nie Rongzhen, *Nie Rongzhen junshi wenxuan* [Selected Military Papers of Nie Rongzhen] (Beijing: Jiefangjun chubanshe, 1992); Marshal Xu Xiangqian, *Xu Xiangqian junshi wenxuan* [Selected Military Papers of Xu Xiangqian] (Beijing: Jiefangjun chubanshe, 1992); Marshal He Long, *He Long junshi wenxuan* [Selected Military Papers of He Long] (Beijing: Jiefangjun chubanshe, 1989); and Marshal Chen Yi, *Chen Yi junshi wenxuan* [Selected Military Papers of Chen Yi] (Beijing: Jiefangjun chubanshe, 1996).

46. The Archives of the PRC Ministry of Foreign Affairs, formerly the Archives Section of the General Office of the Foreign Ministry, have 330,000 volumes of documents, which are mainly in paper form, with some microfilms, photos, audio and video tapes, and compact discs. They record China's foreign policy and diplomatic activities since the founding of the PRC in 1949. The archives declassified about 10,000 volumes of the documents in 2004 and 60,000 in 2006.

47. Among other retired generals and officers are Major General Chai Chengwen; Senior Colonel Guan Zhichao; Colonel Zhao Zuorui; Major Huo Zhenlu; Capts. Wang Xuedong, Zheng Yanman, Zhou Baoshan; and others in Beijing, Shanghai, Guangzhou, Nanjing, Wuhan, and Hangzhou. Part of the research effort resulted in a translated and edited volume: Li, Millett, and Yu, *Mao's Generals Remember Korea*.

48. Some of the generals agreed to use their actual names, and other interviewees' names are not mentioned in this book for understandable reasons.

49. As a result of interviews conducted, some of their stories about the Korean War are included in Richard Peters and Xiaobing Li, *Voices from the Korean War: Personal Stories of American, Korean, and Chinese Soldiers* (Lexington: University Press of Kentucky, 2004).

50. Among the Chinese-border conflicts are the First Taiwan Strait Crisis, September 1954–January 1955; Second Taiwan Strait Crisis, August–October 1958; Sino-Indian War, October–November 1962; and Sino-Soviet Border Conflict, March–August 1969. For more details of these border conflicts, see Xiaobing Li, *A History of the Modern Chinese Army* (Lexington: University Press of Kentucky, 2007), chaps. 6–8.

51. Hu Jintao, speech at a PLA Four Headquarters (Sizongbu; like the Joint Chiefs of Staff in the U.S.) meeting, August 2000, quoted in *Taiyangbao* [The Sun], September 5, 2000.

52. Xi Jinping's speech at the "Sixtieth Anniversary Celebration of the CPVF's Participation in WRUSAK," *Renmin ribao* [People's Daily], October 26, 2010, http://paper.people .com.cn/rmrb/html/2010–10/26.

Chapter 1. From Taiwan to Chosin

1. Xinhuashe, *Renmin ribao*, June 28, 1950, 1–2.
2. Colonel Lee Jong Kan (NKPA, ret.), interview by the author in Harbin, Heilongjiang, in July 2002. See also Jong Kan Lee, "A North Korean Officer's Story," in Peter and Li, *Voices from the Korean War*, 76–84.
3. Major General Xu Yan, *Mao Zedong yu kangmei yuanchao zhanzheng* [Mao Zedong and the WRUSAK], 2nd ed. (Beijing: Jiefangjun chubanshe, 2006), 52.
4. Zhang Guanghua, "The Secret Records of China's Important Decisions to Assist Vietnam and Resist France," in Chinese Military Advisory Group Compilation Team, ed., *Zhongguo junshi guwentuan yuanyue kangfa shilu: Dangshiren de huiyi* [The Records of the Chinese Military Advisory Group in the War to Aid Vietnam and Resist France: Personal Accounts of the Veterans] (Beijing: Zhonggong dangshi chubanshe [CCP Party History Press], 2002), 29.
5. Guo Zhigang, "Foreign Military Assistance after the Founding of the New Republic," in Military History Research Division, PLA-AMS, ed., *Junqi piaopiao: Xinzhongguo 50 nian junshi dashi shushi* [PLA Flag Fluttering: Facts of China's Major Military Events in the Past 50 Years] (Beijing: Jiefangjun chubanshe, 1999), 1:146.
6. Zhongnanhai, translated as "middle and southern seas," was the home of Mao, Zhu, Zhou, and several other top CCP leaders after 1949.
7. Yu Huachen, "Comrade Wei Guoqing in the War to Aid Vietnam and Resist France," in CMAG Compilation Team, *Zhongguo junshi guwentuan yuanyue kangfa shilu*, 38.
8. Xiaobing Li, "Truman and Taiwan: A U.S. Policy Change from Face to Faith," in James I. Matray, ed., *Northeast Asia and the Legacy of Harry S. Truman: Japan, China, and the Two Koreas* (Kirksville, Mo.: Truman State University, 2012), 127–28.
9. Song Chongshi, *Hujiang Song Shilun* [A Tiger General: Song Shilun] (Beijing: Zhishi chanquan chubanshe [Intellectual Rights Publishing], 2013), 159.
10. Mao's telegram to Peng, which was forwarded to Song and Tao on December 17, 1950, in *Mao's Military Manuscripts since 1949*, 1:410–11; Shuguang Zhang and Jian Chen, eds., *Chinese Communist Foreign Policy and the Cold War in Asia: New Documentary Evidence, 1944–1950* (Chicago: Imprint Publications, 1996), 200.
11. Mao's Telegram to Lin Biao, October 31, 1949, "My Suggestions on Your Troops Disposition and Battle Array," in Mao, *Jianguo yilai Mao Zedong wengao, 1949–1976* [Mao Zedong's Manuscripts since the Founding of the State, 1949–1976] (Beijing: Zhongyang wenxian chubanshe, 1989) (hereafter cited as *Mao's Manuscripts since 1949*), 1:107.

12. He Di, "The Last Campaign to Unify China: The CCP's Unrealized Plan to Liberate Taiwan, 1949–1950," in Mark A. Ryan, David M. Finkelstein, and Michael A. McDevitt, eds., *Chinese Warfighting: The PLA Experience since 1949* (Armonk, N.Y.: M. E. Sharpe, 2003), 82–84; Li, *History of the Modern Chinese Army*, 76.

13. Chen Yi was one of ten marshals in 1955, and foreign minister from 1958 to 1965. For more information on Marshal Chen Yi, see Liu Shufa, *Chen Yi nianpu, 1901–1972* [A Chronological Record of Chen Yi, 1901–1972] (Beijing: Renmin chubanshe [People's Press], 1995), 2:632–33; and *Xinghuo liaoyuan* Composition Department, comp., *Zhongguo renmin jiefangjun jiangshuai minglu* [Marshals and Generals of the PLA] (Beijing: Jiefangjun chubanshe, 1992), 1:8–9.

14. For more information on General Su Yu, see *Xinghuo liaoyuan* Composition Department, *Zhongguo renmin jiefangjun jiangshuai minglu*, 1:38–39.

15. For Song's military career, see ibid., 1:100–101; Tan Zheng, *Zhongguo renmin zhiyuanjun renwulu* [Veterans Profile of the CPVF] (Beijing: Zhonggong dangshi chubanshe [CCP Party History Press], 1992), 326–27; and Hu Haibo and Yu Hongjun, *Genzhe Mao Zedong da tianxia* [Follow Mao Zedong to Seize the State Power] (Changsha: Hunan renmin chubanshe [Hunan People's Press], 2009), 57.

16. Defense Ministry, Republic of China, *Guojun houqin shi* [Logistics History of the GMD Armed Forces] (Taipei: Guofangbu shizheng bianyiju [Bureau of History and Political Records of the Defense Ministry], 1992), 6:199–200.

17. Ibid., 6:200–201.

18. Chief General Hao Baicun (GMD Army, ret.), interview by the author in Taipei, Taiwan, in May 1994. Hao served as the GMD Army commander on the offshore islands during the PLA attack on Jinmen in 1949. Then he served as the defense minister of the ROC in the 1980s.

19. Compilation Committee of ROC History, *A Pictorial History of the Republic of China* (Taipei: Modern China Press, 1981), 2:297. The GMD Army officially claimed PLA casualties of about 20,000 men, including 7,200 prisoners. According to the author's interviews in both Taiwan and China, 10,000 PLA casualties seems closer to the truth.

20. General Jiang Weiguo (GMD Army, ret.), interview by the author at Rongzong [Glory General] Hospital in Taipei, Taiwan, on May 25–27, 1994.

21. CMC document, "Circular on the Setback of Jinmen Battle, October 29, 1949." This circular was sealed and issued by the CMC. In 1987, the Archives and Research Division of the CCP Central Committee found that Mao had drafted the original document. The division reprinted it from Mao's manuscript and included it in *Mao's Manuscripts since 1949*, 1:100–101.

22. Ibid.

23. Two of these CMC telegrams were drafted by Mao to Su Yu. The first one is titled "Telegram for the Operation Plan of the Dinghai Campaign, November 4, 1949," and

the second, "Telegram: The Disposition of the Dinghai Campaign, November 14, 1949." The latter reads, "In view of the military failure on Jinmen, you must check out closely and seriously all problems, such as boat transportation, troop reinforcements, and attack opportunity on the Dinghai Landing. If it is not well prepared, we could rather postpone the attack than feel sorry about it later." *Mao's Manuscripts since 1949*, 1:118, 120, 137.

24. General Ye Fei, *Ye Fei huiyilu* [Memoirs of Ye Fei] (Beijing: Jiefangjun chubanshe, 1988), 608; interview by the author of the staff member of the 10th Army Group HQ at Hangzhou, Zhejiang, July 6, 2006. Ye was the commander of the 10th Army Group in 1949–1955. *Xinghuo liaoyuan* Composition Department, *Zhongguo renmin jiefangjun jiangshuai minglu*, 1:58–59.

25. Yang Guoyu, *Dangdai Zhongguo haijun* [Contemporary Chinese Navy] (Beijing: Zhongguo shehui kexue chubanshe [China Social Sciences Press], 1987), 17.

26. The first group of eighty-nine PLA Air Force pilots graduated from the training schools in May 1950. The PLA Air Force (PLAAF) organized its first division in Nanjing with fifty Soviet-made fighters and bombers. The GMD Air Force on Taiwan had about two hundred fighters and bombers at that time. Meanwhile, the PLAN expanded to fifty-one medium warships, fifty-two landing boats, and thirty support vessels, totaling 43,000 tons. The GMD Navy had a total tonnage of 100,000 at that time. Defense Ministry, ROC, *Guojun houqin shi*, 6:262, 277.

27. Ibid., 6:277.

28. Chen, *China's Road to the Korean War*, 3.

29. Zhou Enlai Military Record Compilation Team, comp., *Zhou Enlai junshi huodong jishi* [The Records of Zhou Enlai's Military Affairs] (Beijing: Zhongyang wenxian chubanshe, 2000), 2:117–18.

30. For the Sino-Soviet alliance, see Shen Zhihua and Yafeng Xia, *Mao and the Sino-Soviet Partnership, 1945–1959: A New History* (Lanham, Md.: Lexington Books, 2017); Shen Zhihua and Danhui Li, *After Leaning to One Side: China and Its Allies in the Cold War* (Stanford, Calif.: Stanford University Press, 2011); Thomas P. Bernstein and Hua-yu Li, *China Learns from the Soviet Union, 1949–present* (Lanham, Md.: Lexington Books, 2010); Lorenz M. Luthi, *The Sino-Soviet Split: Cold War in the Communist World* (Princeton, N.J.: Princeton University Press, 2008); Chen, *Mao's China and the Cold War*; Odd Arne Westad, ed., *Brothers in Arms: The Rise and Fall of the Sino-Soviet Alliance, 1945–1963* (Stanford, Calif.: Stanford University Press, 1998); Michael M. Sheng, *Battling Western Imperialism: Mao, Stalin, and the United States* (Princeton, N.J.: Princeton University Press, 1997); Vladislav Zubok and Constantine Pleshakov, *Inside the Kremlin's Cold War: From Stalin to Khrushchev* (Cambridge, Mass.: Harvard University Press, 1996); and Gordon H. Chang, *Friends and Enemies: The United States, China, and the Soviet Union* (Stanford, Calif.: Stanford University Press, 1990).

31. Shu Guang Zhang, *Deterrence and Strategic Culture: Chinese-American Confrontations, 1949–1958* (Ithaca, N.Y.: Cornell University, 1992), 32; Li, *History of the Modern Chinese Army*, 120.

32. Lieutenant Colonel Shuang Shi, *Kaiguo diyi zhan: kangmei yuanchao zhanzheng quanjing jishi* [The First War since the Founding of the State: The Complete Story of the WRUSAK] (Beijing: Zhonggong dangshi chubanshe [CCP Party History Press], 2004), 1:46.

33. Mao's telegram to Liu Shaoqi, "Approval of Disposing Four Divisions for Landing Campaign, February 10, 1950," Mao's comments on the "Proposal of Attacking Dinghai First, Jinmen Second, March 28, 1950," and Mao to Su Yu, "Instructions on Paratroops Training," in *Mao's Manuscripts since 1949*, 1:256–57, 282.

34. Grand General Xiao Jinguang, *Xiao Jinguang huiyilu* [Memoirs of Xiao Jinguang] (Beijing: Jiefangjun chubanshe, 1988), 2:8, 26.

35. He, "Last Campaign to Unify China," 82–83.

36. General Jiang Weiguo (Chiang Wei-kuo) (GMD Army, ret.), interview by the author at the Rongzong Hospital in Taipei, Taiwan, on May 23, 1994. Jiang recalled that his father, Jiang Jieshi (Chiang Kai-shek), and GMD intelligence had the information on the PLA landing preparations in the spring of 1950.

37. CCP Party History Research Division, *Zhongguo gongchandang lishi dashiji, 1919–1987* [Major Historical Events of the CCP, 1919–1987] (Beijing: Renmin chubanshe [People's Press], 1989), 191–92.

38. General Ye Fei, interview by the author in Hangzhou, Zhejiang, in July 1996. Ye served as the commander of the 10th Army Group, 3rd Field Army of the PLA, in 1949–1951.

39. Zhou, "The Statement of Protest against American Armed Invasion of Chinese Territory Taiwan," in *Zhou Enlai junshi wenxun* [Selected Military Works of Zhou Enlai] (Beijing: Renmin chubanshe [People's Press], 1997) (hereafter cited as *Selected Military Works of Zhou*), 4:29–31; it is also quoted in Li Changjiu and Shi Lujia, eds., *Zhongmei guanxi erbainian* [History of Sino-American Relations] (Beijing: Xinhua chubanshe [New China Press], 1984), 170; CCP Central Archival and Manuscript Research Division, *Zhou Enlai nianpu, 1949–1976* [A Chronological Record of Zhou Enlai, 1949–1976] (Beijing: Zhongyang wenxian chubanshe, 1997), 1:51.

40. Mao, "Unite and Defeat Any Provocation of U.S. Imperialism," speech at the Eighth Plenary Session of the Central People's Governmental Council, June 28, 1950, in *Mao's Military Manuscripts since 1949*, 1:154–55; Mao, *Mao Zedong on Diplomacy* (Beijing: Foreign Languages Press, 1998), 106.

41. Maj. Gen. William C. Chase arrived in Taiwan on May 1, 1951, to establish JUSMAAG (Joint U.S. Military Assistance Advisory Group)-China. For more details, see David M. Finkelstein, *Washington's Taiwan Dilemma, 1949–1950: From Abandonment to Salvation* (Fairfax, Va.: George Mason University Press, 1993), 336.

42. Vice Adm. Arthur D. Struble, "The Commander of the Seventh Fleet to the Commander of Naval Forces, Far East, February 27, 1951," in U.S. Department of State, *Foreign Relations of the United States: China, 1951* (Washington, D.C.: Government Printing Office, 1982), 7:1509.

43. Finkelstein, *Washington's Taiwan Dilemma*, 332–33.

44. Chief General Hao Bocun (Hau Pei-stun) (GMD Army, ret.), interview by the author in Taipei, Taiwan, on May 23–24, 1994. Hao, as the commander of the front artillery force on Jinmen (Quemoy) Island, felt released when he was informed of the U.S. Seventh Fleet's patrol in the Taiwan Strait in June 1950. See also Xiao, *Xiao Jinguang huiyilu*, 2:26.

45. Chief General Hao Bocun, interview by the author in Taipei, Taiwan, on May 23–24, 1994. Hao served as the commander of the GMD front artillery force on Jinmen Island in 1950.

46. MacArthur is quoted in Ridgway, *Korean War*, 37.

47. Xiao, *Xiao Jinguang huiyilu*, 2:26; Zhou Military Record Compilation Team, *Zhou Enlai junshi huodong jishi*, 2:128–29.

48. Mao, "The Great Achievements of the Three Glorious Movements," a speech at the Third Plenary Session of the First National Committee of the Chinese People's Political Consultative Conference, October 23, 1951, in *Mao's Manuscripts since 1949*, 2:481–86; also in *Mao Zedong xuanji* [Selected Works of Mao Zedong] (Beijing: Renmin chubanshe [People's Press], 1977) (hereafter cited as *Selected Works of Mao*), 5:50–52.

49. Ye, *Ye Fei huiyilu*, 613–14.

50. Li, "Truman and Taiwan," 119–20.

51. Mao's quote is in Military History Research Division, *Zhongguo renmin zhiyuanjun kangmei yuanchao zhanshi*, 60. Mao also made the same point in his directive to the ECMR Command on August 11, 1950, in *Mao's Military Manuscripts since 1949*, 1:181–82.

52. Mao's opening speech at the Third Plenary of the First Chinese People's Political Consultative Conference on October 23, 1951, in *Collected Military Works of Mao*, 6:184. Mao's speech is also in *Renmin ribao*, October 24, 1951, 1–2.

53. Mao's conversations with Wang Jifan and Zhou Shizhao on October 27, 1950, from the recollections of Wang Yuqing, grandson of Wang Jifan, in *Junshi lishi* [Military History]: 88–93; *Guandong zhuojia* [Authors from Northeast China] 9 (2003); and *Zhiqingzhe shuo* [The Inside Stories] 2 (2005): 3–4. See also Xu, *Mao Zedong yu kangmei yuanchao zhanzheng*, 146.

54. Zhou's speech at the CPVF commanders meeting on February 17, 1958, in *Selected Military Works of Zhou*, 4:394–96.

55. Xu, *Mao Zedong yu kangmei yuanchao zhanzheng*, 59.

56. After he received Roshchin's telegram to Moscow, Stalin confirmed the CCP leaders' concerns of a possible UNF invasion of North Korea. In his telegram to Zhou Enlai on July 5, 1950, Stalin agreed: "We consider it correct to concentrate immediately nine Chinese divisions on the Chinese-Korean border for volunteer actions in North Korea in case the enemy crosses the 38th parallel. We will try to provide air cover for these units." "Filippov (Stalin) to Chinese Foreign Minister Zhou Enlai (via Soviet ambassador to the PRC N. V. Roshchin)," ciphered telegram no. 3172, Archives of the President of the Russian Federation, Fond 45, Opis 1, Delo 331, List 79, in "New Russian Documents on the Korean War," trans. and ed. Kathryn Weathersby, in *Bulletin: Cold War International History Project* 6–7 (Winter 1995–96): 43 (Washington, D.C.: Woodrow Wilson International Center for Scholars).

57. "The CMC National Defense Report to Mao from Nie Rongzhen, July 7, 1950," *Mao's Manuscripts since 1949*, 1:428; *Mao's Military Manuscripts since 1949*, 1:159n1; Zhang and Chen, *Chinese Communist Foreign Policy*, 156; Marshal Nie Rongzhen, "Beijing's Decision to Intervene," in Li, Millet, and Yu, *Mao's Generals Remember Korea*, 39–40.

58. Mao, "Approval of the CMC National Defense Report, July 8, 1950," *Mao's Military Manuscripts since* 1949, 1:158–59; Xu, *Mao Zedong yu kangmei yuanchao zhanzheng*, 65.

59. Major General Lei Yingfu, "The Establishment of the Northeast Border Defense Army, July 1950," trans. and ed. Xiaobing Li, Don Duffy, and Zujian Zhang, "Chinese Generals Recall the Korean War," *Chinese Historians* 7, nos. 1–2 (Spring and Fall 1994): 127–29. Lei was director of the Operation Department of the PLA General Staff and Premier Zhou's military secretary. See also Feng Xianzhi and Li Jie, *Mao Zedong yu kangmei yuanchao* [Mao Zedong and the Resistance against the U.S. and Assistance to Korea] (Beijing: Zhongyang wenxian chubanshe, 2000), 4; and Major General Xu Yan, *Diyici jiaoliang: Kangmei yuanchao zhanzheng de lishi huigu yu fansi* [The First Encounter: A Historical Retrospective of the WRUSAK] (Beijing: Zhongguo guangbo dianshi chubanshe [China's Radio and Television Press], 1990), 16–18.

60. Lei, "Establishment of the Northeast Border Defense Army," 127–29; Feng and Li, *Mao Zedong yu kangmei yuanchao*, 4.

61. According to the CMC order, the main task of the NEBDA was "to defend the borders of the Northeast." For more details, see Zhang and Chen, *Chinese Communist Foreign Policy*, 156n16; and Chen, *China's Road to the Korean War*, 135–37.

62. Du, *Zai zhiyuanjun zongbu*, 15, 17–18. Du served as director of the Political Department of the CPVF General HQ in 1950–1953. The quotation is from Xu, *Mao Zedong yu kangmei yuanchao zhanzheng*, 59.

63. Mao's quote was omitted when his telegram of October 14, 1950, was included and published in *Collected Military Works of Mao*, 6:122–23. The omitted sentences were published for the first time in CCP Central Archival and Manuscript Research Division, *Dang de wenxian* 5 (2000): 8.

64. Bo Yibo, *Ruogan zhongda juece yu shijian de huigu* [Recollections of Certain Important Decisions and Events] (Beijing: Zhonggong zhongyang dangxiao chubanshe [CCP Central Party Academy Press], 1991), 1:43.

65. The CMC document "CMC Telegram to Gao Gang, August 5, 1950," drafted by Mao, is in "Mao's Dispatch of Chinese Troops to Korea: Forty-six Telegrams, July–October 1950," trans. and ed. Xiaobing Li, Xi Wang, and Chen Jian, *Chinese Historians* 5, no. 1 (Spring 1992): 64; Zhang and Chen, *Chinese Communist Foreign Policy*, 157.

66. Lieutenant General Du Ping, "Political Mobilization and Control," in *Mao's Generals Remember Korea*, 62; Zhang, *Mao's Military Romanticism*, 81.

67. Military History Research Division, *Zhongguo renmin zhiyuanjun kangmei yuanchao zhanshi*, 6.

68. Mao, "Korean War Situation and Our Policy," speech at the Ninth Plenary of the PRC Central Government, September 5, 1950, in *Mao's Military Manuscripts since 1949*, 1:201–3; *Collected Military Works of Mao*, 6:93–94.

69. Major General Xu Changyou, interview by the author in Shanghai on April 26–27, 2000. Xu served as the deputy secretary general of the CCP Central Military Commission.

70. Stalin's telegram in Archives of the President of the Russian Federation, Fond 45, Opis 1, Delo 337, List 167, quoted in Shen Zhihua, "China Sends Troops to Korea: Beijing's Policy-making Process," in *China and the United States: A New Cold War History*, ed. Xiaobing Li and Hongshan Li (Lanham, Md.: University Press of America, 1998), 28; Shen Zhihua, *Mao Zedong, Stalin he chaoxian zhanzheng* [Mao Zedong, Stalin, and the Korean War] (Guangzhou: Guangdong renmin chubanshe [Guangdong People's Press], 2004), 221.

71. Mao talked about this difficult decision a couple of times during and after the Korean War. See Marshal Nie Rongzhen, *Nie Rongzhen huiyilu* [Memoir of Nie Rongzhen] (Beijing: Jiefangjun chubanshe, 1984), 2:935; Xu, *Mao Zedong yu kangmei yuanchao zhanzheng*, 4.

72. Feng and Li, *Mao Zedong yu kangmei yuanchao*, 7.

73. Mao's conversation with the delegation of the Central Committee of the Communist Party in Beijing, September 23, 1956, in ibid., 7–8.

74. For more detailed discussions on the Soviet factors in recent works, see Li, *Juezhan chaoxian*, 152–56; Niu Jun, *Lengzhan yu xin zhongguo waijiao de yuanqi, 1949–1955* [The Cold War and Origin of Diplomacy of People's Republic of China, 1949–1955], rev. ed. (Beijing: Shehui kexue wenxian chubanshe [Archival and Manuscript Materials of Social Sciences Publishing], 2013), 280–302; Deng Feng, *Lengzhan chuqi dongya guoji guanxi yanjiu* [International Relations in East Asia during the Early Cold War Era] (Beijing: Jiuzhou chubanshe [Jiuzhou Press], 2015), 21–23; Shen, *Lengzhan zai yazhou*, 135–72; Tao Wenzhao, *Zhongmei guanxishi, 1949–1972* [PRC-U.S. Relations,

1949–1972] (Shanghai: Shanghai renmin chubanshe [Shanghai People's Press], 1999), 24–25; Major General Qi Dexue, "Several Issues on the Resisting U.S. and Aiding Korea War," in *Zhonggong dangshi yanjiu* [CCP Party History Research] 1 (1998): 75–76; and Andrew Scobell, *China's Use of Military Force: Beyond the Great Wall and the Long March* (Cambridge: Cambridge University Press, 2003), 82–89.

75. The PRC and the Soviet Union signed the Sino-Soviet alliance treaty on February 14, 1950, in Moscow. The treaty stated that if one side was attacked by a third country, the other side "must go all out to provide military and other assistance." Mao, "Telegram to Liu Shaoqi, January 25, 1950," *Mao's Manuscripts since 1949*, 1:251–52; Zhang and Chen, *Chinese Communist Foreign Policy*, 140–41.

76. Wang Yan et al., *Peng Dehuai zhuan* [Biography of Peng Dehuai] (Beijing: Dangdai zhongguo chubanshe [Contemporary China Publishing], 1993), 372, 388; *Xinghuo Liaoyuan* Composition Department, *Zhongguo renmin jiefangjun jiangshuai minglu*, 1:20; Peng, "My Story," 30.

77. Peng, "My Story," 32.

78. Senior Colonel Yang Feng'an and Wang Tiancheng, *Beiwei 38 duxian: Peng Dehuai yu chaoxian zhanzheng* [The North Latitude 38th Parallel: Peng Dehuai and the Korean War] (Beijing: Zhongyang wenxian chubanshe, 2009), 90. Yang was Peng's military assistant and deputy director of Peng's Executive Office at the CPVF General HQ in 1950–1953. See also Peng Dehuai Biography Compilation Team, *Yige zhanzheng de ren* [A Real Man] (Beijing: Renmin chubanshe [People's Press], 1994), 237–53, 313–35; and Allan R. Millett, *Their War for Korea: American, Asian, and European Combatants and Civilians, 1945–1953* (Washington, D.C.: Brassey's, 2002), 106–11.

79. Peng, "My Story," 33; Peng Dehuai Biography Compilation Team, *Yige zhanzheng de ren*, 166–67.

80. Nie, "Beijing's Decision to Intervene," 42; Wang et al., *Peng Dehuai zhuan*, 402–3; Bruce A. Elleman, *Modern Chinese Warfare, 1795–1989* (London: Routledge, 2001), 246–47.

81. Nie, "Beijing's Decision to Intervene," 42; Feng and Li, *Mao Zedong yu kangmei yuanchao*, 18–22.

82. Among the major works by leading Chinese military historians are Xu, *Mao Zedong yu kangmei yuanchao zhanzheng*; Feng and Li, *Mao Zedong yu kangmei yuanchao*; Yang and Wang, *Beiwei 38 duxian*; and Major General Chai Chengwen, *Banmendian tanpan jishi* [The True Stories of the Panmunjom Negotiations] (Beijing: Shishi chubanshe [Current Affairs Press], 2000). Chai served as chargé d'affaires of the PRC to the DPRK from July 10 to August 12, 1950, when China opened its embassy at Pyongyang. Chai was then head of the PRC military mission to North Korea from August 1950 to January 1955.

83. Andrew B. Kennedy, "Military Audacity: Mao Zedong, Liu Shaoqi, and China's Adventure in Korea," in *History and Neorealism, ed.* Ernest May, Richard Rosecrance,

and Zara Steiner (Cambridge: Cambridge University Press, 2010); Yuan Xi, "The Truth," *Suibi* (Daily Records), no. 6, 1999.

84. Shen, *Mao Zedong, Stalin he chaoxian zhanzheng*; William W. Stueck, *The Korean War: An International History* (Princeton, N.J.: Princeton University Press, 1995); Chen, *China's Road to the Korean War.*

85. Simei Qing, "The US-China Confrontation in Korea, Assessment of Intention in Time of Crisis," in Matray, *Northeast Asia and Truman,* 109.

86. Mao, "CMC Order to Establish the Chinese People's Volunteer Force," in *Collected Military Works of Mao,* 6:117; *Collected Works of Mao,* 6:100–101; Zhang and Chen, *Chinese Communist Foreign Policy,* 164–65.

87. Mao's conversation with Kim Il-sung quoted in CCP Central Archival and Manuscript Research Division, *Dang de wenxian* 5 (2000): 13.

88. Yang and Wang, *Beiwei 38 duxian,* 106; Xu Yan, "Chinese Forces and Their Casualties in the Korean War," trans. Xiaobing Li, *Chinese Historians* 6, no. 2 (Fall 1993): 48.

89. Mao's telegram to Chen Yi at 1:00 A.M. on October 14, 1950, in *Mao's Military Manuscripts since 1949,* 1:255.

90. The quote from X Corps intelligence is in Roy E. Appleman, *South to the Naktong, North to the Yalu (June–November 1950): U.S. Army in the Korean War* (Washington, D.C.: Office of the Chief of Military History and U.S. Government Printing Office, 1961), 756.

91. Mao's telegram to Peng and Gao [Gang] at 6:00 A.M. on October 29, 1950, in *Mao's Military Manuscripts since 1949,* 1:306–7.

92. Mao's quote is from Song, *Hujiang Song Shilun,* 154–55.

93. Chu Yun, *Chaoxian zhanzheng neimu quangongkai* [Declassifying the Korean War] (Beijing: Shishi chubanshe [Current Affairs Publishing], 2005), 161; Shen, "China Sends Troops to Korea," 13.

94. Peng concentrated a superior force to outnumber the enemy wherever the situation permitted in order to eliminate entire enemy battalions, regiments, or divisions, rather than to simply repel the enemy from the peninsula. Peng Dehuai Biography Compilation Team, *Yige zhanzheng de ren,* 178; Peng, "My Story," 32–33; Military History Research Division, *Zhongguo renmin zhiyuanjun kangmei yuanchao zhanshi,* 11; Feng and Li, *Mao Zedong yu kangmei yuanchao,* 30.

95. Peng, "Speech at the CPVF Army and Division Commanders Meeting, October 14, 1950," in *Selected Military Papers of Peng,* 324.

96. Mao's telegram to Peng and Gao [Gang] at 10:00 A.M. on October 27, 1950, in *Mao's Military Manuscripts since 1949,* 1:317.

97. Mao's telegram to Chen [Yi] and Zhang [Zhen] on October 23, 1950, in ibid., 1:286.

98. CCP Central Archival and Manuscript Research Division, *Zhu De nianpu, 1886–1976* [A Chronological Record of Zhu De, 1886–1976] (Beijing: Renmin chubanshe [People's Press], 1986), 350.

99. Mao's telegram to Song and Tao at 10:00 A.M. on October 31, 1950, in *Collected Military Works of Mao*, 6:183–84; Zhang and Chen, *Chinese Communist Foreign Policy*, 200.

100. He, Feng, and Lu, *Xuezhan Changjin hu*, 87.

101. Song, *Hujiang Song Shilun*, 155–57.

102. Ibid., 155.

103. Mao, *Collected Military Works of Mao*, 1:197.

104. Captain Wang Xuedong, interview by the author at Harbin, Heilongjiang, April 2000. See also Wang Xuedong, "The Chosin Reservoir: A Chinese Captain's Story," in Peters and Li, *Voices from the Korean War*, 119. Captain Wang served in the 1st Company, 172nd Regiment, 58th Division, 20th Army, 9th Army Group of the CPVF in 1950–53.

105. For more information on Lieutenant General Zhang Yixiang, see *Xinghuo liaoyuan* Composition Department, *Zhongguo renmin jiefangjun jiangshuai minglu*, 1:334–35; and Tan, *Zhongguo renmin zhiyuanjun renwulu*, 385–86.

106. He, Feng, and Lu, *Xuezhan Changjin hu*, Appendix 2: Charts of the Equipment and Weapons of the CPVF 9th Army Group, 299.

107. Hu Haibo, *Liangjian Changjin hu: Dierci zhanyi zhanshi baogao* [Waving the Sword at the Chosin Lake: The Combat Report on the Second Campaign] (Beijing: Junshi kexue chubanshe), 193–95.

108. For more information on Major General He Jinnian, see Tan, *Zhongguo renmin zhiyuanjun renwulu*, 502–3; and *Xinghuo liaoyuan* Composition Department, *Zhongguo renmin jiefangjun jiangshuai minglu*, 3:337.

109. For more information on Major General Peng Deqing, see Tan, *Zhongguo renmin zhiyuanjun renwulu*, 615–16; and *Xinghuo liaoyuan* Composition Department, *Zhongguo renmin jiefangjun jiangshuai minglu*, 3:525.

110. The CPVF 27th Army Command, *Zhongguo renmin zhiyuanjun di 27 jun kangmei yuanchao zhanzheng shi* [Combat History of the CPVF 27th Army in the WRUSAK] (April 1954), 2, PLA Twenty-Seventh Army Archives.

111. He, Feng, and Lu, *Xuezhan Changjin hu*, 88.

112. For more information on Lieutenant General Zhang Renchu, see *Xinghuo liaoyuan* Composition Department, *Zhongguo renmin jiefangjun jiangshuai minglu*, 1:316–17; and Tan, *Zhongguo renmin zhiyuanjun renwulu*, 342.

113. He, Feng, and Lu, *Xuezhan Changjin hu*, Appendix 2: Charts of the Equipment and Weapons of the CPVF 9th Army Group, 299.

114. Ibid., 88; Zhou Zhong, *Kangmei yuanchao zhanzheng huoqinshi jianbianben* [A Concise History of the Logistics in the WRUSAK] (Beijing: Jindun chubanshe [Golden Shield Press], 1993), 43.

115. Mao's telegram to Peng Dehuai, Deng Hua, and Pak [Il-yu] on November 9, 1950, in *Mao's Military Manuscripts since 1949*, 1:342.

116. Mao's telegram to Peng, Deng, and Pak on November 12, 1950, in ibid., 1:347.

Chapter 2. A Deception with Three Problems

1. Military History Institute, PLA Academy of Military Science, *Kangmei yuanchao zhanzheng shi* [History of the WRUSAK], 3rd ed. (Beijing: Junshi kexue chubanshe, 2014), 1:465.

2. CPVF 27th Army Command, *Zhongguo renmin zhiyuanjun di 27 jun kangmei yuanchao zhanzheng shi*, 3.

3. General Hong Xuezhi, *Kangmei yuanchao zhanzheng huiyi* [Recollections of the WRUSAK] (Beijing: Jiefangjun wenyi chubanshe [PLA Literature Press], 1990), 90–91; Wang et al., *Peng Dehuai zhuan*, 423.

4. Military History Institute, *Kangmei yuanchao zhanzheng shi*, 1:454–55.

5. Yu, "What China Learned," 17.

6. Mao's telegram to Song and Tao at 10:00 A.M. on October 31, 1950, in *Collected Military Works of Mao*, 6:183–84; Zhang and Chen, *Chinese Communist Foreign Policy*, 200.

7. He, Feng, and Lu, *Xuezhan Changjin hu*, 101.

8. Shuang, *Kaiguo diyi zhan*, 1:189.

9. "The Central Military Commission's Circular on the Combat Characteristics of South Korean Troops, October 30, 1950," CMC document drafted by Mao, in *Mao's Manuscripts since 1949*, 1:630–31; "Mao's Telegrams during the Korean War," trans. Xiaobing Li and Glenn Tracy, *Chinese Historians* 5, no. 2 (Fall 1992): 66–67.

10. Military History Research Division, *Zhongguo renmin zhiyuanjun kangmei yuanchao zhanshi*, 24; Appleman, *East of Chosin*, 689–708.

11. Feng and Li, *Mao Zedong yu kangmei yuanchao*, 38.

12. Peng, "Speech at the First Expanded Meeting of the CPVF Party Committee, November 13, 1950," in *Selected Military Papers of Peng*, 337–38.

13. Mao's telegram to Peng and Deng Hua at 1:00 A.M. on November 5, 1950, in *Collected Military Works of Mao*, 6:194–95; Zhang and Chen, *Chinese Communist Foreign Policy*, 201–2.

14. Mao's telegram to Peng and Deng Hua at 10:00 P.M. on November 5, 1950, in *Collected Military Works of Mao*, 6:197; Zhang and Chen, *Chinese Communist Foreign Policy*, 202–3.

15. Xu, *Mao Zedong yu kangmei yuanchao zhanzheng*, 170.

16. Peng, "My Story," 33.

17. Mao's telegram to Peng, Deng, and Pak, "Approval of the CPVF's Plan and Deployment for the Next Campaign," November 9, 1950, in *Collected Military Works of Mao*, 6:198; *Mao's Military Manuscripts since 1949*, 1:342–43.

18. Hong, *Hong Xuezhi Huiyilu*, 408–10; Du, "Political Mobilization and Control," 73–74.

19. Peng, "Speech at the First Expanded Meeting of the CPVF Party Committee, November 13, 1950," in *Selected Military Papers of Peng*, 337–38.

20. Ibid., 337; Du, "Political Mobilization and Control," 74–75.

21. MacArthur quoted in Weintraub, *Christmas Far from Home*, 231.

22. Major General Xu Yan, "Chinese Forces and Their Casualties in the Korean War," trans. Xiaobing Li, *Chinese Historians* 6, no. 2 (Fall 1993): 48.

23. Mao's telegram to Song and Tao at 10:00 A.M. on October 31, 1950, in *Collected Military Works of Mao*, 6:183–84; Zhang and Chen, *Chinese Communist Foreign Policy*, 200.

24. "Army Group Operation Order No. 7" of the CPVF 9th Army Group, quoted in CPVF 27th Army Command, *Zhongguo renmin zhiyuanjun di 27 jun kangmei yuanchao zhanzheng shi*, 1.

25. Mao changed the entry date of the 9th Army Group three times—October 31, November 2, and November 5, 1950—in his telegrams to Peng, Song, and Tao, in *Collected Military Works of Mao*, 6:183–84, 188–89, 197; Zhang and Chen, *Chinese Communist Foreign Policy*, 200.

26. Hu, *Liangjian Changjin hu*, 193.

27. Mao's telegram to Peng and Deng at 7:00 P.M. on November 2, 1950, in *Collected Military Works of Mao*, 6:188–89.

28. Mao's telegram to Peng and Deng Hua at 10:00 P.M. on November 5, 1950, in *Collected Military Works of Mao*, 6:197; Zhang and Chen, *Chinese Communist Foreign Policy*, 202–3.

29. Peng's telegram to Song and Tao Yong and copied to the CMC at 10:00 A.M. on November 6, 1950, in *Selected Military Papers of Peng*, 343–44.

30. Noboru Kojima, *Chosen Senso* [The Korean War] (Tokyo: Bungeishun, 1977); trans. Zhou Xiaoyin et al., *Zui hanleng de dongtian* [The Coldest Winter] (Chongqing, Sichuan: Chongqing chubanshe [Chongqing Publishing House], 2015), 1:297.

31. Appleman, *South to the Naktong*, 746.

32. Ibid., 736; Clay Blair, *The Forgotten War: America in Korea, 1950–1953* (New York: Times Books, 1987), 418.

33. Senior Colonel Li Qingshan, *Zhiyuanjun yuanchao jishi* [The CPVF Records of Aiding Korea] (Beijing: Zhonggong dangshi chubanshe [CCP Party History Press], 2008), 193; Luo Xuanyou, *Chaoxian zhanzheng: Zhengzhan jishi* [The Korean War: The Battle Records] (Beijing: Jiefangjun wenyi chubanshe, 2007), 176.

34. Xu, *Mao Zedong yu kangmei yuanchao zhanzheng*, 174.

35. He, Feng, and Lu, *Xuezhan Changjin hu*, 68.

36. Ibid., 69.

37. Peng had scheduled the attack in the evening of November 25. Peng's order to all the CPVF armies at 11:00 P.M. on November 22, 1950, in *Selected Military Papers of Peng*, 347.

38. Military History Institute, *Kangmei yuanchao zhanzheng shi*, 1:511; Song, *Hujiang Song Shilun*, 157–58.

39. Hu, *Liangjian Changjin hu*, 206.

40. Wang, "Chosin Reservoir," 119. Wang served in the First Company, 172nd Regiment, 58th Division, 20th Army of the CPVF.

41. Song's telegram to the CPVF 20th and 27th Armies at 8:00 P.M. on November 24, 1950, quoted in Military History Institute, *Kangmei yuanchao zhanzheng shi*, 1:517.

42. CPVF 27th Army Command, "Instruction on Several Tactical Issues in Attacking the U.S. and ROK Armies, November 13, 1950, Linjiang," in *Collection of the Orders, Instructions, and Documents for All Operations and Battles in Korea, 1950–1952*, 113–15. *The PLA Twenty-Seventh Army Archives*, Army Headquarters, Shijiazhuang, Hebei.

43. Joseph C. Goulden, *Korea: The Untold Story of the War* (New York: Times Books, 1982), 328.

44. CPVF 27th Army Command, *Zhongguo renmin zhiyuanjun di 27 jun kangmei yuanchao zhanzheng shi*, 3.

45. Ibid.

46. Hu, *Liangjian Changjin hu*, 201.

47. Li Zhuang, "CPVF Combat around the Chosin Lake," in National Committee of Chinese People to Support World Peace against American Invasion, ed., *Zhandou zai Changjin hupan* [War-fighting around the Chosin Lake] (Beijing: Renmin chubanshe [People's Press], 1951), 7.

48. Wang Shuzeng, *Juezhan chaoxian: Chaoxian zhanchang shi wojun tong meijun jiaoliang de lianbingchang* [The Showdown in Korea: The Battleground for a Competition between the Chinese Army and American Army] (Beijing: Jiefangjun wenyi chubanshe, 2007), 214.

49. Du, *Zai zhiyuanjun zongbu*, 122; Yang, *Zai zhiyuanjun silingbu de suiyueli*, 74; Captain Wang, interview by the author; Wang, "Chosin Reservoir," 121–22.

50. Captain Wang, interview by the author; Wang, "Chosin Reservoir," 119.

51. Cui Xianghua and Chen Dapeng, *Tao Yong jiangjun zhuan* [Biography of General Tao Yong] (Beijing: Jiefangjun chubanshe, 1989), 393.

52. Colonel Sherman Xiaogang Lai, interview by the author at Jacksonville, Fla., in April 2017. Professor Lai has shared with the author his interview with his father-in-law, General Li Gelin. Li was the operation chief of the 81st Division, 27th Army of the CPVF in the Korean War.

53. Major Song Xiesheng, interview by the author at Nanjing, March 2008. Song served in the 7th Company, 3rd Battalion, 238th Regiment, 80th Division, 27th Army of the CPVF, during the Battle of Chosin.

54. CPVF 27th Army Command, *Zhongguo renmin zhiyuanjun di 27 jun kangmei yuanchao zhanzheng shi*, 17.

55. Chen Fu and Zhu Jinhui, "Army Commander Liao Zhengguo Recalls the Battle of Chosin Lake," *Zhiwang kangjian* [Digital Library], 228–29, http://www.cnki.net.

56. Xiaobing Li, *China's Battle for Korea: The 1951 Spring Offensive Campaign* (Bloomington: Indiana University Press, 2014), 58–59.

57. Captain Wang, interview by the author; Wang, "Chosin Reservoir," 119.

58. Chen and Zhu, "Army Commander Liao Zhengguo Recalls."

59. He, Feng, and Lu, *Xuezhan Changjin hu*, 74.

60. Song, *Hujiang Song Shilun*, 159.

61. The stir-fried flour was a mixture of 70 percent wheat, 30 percent soybean and sorghum, and 0.5 percent salt. From the Second Offensive Campaign (November 1950) to the end of the Fifth Offensive Campaign (June 1951), it was the main staple food for the 1 million Chinese forces in the Korean War. For more details, see Zhou, *Kangmei yuanchao zhanzheng huoqinshi jianbianben*, 34–35.

62. Song and Tao's telegram to Peng and Deng at 5:10 P.M. on November 21, 1950, quoted in Zhao Yihong, *27 jun chuanqi* [The Legacy of the 27th Army] (Jilin: Jilin renmin chubanshe [Jilin People's Press], 1995), 415; Hong, *Hong Xuezhi Huiyilu*, 427; Xu, *Diyici jiaoliang*, 58–59.

63. Major General Jiang Yonghui, *38 jun zai chaoxian* [The 38th Army in Korea], 2nd ed. (Shenyang: Liaoning renmin chubanshe [Liaoning People's Press], 2009), 153–54. Jiang was deputy commander of the 38th Army of the CPVF. See also Du, *Zai zhiyuanjun zongbu*, 103–4.

64. Ibid.

65. Guo Baoheng and Hu Zhiyuan, *Chipin hanjiang nanbei: 42 jun zai chaoxian* [Fighting over the Han River: the 42nd Army in Korea] (Shenyang: Liaoning renmin chubanshe [Liaoning People's Press], 1996), 110–11; Jiang, *38 jun zai chaoxian*, 118–21.

66. Hong, *Hong Xuezhi Huiyilu*, 421–23; Yang, *Zai zhiyuanjun silingbu de suiyueli*, 51–52; Jiang, *38 jun zai chaoxian*, 166–71, 194–95, 218–19.

67. Lieutenant General Wu Xinquan, *Chaoxian zhanchang 1000 tian: 39 jun zai chaoxian* [One Thousand Days on the Korean Battleground: The 39th Army in Korea] (Shenyang: Liaoning renmin chubanshe [Liaoning People's Press], 1996), 164–74. Wu was the commander of the 39th Army of the CPVF. See also Du, *Zai zhiyuanjun zongbu*, 120.

68. Li, *China's Battle for Korea*, 49–50.

69. Mao's telegram to Peng and Deng, November 5, 1950, in *Collected Military Works of Mao*, 6:197; Zhang and Chen, *Chinese Communist Foreign Policy*, 203.

70. Peng's telegram to Song and Tao Yong and copied to the CMC at 10:00 A.M. on November 6, 1950, in *Selected Military Papers of Peng*, 343–44.

71. Peng's telegram to Song and Tao at 10:30 A.M. on November 12, 1950, quoted in Military History Institute, *Kangmei yuanchao zhanzheng shi*, 1:514.

72. Mao's telegram to Peng, Deng [Hua], and Pak [Il-yu], November 12, 1950, in *Mao's Manuscripts since 1949*, 1:657; Zhang and Chen, *Chinese Communist Foreign Policy*, 203–4.

73. Song and Tao's telegram to Peng and Deng at 6:00 P.M. on November 19, 1950, quoted in Military History Institute, *Kangmei yuanchao zhanzheng shi*, 1:514–15.

74. Millett, *War for Korea*, 335.

75. Lieutenant Colonel Sherman Xiaogang Lai (PLA, ret.), interview by the author at Jacksonville, Fla., on April 1, 2017. Lieutenant Colonel Lai worked in the Department of Foreign Military Studies, PLA-AMS, Beijing, from 1987 to 1996.

76. Lynn Montross and Nicholas A. Canzona, *U.S. Marine Operations in Korea, 1950–1953*, vol. 3, *The Chosin Reservoir Campaign* (Washington, D.C.: Marine Corps Headquarters, 1957), 129; Millett, *War for Korea*, 318.

77. *Song Shilun Zhuan* Compilation Team, PLA-AMS, *Song Shilun Zhuan* [Biography of Song Shilun] (Beijing: Junshi kexue chubanshe), 268.

78. Montross and Canzona, *U.S. Marine Operations in Korea*, 3:163.

79. Song and Tao's telegram to Peng and Deng at 6:00 P.M. on November 19, 1950, quoted in Military History Institute, *Kangmei yuanchao zhanzheng shi*, 1:514–15.

80. Telegram from Peng and Deng to the commanders of the 9th Army Group on November 20, 1950, quoted in *Kangmei yuanchao zhanzheng shi*, 1:515.

81. Song's quote from Chen Guanren, *Bingtuan silingyuan* [PLA Commanders of the Army Groups] (Beijing: Zhonggong dangshi chubanshe [CCP Party History Press], 2015), 236.

82. Telegram from Peng and Deng to the commanders of the 9th Army Group on November 20, 1950, quoted in Military History Institute, *Kangmei yuanchao zhanzheng shi*, 1:515.

83. "The Political Mobilization Instruction" issued by the Political Department of the CPVF Command, November 24, 1959, quoted in *Song Shilun Zhuan* Compilation Team, *Song Shilun Zhuan*, 274.

84. Ibid., 273.

85. Lin Wei, "Hand Combat in the Snow," in National Committee of Chinese People to Support World Peace against American Invasion, *Zhandou zai Changjin hupan*, 14.

86. Zhou Maofang, "Unforgettable Years of the War," in Ge Chumin, ed., *Laozhanshi yishi* [Personal Stories of the Veterans] (Beijing: Zhongguo duiwai fanyi chuban gongsi [China Outreach and Translation Publishing Company], 2000), 487.

87. Roy E. Appleman, *Escaping the Trap: The US Army X Corps in Northeast Korea, 1950* (College Station: Texas A&M University Press, 1990), 24.

88. Zhou, "Unforgettable Years of the War," 487. Zhou worked at the 9th Army Group headquarters as a communication staff member in 1950–52.

89. Telegram from Song, Tao Yong, and Qin Jian to the commanders of the 20th and 27th Armies, copying to Peng, Deng, and the CMC at 8:00 P.M. on November 24, 1950, quoted in PLA-AMS, "The Unforgotten Korean War: Chinese Perspective and Appraisals," 180–81. "The Unforgotten Korean War" is an unpublished manuscript written by retired PLA officers and officer-historians and sponsored by the Office of

Net Assessment, Office of the U.S. Secretary of Defense, in 2006. I received a copy of the entire manuscript from Allan R. Millett and the chapters from Steven Levine. Millett believes that this manuscript is "an invaluable source on the war from the PLA's perspective for 1950–51 and covers the five major Chinese offensives of that period, complete with maps." Millett, *War for Korea*, 589.

90. CPVF 27th Army Command, "The Instruction on Tactic Issues on Fighting the U.S. and ROK Armies, November 13, 1950," in *The Collection of the Army Instructions, Orders, and Documents in Korea (1950–1954), PLA Twenty-Seventh Army Archives*, Shijiazhuang, Hebei: 27th Army Headquarters, 114.

Chapter 3. Massed Attack on the Marines

1. Wang, *Juezhan chaoxian*, 213.

2. Ibid.

3. Song Shilun and Tao Yong's telegram to Peng Dehuai and Deng Hua at 6:00 P.M. on November 19, 1950, quoted in Military History Institute, *Kangmei yuanchao zhanzheng shi*, 1:514–15.

4. *Song Shilun Zhuan* Compilation Team, *Song Shilun Zhuan*, 267.

5. Ibid., 273.

6. Song's telegram to Peng and the CPVF headquarters on November 29, 1950, quoted in PLA-AMS, "Unforgotten Korean War," 1:187–88.

7. Captain Wang, interview by the author; see also Wang, "Chosin Reservoir," 121.

8. Yao Youzhi and Li Qingshan, *Zhiyuanjun yongcuo qiangdi de 10 da zhanyi* [The Ten Major Battles of the CPVF against a Strong Enemy] (Shenyang: Baishan chubanshe [White Mountain Publishing], 2009), 80; Li, *Zhiyuanjun yuanchao jishi*, 183.

9. Shuang, *Kaiguo diyi zhan*, 1:181.

10. Ibid.

11. CPVF 27th Army Command, *Collection of the Orders, Instructions, and Documents for All Operations and Battles in Korea, 1950–1952*, in *PLA Twenty-Seventh Army Archives*, 22; Hu, *Liangjian Changjin hu*, 227.

12. Chen and Zhu, "Army Commander Liao Zhengguo Recalls," 238.

13. Chu, *Chaoxian zhanzheng neimu quangongkai*, 192; Zhao, *27 jun chuanqi*, 338–39, 359.

14. Montross and Canzona, *U.S. Marine Operations in Korea*, 3:161–62; Millett, *War for Korea*, 339.

15. Montross and Canzona, *U.S. Marine Operations in Korea*, 158.

16. Composition Committee, *38 xian shangde jiaofeng: Kangmei yuanchao zhanzheng jishi* [The War-Fighting over the 38th Parallel: The True Records of the WRUSAK] (Beijing: Jiefangjun wenyi chubanshe, 2010), 152.

17. For more details on Major General Xiao Jinghai, see *Xinghuo liaoyuan* Composition Department, *Zhongguo renmin jiefangjun jiangshuai minglu*, 2:328; and Tan, *Zhongguo renmin zhiyuanjun renwulu*, 281.

18. Zhao, *27 jun chuanqi*, 311–13, 338–39, 359.

19. He, Feng, and Lu, *Xuezhan Changjin hu*, 154–55; Montross and Canzona, *U.S. Marine Operations in Korea*, 3:167.

20. He, Feng, and Lu, *Xuezhan Changjin hu*, 156.

21. 1st Lieutenant Yang Yizhi, interview by the author in the Rongjia Zhongxin (Glorious Retirement Center for Veterans) in Taipei, Taiwan, July 2008. Yang served in the 1st Battalion, 237th Regiment, 79th Division, 27th Army, 9th Army Group of the CPVF. He and his platoon entered Korea in mid-November 1950 and participated in the Second Offensive Campaign. He was captured by the UNF during the CPVF Fifth Campaign in May 1951. After the armistice was signed in July 1953, he decided to go to Taiwan rather than return to China.

22. The 9th Army Group came from Southeast China, where the average annual temperature is about 72°F. Captain Wang, interview by the author; see also Wang, "Chosin Reservoir," 119.

23. 1st Lieutenant Yang, interview by the author; Montross and Canzona, *U.S. Marine Operation in Korea*, 3:163.

24. Xinhua News Agency, "So Much about the Best American Division," in National Committee of Chinese People to Support World Peace against American Invasion, *Zhandou zai Changjin hupan*, 36–37.

25. Montross and Canzona, *U.S. Marine Operations in Korea*, 3:164, 168.

26. The entire 27th Army had only 180 pieces of artillery. See CPVF 27th Army Command, *Collection of Orders, Instructions, and Documents*, 18.

27. Wang, *Juezhan chaoxian*, 214; Hu, *Liangjian Changjin hu*, 213.

28. Wang, *Juezhan chaoxian*, 215; Yao and Li, *Zhiyuanjun yongcuo qiangdi de 10 da zhanyi*, 85.

29. Hu, *Liangjian Changjin hu*, 214; Shuang, *Kaiguo diyi zhan*, 1:181.

30. Chen Wenhan, "The Heroic Story of Comrade Tang Yun," in *Zhongguo renmin zhiyuanjun 20 jun kanmei yuanchao yingmo ji'nianji* [Memorial Collection of the Heroes of the CPVF 20th Army in the WRUSAK], *The Twentieth Army Archives*, Kaifeng, Henan (1953), 65–66. Tang Yun served in the 3rd Company, 1st Battalion, 237th Regiment, 59th Division, 27th Army, CPVF 9th Army Group.

31. Zou Shiyong is quoted in Zhang Xiaowu and Li Xianming, "On the Reasons Why the CPVF Failed to Annihilate the American Divisions in the Battle of the Changjin Lake," *Gaige yu kaifang* [The Reform and Opening] 13 (2015): 83.

32. Shuang, *Kaiguo diyi zhan*, 1:181.

33. He, Feng, and Lu, *Xuezhan Changjin hu*, 167, 201.

34. Ibid., 155.

35. Ibid., 167; Wang, *Juezhan chaoxian*, 214.

36. He, Feng, and Lu, *Xuezhan Changjin hu*, 175.

37. Montross and Canzona, *U.S. Marine Operations in Korea*, 3:168.

38. Shuang, *Kaiguo diyi zhan*, 1:181–82.

39. Montross and Canzona, *U.S. Marine Operations in Korea*, 3:168.

40. For more details on Major General Dai Kelin, see *Xinghuo liaoyuan* Composition Department, *Zhongguo renmin jiefangjun jiangshuai minglu*, 3:695; and Tan, *Zhongguo renmin zhiyuanjun renwulu*, 693.

41. Captain Wang, interview by the author; Wang, "Chosin Reservoir," 121.

42. Millett, *War for Korea*, 339.

43. Li, "CPVF Combat around Chosin Lake," 9–10.

44. Hu, *Liangjian Changjin hu*, 227.

45. CPVF 27th Army Command, *Zhongguo renmin zhiyuanjun di 27 jun kangmei yuanchao zhanzheng shi*, 18.

46. Zhang and Li, "Why the CPVF Failed," 83.

47. Jeff Kinard, "Human Wave Attacks," in *The Encyclopedia of the Korean War*, 2nd ed., ed. Spencer C. Tucker (Santa Barbara, Calif.: ABC-CLIO, 2010), 1:343–44. For more details on the "human wave," see Sandler, *Korean War*, 142–43; and Hastings, *Korean War*, 81, 96, 335.

48. Edward C. O'Dowd, *Chinese Military Strategy in the Third Indochina War: The Last Maoist War* (London: Routledge, 2007), 144.

49. Brian Steed, *Armed Conflict: The Lessons of Modern Warfare* (New York: Ballantine Books, 2003), 59.

50. Ibid., 59–60.

51. Elleman, *Modern Chinese Warfare*, 247.

52. Captain Wang, interview by the author. For more details of the early Chinese attacks, see also Wang, "Chosin Reservoir," 117–24; and Yu, "What China Learned," 14, 15–17.

53. Brian R. Cornell, "The Origins of the Human Wave Phenomenon in Chinese Military History and the Korean War (1950–1953)," term paper for Graduate Seminar: Non-Western Military History, *MMH Seminar 4* (Norwich, Vt.: Norwich University, 2011), 9.

54. O'Dowd, *Chinese Military Strategy*, 145.

55. Mao, "On Protracted War," lecture series delivered by Mao May 26–June 3, 1938, at Yan'an Association for the Study of the Anti-Japanese War, in *Selected Works of Mao Tse-tung*, 2:156.

56. Ibid.

57. Peng, "The Summary of the First Campaign and Principles for the Second Offensive Campaign," speech at the enlarged CPVF's First Party Committee meeting, November 13, 1950, in *Selected Military Papers of Peng*, 341–42.

58. Ibid., 338.

59. Peng's campaign instruction to all CPVF armies and the CMC at 1:30 P.M. on November 28, 1950, in ibid., 348.

60. CPVF Political Mobilization Order of the Second Campaign, November 24, 1950, quoted in Du, *Zai zhiyuanjun zongbu*, 82.

61. Ibid., 83.

62. *Song Shilun Zhuan* Compilation Team, *Song Shilun Zhuan*, 274–75.
63. Li, "CPVF Combat around Chosin Lake," 8; Du, "Political Mobilization and Control," 68.
64. For example, see Peng Renlong, "A Few Stories about Resisting the U.S. and Aiding Korea," in Ge Chumin, ed., *Laozhanshi yishi* [Personal Stories of the Veterans] (Beijing: Zhongguo duiwai fanyi chuban gongsi [China Outreach and Translation Publishing Company], 2000), 443–44; and He, Feng, and Lu, *Xuezhan Changjin hu*, 114.
65. O'Dowd, *Chinese Military Strategy*, 144.
66. He, Feng, and Lu, *Xuezhan Changjin hu*, 10.
67. CPVF 27th Army Command, "The Instruction on Tactic Issues on Fighting the U.S. and ROK Armies, November 13, 1950," in *The Collection of the Army Instructions, Orders, and Documents in Korea (1950–1954)*, the 27th Army Archives (Shijiazhuang, Hebei: 27th Army Headquarters), 113.
68. Shuang, *Kaiguo diyi zhan*, 1:189.
69. CPVF 27th Army Command, *Collection of Orders, Instructions, and Documents*, 18–19.
70. Ibid., 21.
71. Shuang, *Kaiguo diyi zhan*, 1:181.
72. He, Feng, and Lu, *Xuezhan Changjin hu*, 157–58.
73. Shuang, *Kaiguo diyi zhan*, 1:373.
74. *Xinghuo liaoyuan* Composition Department, *Zhongguo renmin jiefangjun jiangshuai minglu*, 3:695; and Tan, *Zhongguo renmin zhiyuanjun renwulu*, 693.
75. For more details on Major General Huang Chaotian, see *Xinghuo liaoyuan* Composition Department, *Zhongguo renmin jiefangjun jiangshuai minglu*, 3:468; and Tan, *Zhongguo renmin zhiyuanjun renwulu*, 578.
76. Cpl. Harold L. Mulhausen (USMC, ret.), interviews by the author in Edmond, Oklahoma, in September 2005 and March 2006. Corporal Mulhausen served in A Company, 7th Regiment, U.S. 1st Marine Division in 1950–1952. See also Harold L. Mulhausen, "The Chosin Reservoir: A Marine's Story," in Peters and Li, *Voices from the Korean War*, 98–116; Gugeler, *Combat Actions in Korea*, 54–79; Robert Leckie, *Conflict: The History of the Korean War* (New York: Da Capo Press, 1996), 209–11, 219–20; and Burton I. Kaufman, *The Korean Conflict* (Westport, Conn.: Greenwood Press, 1999), 48–49.
77. Hu, *Liangjian Changjin hu*, 214.
78. For more details on Major General Zhu Qixiang, see *Xinghuo liaoyuan* Composition Department, *Zhongguo renmin jiefangjun jiangshuai minglu*, 2:238; and Tan, *Zhongguo renmin zhiyuanjun renwulu*, 118.
79. Wang Ping, "Opening the Path of Attacks," in National Committee of Chinese People to Support World Peace against American Invasion, *Zhandou zai Changjin hupan*, 53–54.
80. Hu, *Liangjian Changjin hu*, 215.

81. CPVF 27th Army Command, *Zhongguo renmin zhiyuanjun di 27 jun kangmei yuanchao zhanzheng shi*, 19–20.

82. China National Military Museum, ed., *Kangmei yuanchao zhanzheng fengyunlu* [The Operational Files of the WRUSAK] (Beijing: Huacheng chubanshe [Huacheng Publishing], 1999), 45; He, Feng, and Lu, *Xuezhan Changjin hu*, 228–29.

83. Captain Yang Gensi became the first Chinese national hero of the Korean War. In 1952, the Chinese government gave him the honorary title of "super military hero." The Yang Gensi Memorial Park was established at the Chosin Reservoir in North Korea in 1955. Composition Committee, *38 xian shang de jiaofeng*, 166–69.

84. Captain Wang, interview by the author; Wang, "Chosin Reservoir," 122–24.

85. Ibid.

86. Ibid.

87. He, Feng, and Lu, *Xuezhan Changjin hu*, 191–93.

88. Du, *Zai zhiyuanjun zongbu*, 122; Yang, *Zai zhiyuanjun silingbu de suiyueli*, 74; Captain Wang, interview by the author; Wang, "Chosin Reservoir," 121–22.

89. Zhang Yong, "Deadly Battle at Chosin," in National Committee of Chinese People to Support World Peace against American Invasion, *Zhandou zai Changjin hupan*, 25.

90. Zhang and Li, "Why the CPVF Failed," 83.

91. CPVF 27th Army Command, *Collection of Orders, Instructions, and Documents*, 41–42.

92. Chen Wenhan, "Brave Battle Fighting of Heroic Tang Yun," in *Zhongguo renmin zhiyuanjun 20 jun kangmei yuanchao yingmo ji'nianji* [The Commemorative Collection of the Heroes and Models of the CPVF 20th Army in WRUSAK] (Shanghai: The PLA 20th Army Headquarters, 1953): 65.

93. Ni Gongluan, "The Iron Division: The 60th Division in Resisting the U.S. and Aiding Korea," in *Ji'nin Li Xiannian tongzhi danchen 100 zhunian huiyi wenxian* [Conference Proceeding for the 100th Anniversary of Comrade Li Xiannian's Birthday], Beijing, June 2009, 341–78; He, Feng, and Lu, *Xuezhan Changjin hu*, 10.

94. Chen, "Brave Battle Fighting," 65.

95. Ibid.

96. Chen and Zhu, "Army Commander Liao Zhengguo Recalls," 230.

97. Peng's telegram to Song and commanders of the 9th Army Group at 3:00 P.M. on November 28, 1950, quoted in PLA-AMS, "Unforgotten Korean War," 1:187.

98. For more details on Major General Peng Fei, see *Xinghuo liaoyuan* Composition Department, *Zhongguo renmin jiefangjun jiangshuai minglu*, 3:515; and Tan, *Zhongguo renmin zhiyuanjun renwulu*, 608–9.

99. Appleman, *Escaping the Trap*, 187–88.

100. Millett, *War for Korea*, 340.

101. Xia Jicheng, "The True Story of the U.S. Tasking Team's Surrender," *Dajiang nanbei* [North and South of the Great River] 10 (2010): 205.

102. Millett, *War for Korea*, 340.

103. For more details on Senior Colonel Xu Fang, see Tan, *Zhongguo renmin zhiyuanjun renwulu*, 531.

104. He, Feng, and Lu, *Xuezhan Changjin hu*, 244–45.

105. U.S. Department of State, *Foreign Relations of the United States: Korea, 1950* (Washington, D.C.: Government Printing Office, 1982), vol. 7.

106. Ibid.

107. Hu and Li, *Zhongguo renmin zhiyuanjun zhengzhan chuanqi*, 94–95.

108. PLA-AMS, "Unforgotten Korean War," 1:187.

109. Telegram from Song and Qin Jian, chief of staff of the 9th Army Group, to Peng and other commanders of the CPVF at 2:00 P.M. on November 29, 1950, quoted in ibid., 188.

Chapter 4. Annihilate the U.S. 31st Regiment

1. Hu and Li, *Zhongguo renmin zhiyuanjun zhengzhan chuanqi*, 99; Hu, *Liangjian Changjin hu*, 230–31.

2. Military History Institute, *Kangmei yuanchao zhanzheng shi*, 1:525–26; *Song Shilun Zhuan* Compilation Team, *Song Shilun Zhuan*, 276–77.

3. Composition Committee, *38 xian shang de jiaofeng*, 171–73.

4. Hu, *Liangjian Changjin hu*, 231.

5. Song, *Hujiang Song Shilun*, 160; Shuang, *Kaiguo diyi zhan*, 1:182.

6. Song Shilun and Qin Jian to Peng Dehuai and the CPVF Command at 2:00 P.M. on November 29, 1950, quoted in PLA-AMS, "Unforgotten Korean War," 1:188; also in Military History Institute, *Kangmei yuanchao zhanzheng shi*, 1:526.

7. Cui and Chen, *Tao Yong jiangjun zhuan*, 391; Shuang, *Kaiguo diyi zhan*, 1:184.

8. For more details on Major General Zhan Da'nan, see *Xinghuo liaoyuan* Composition Department, *Zhongguo renmin jiefangjun jiangshuai minglu*, 3:623; and Tan, *Zhongguo renmin zhiyuanjun renwulu*, 659–60.

9. Commander Zhan's misinformation is recorded in the diary entry of Zhu Yulin, *Zhu Yulin riji, 1950–1953* [Diary of Zhu Yulin, 1950–1953], on November 29, 1950. Zhu served as the English translator in the Intelligence Office of the 80th Division Command, 27th Army, 9th Army Group of the CPVF, during the Battle of Chosin. See Chen Shuang, "A Touchable War Memory: A Newly Discovered Combat Diary of a CPVF Officer," *Shu Cheng* [Book City] (November 2010): 6, 12.

10. Appleman, *Escaping the Trap*, 75–76; Taaffe, *MacArthur's Korean Generals*, 133.

11. Montross and Canzona, *U.S. Marine Operations in Korea*, 3:243.

12. Mossman, *U.S. Army in the Korean War*, 92; Roe, *Dragon Strikes*, 297.

13. For more information on Senior Colonel Zhang Yingbuo, see Tan, *Zhongguo renmin zhiyuanjun renwulu*, 362–63; CPVF 27th Army Command, *Zhongguo renmin zhiyuanjun di 27 jun kangmei yuanchao zhanzheng shi*, 18.

14. For more details on Senior Colonel Peng Hui, see Tan, *Zhongguo renmin zhiyuanjun renwulu*, 611.

15. For more information on Rao Huitan, see ibid., 503–4.

16. See "Yan Chuanye," accessed October 23, 2017, https://baike.baidu.com/item/%E9 %98%8E%E5%B7%fr=aladdin.

17. He, Feng, and Lu, *Xuezhan Changjin hu*, 115–16, 124.

18. CPVF 27th Army Command, *Zhongguo renmin zhiyuanjun di 27 jun kangmei yuanchao zhanzheng shi*, 18.

19. Colonel Yan Chuanye, interview by Wang Yang, in Wang Yang, "Bloody Attack at Sinhung-ni and the Destruction of 'Polar Bear,'" in *Wenshi jinhua* [The Essence of Historical Literature] 166, no. 3 (2004): 44–51; Hu, *Liangjian Changjin hu*, 232. Ye served as the commander of the 238th Regiment, 80th Division, 27th Army, 9th Army Group of the CPVF, during the Battle of Chosin. He became the commander of the PLA 27th Army from 1970 to 1983.

20. Lieutenant Colonel Zhang Guijin, interview by the author in Wuxi, Jiangsu, March 14–15, 2008. Zhang was political commissar of the 2nd Battalion, 239th Regiment, 80th Division, 27th Army, 9th Army Group of the CPVF, during the Battle of Chosin.

21. Major Song, interview by the author. Song was assistant captain of the 7th Company, 3rd Battalion, 238th Regiment, 80th Division, 27th Army, 9th Army Group of the CPVF, during the Battle of Chosin.

22. He, Feng, and Lu, *Xuezhan Changjin hu*, 117.

23. For more information on CPVF interrogations of American POWs, see Zhu, *Zhu Yulin riji*, diary entries from Chen, "Touchable War Memory," 14.

24. Lieutenant Colonel Zhang, interview by the author.

25. CPVF 27th Army Command, *Zhongguo renmin zhiyuanjun di 27 jun kangmei yuanchao zhanzheng shi*, 3.

26. He, Feng, and Lu, *Xuezhan Changjin hu*, 118; Appleman, *Escaping the Trap*, 89.

27. Lieutenant Colonel Zhang, interview by the author; see also Lin, "Hand Combat in the Snow," 15–16.

28. For more information on the American POWs, see Zhu, *Zhu Yulin riji*, diary entries, 14.

29. Lieutenant Colonel Zhang, interview by the author; see also Xinhua News Agency, "Best American Division," 39.

30. He, Feng, and Lu, *Xuezhan Changjin hu*, 121.

31. Qu Zhongyi, "The Battle of Sinhung-ni: Annihilation of an Entire Regiment of the U.S. Seventh Division," in National Committee of Chinese People to Support World Peace against American Invasion, *Zhandou zai Changjin hupan*, 29.

32. Zhang and Li, "Why the CPVF Failed," 83.

33. CPVF 27th Army Command, "The Successful Combat Experience of the Fourth Company at Sinhung-ni," in *Zhongguo renmin zhiyuanjun di 27 jun kangmei yuanchao zhanzheng shi*, 185–88.

34. Appleman, *Escaping the Trap*, 90.

35. Hu and Li, *Zhongguo renmin zhiyuanjun zhengzhan chuanqi*, 108–9; He, Feng, and Lu, *Xuezhan Changjin hu*, 120, 126–27; Mossman, *U.S. Army in the Korean War*, 97; Roe, *Dragon Strikes*, 304.

36. Hu, *Liangjian Changjin hu*, 232–33; Roe, *Dragon Strikes*, 306.

37. Luan Kechao, *Xue yu huo de jiaoliang: Kangmei yuanchao jishi* [The Contest: Blood vs. Fire: The Records of Resisting America and Aiding Korea] (Beijing: Huayi chubanshe [China Literature Publishing House], 2008), 138.

38. Colonel Yan Chuanye, interview by Wang, in "Bloody Attack at Sinhung-ni," 46–47.

39. Major Song, interview by the author.

40. Kong Qingsan was awarded by the CPVF Command the Special-Class Medal and the First-Class Combat Hero, posthumously, on September 24, 1952. For more details, see Hu, *Liangjian Changjin hu*, 233–36.

41. China National Military Museum, *Kangmei yuanchao zhanzheng fengyunlu*, 149; Song, *Hujiang Song Shilun*, 161.

42. Qu, "Battle of Sinhung-ni," 30–31. Shao Mingze was commander of the 1st Battalion, 240th Regiment, 80th Division, 27th Army, 9th Army Group of the CPVF, during the Battle of Chosin. He became a major general and deputy commander of the 27th Army in the 1960s. See Ba Tanshan, "Nisuo buzhidao de chaoxian zhanzheng: Bingxue Changjin hu" [The Korean War You Don't Know: Snow and Blood in the Chosin Lake], accessed April 24, 2017, http://www.360doc.com/content/11/0525/00 /2984805–119180423.shtml.

43. CPVF 27th Army Command, "Successful Defense by One Soldier Wu Jiangwei, Second Platoon, Ninth Company, 240th Regiment, during the Second Offensive Campaign," in *Zhongguo renmin zhiyuanjun di 27 jun kangmei yuanchao zhanzheng shi*, 220.

44. Military History Research Division, PLA-AMS, *Zhongguo renmin zhiyuanjun kangmei yuanchao zhanshi*, 43–44; China National Military Museum, ed., *Kangmei yuanchao zhanzheng jishi* [A Chronological Record of the WRUSAK] (Beijing: Jiefangjun chubanshe, 2008), 43–44.

45. He, Feng, and Lu, *Xuezhan Changjin hu*, 146.

46. Ibid., 126–27; Appleman, *Escaping the Trap*, 106–7.

47. General Shao Mingze, interview by Wang Yang, in Wang, "Bloody Attack at Sinhung-ni," 47.

48. Wang, *Juezhan chaoxian*, 215.

49. He, Feng, and Lu, *Xuezhan Changjin hu*, 130.

50. CPVF 27th Army Command, *Zhongguo renmin zhiyuanjun di 27 jun kangmei yuanchao zhanzheng shi*, 23.

51. *Song Shilun Zhuan* Compilation Team, *Song Shilun Zhuan*, 275; Hu, *Liangjian Changjin hu*, 226.

52. Wang, "Bloody Attack at Sinhung-ni," 47; He, Feng, and Lu, *Xuezhan Changjin hu*, 132.

53. Lieutenant Colonel Zhang, interview by the author.

54. Appleman, *Escaping the Trap*, 103.

55. China National Military Museum, *Kangmei yuanchao zhanzheng fengyunlu*, 147.

56. Qu, "Battle of Sinhung-ni," 31–32; Hu and Li, *Zhongguo renmin zhiyuanjun zhengzhan chuanqi*, 110.

57. Hu, *Liangjian Changjin hu*, 236.

58. Lin, "Hand Combat in the Snow," 17–18; Appleman, *Escaping the Trap*, 103–5.

59. Roe, *Dragon Strikes*, 312–13.

60. Halberstam, *Coldest Winter*, 439; Taaffe, *MacArthur's Korean Generals*, 133; Appleman, *Escaping the Trap*, 103.

61. Sandler, *Korean War*, 122.

62. Appleman, *Escaping the Trap*, 106.

63. He, Feng, and Lu, *Xuezhan Changjin hu*, 133.

64. Lieutenant Colonel Zhang, interview by the author.

65. Major Song, interview by the author.

66. Roe, *Dragon Strikes*, 315.

67. Ba, "Nisuo buzhidao de chaoxian zhanzheng," accessed April 24, 2017, http://www .360doc.com/content/11/0525/00/2984805–119180423.shtml.

68. Mossman, *U.S. Army in the Korean War*, 99.

69. Commander Zhan's order recorded in Zhu, *Zhu Yulin riji*, November 29, 1950; see Chen, "Touchable War Memory," 6.

70. China National Military Museum, *Kangmei yuanchao zhanzheng fengyunlu*, 148.

71. Hu, *Liangjian Changjin hu*, 240.

72. He, Feng, and Lu, *Xuezhan Changjin hu*, 134.

73. Ibid., 133–34.

74. Roe, *Dragon Strikes*, 315–16.

75. Luan, *Xue yu huo de jiaoliang*, 137; Halberstam, *Coldest Winter*, 439; Appleman, *Escaping the Trap*, 114.

76. Appleman, *Escaping the Trap*, 123.

77. Taaffe, *MacArthur's Korean Generals*, 133.

78. CPVF 27th Army Command, "The Anti-tank Cases of the 242nd Regiment in the Second Offensive Campaign," in *Zhongguo renmin zhiyuanjun di 27 jun kangmei yuanchao zhanzheng shi*, 23.

79. Appleman, *Escaping the Trap*, 118–19.

80. Roe, *Dragon Strikes*, 312.

81. *Song Shilun Zhuan* Compilation Team, *Song Shilun Zhuan*, 276; Hu, *Liangjian Changjin hu*, 230.

82. Hu and Li *Zhongguo renmin zhiyuanjun zhengzhan chuanqi*, 110.

83. He, Feng, and Lu, *Xuezhan Changjin hu*, 131.

84. This statement explains the CPVF commanders' perception of the U.S. forces. The Chinese believed, for example, that U.S. mechanized units had tremendous firepower and mobility but depended considerably on roads and bridges, and that, therefore, the U.S. troops tended to stay near the roads and lacked flexibility to occupy advantageous terrain, thus providing the CPVF opportunities to cut them to pieces. CPVF 27th Army Command, "Instruction on Several Tactical Issues in Attacking the U.S. and ROK Armies, November 13, 1950, Linjiang," in *Collection of Orders, Instructions, and Documents*, 114; Li, *Zhiyuanjun yuanchao jishi*, 142.

85. Lieutenant Colonel Zhang, interview by the author.

86. CPVF 27th Army Command, *Zhongguo renmin zhiyuanjun di 27 jun kangmei yuanchao zhanzheng shi*, 4.

87. Luan, *Xue ye huo de jiaoliang*, 137.

88. China National Military Museum, *Kangmei yuanchao zhanzheng fengyunlu*, 148.

89. For more details on Major General Sun Ruifu, see *Xinghuo liaoyuan* Composition Department, *Zhongguo renmin jiefangjun jiangshuai minglu*, 3:623; and Tan, *Zhongguo renmin zhiyuanjun renwulu*, 184.

90. China National Military Museum, *Kangmei yuanchao zhanzheng fengyunlu*, 148.

91. Su Changjie, Wang Qinjun, and Jiang Xiangqin, *Jinluu: 27 jun zhandou lichen* [Mighty Military Force: the Combat History of the PLA 27th Army] (Beijing: Jiefangjun wenyi chubanshe, 2004), 203–6.

92. China National Military Museum, *Kangmei yuanchao zhanzheng fengyunlu*, 148; Military History Institute, *Kangmei yuanchao zhanzheng shi*, 1:527.

93. Military History Institute, *Kangmei yuanchao zhanzheng shi*, 1:526; Li, *Zhiyuanjun yuanchao jishi*, 183.

94. Hu, *Liangjian Changjin hu*, 245.

95. CPVF 27th Army Command, *Zhongguo renmin zhiyuanjun di 27 jun kangmei yuanchao zhanzheng shi*, 19.

96. Hu, *Liangjian Changjin hu*, 249.

97. Shuang, *Kaiguo diyi zhan*, 1:184–85.

98. Cui and Chen, *Tao Yong jiangjun zhuan*, 393–94.

99. Montross and Canzona, *U.S. Marine Operations in Korea*, 3:244.

100. Military History Research Division, *Zhongguo renmin zhiyuanjun kangmei yuanchao zhanshi*, 45.

101. Hu, *Liangjian Changjin hu*, 249.

102. Military History Institute, *Kangmei yuanchao zhanzheng shi*, 1:527.

103. China National Military Museum, *Kangmei yuanchao zhanzheng fengyunlu*, 148.

104. Military History Institute, *Kangmei yuanchao zhanzheng shi*, 1:527; CPVF 27th Army Command, *Zhongguo renmin zhiyuanjun di 27 jun kangmei yuanchao zhanzheng shi*, 46.

105. President Truman awarded the Congressional Medal of Honor, posthumously, to Lt. Col. Donald C. Faith on June 21, 1951. Mossman, *U.S. Army in the Korean War*, 152.

106. Ibid., 135.

107. Appleman, *Escaping the Trap*, 128–29.

108. Mossman, *U.S. Army in the Korean War*, 136.

109. Qu, "Battle of Sinhung-ni," 33; China National Military Museum, *Kangmei yuanchao zhanzheng fengyunlu*, 148–49.

110. Lin, "Hand Combat in the Snow," 18–19; Li, *Zhiyuanjun yuanchao jishi*, 184.

111. Military History Institute, *Kangmei yuanchao zhanzheng shi*, 1:528; Hu and Li, *Zhongguo renmin zhiyuanjun zhengzhan chuanqi*, 100.

112. Taaffe, *MacArthur's Korean Generals*, 133.

113. Hong, *Hong Xuezhi Huiyilu*, 427; Mossman, *U.S. Army in the Korean War*, 132–37.

114. He, Feng, and Lu, *Xuezhan Changjin hu*, 146.

115. PLA-AMS, "Unforgotten Korean War," 1:207.

116. Wang Jun, *Changjin Hu* [The Chosin Lake] (Changsha: Hunan wenyi chubanshe [Hunan Literature Publishing], 2011), 256; Ba, "Nisuo buzhidao de chaoxian zhanzheng."

117. Telegram from the 9th Army Group to the CPVF Command on December 2, 1950, quoted in *Song Shilun Zhuan* Compilation Team, *Song Shilun Zhuan*, 278.

118. Mao's telegram to Peng and Deng [Hua], copied to Song [Shilun] and Qin [Jian], at 2400 hours on December 3, 1950, in *Mao's Manuscripts since 1949*, 1:379; Zhang and Chen, *Chinese Communist Foreign Policy*, 203–4.

119. Mao's telegram to Peng, Deng [Hua], Song [Shilun], and Qin [Jian], at 1:00 A.M. on December 3, 1950, in *Mao's Military Manuscripts since 1949*, 1:385–86; Zhang and Chen, *Chinese Communist Foreign Policy*, 210.

120. Peng, "My Story," 36.

Chapter 5. Failed Roadblocks and Pursuit

1. Telegram from Song and Qin Jian to Peng Dehuai and Deng Hua at 9:00 A.M., December 1, 1950, quoted in PLA-AMS, "Unforgotten Korean War," 1:191.

2. Telegram from Peng and other CPVF commanders to Song and Qin at 5:00 P.M., December 1, 1950, quoted in Military History Institute, *Kangmei yuanchao zhanzheng shi*, 1:529.

3. Ibid., 1:191.

4. CMC telegram to Peng and other CPVF commanders and copied to Song and Tao, drafted by Mao, at 1:00 P.M., December 2, 1950, quoted in *Collected Military Works of Mao*, 6:198.

5. CPVF 27th Army Command, *Zhongguo renmin zhiyuanjun di 27 jun kangmei yuanchao zhanzheng shi*, 20; Song, *Hujiang Song Shilun*, 161, 162–63.

6. *Song Shilun Zhuan* Compilation Team, *Song Shilun Zhuan*, 289, 297.

7. Bob Drury and Tom Clavin, *The Last Stand of Fox Company: A True Story of U.S. Marines in Combat* (New York: Grove, 2009), 304–5; Millett, *War for Korea*, 354.

8. Major General Zhang Zhixiu, *Junluu shengya* [My Military Career in the Chinese Army] (Beijing: Jiefangjun chubanshe, 1998), 312–14; Li, *Zhiyuanjun yuanchao jishi*, 184.

9. For examples, see Xu, *Diyici jiaoliang*, 58; and Wang, *Juezhan chaoxian*, 214.

10. Appleman, *Escaping the Trap*, 287–88.

11. Song reported his encirclement and annihilation plan in his telegram to Peng and Deng Hua at 9:00 A.M. on December 1, 1950, quoted in Military History Institute, *Kangmei yuanchao zhanzheng shi*, 1:529.

12. Military History Research Division, *Zhongguo renmin zhiyuanjun kangmei yuanchao zhanshi*, 45; Li, *Zhiyuanjun yuanchao jishi*, 186.

13. Mossman, *U.S. Army in the Korean War*, 129.

14. Montross and Canzona, *U.S. Marine Operations in Korea*, 3:249–50.

15. CPVF 27th Army Command, *Zhongguo renmin zhiyuanjun di 27 jun kangmei yuanchao zhanzheng shi*, 19; Xinhua News Agency, "Best American Division," 38.

16. Appleman, *Escaping the Trap*, 213, 215.

17. Li, "CPVF Combat around Chosin Lake," 11–12; Millett, *War for Korea*, 348.

18. Zhang, "Deadly Battle at Chosin," 22; Composition Committee, *38 xian shang de jiaofeng*, 175; Shuang, *Kaiguo diyi zhan*, 1:186.

19. Major Zhou Wenjiang, interview by the author at Jinhua, Zhejiang, July 2009. Zhou served as assistant commander of the 2nd Battalion, 177th Regiment, 59th Division, 20th Army, 9th Army Group of the CPVF, during the Battle of Chosin.

20. Major Zhou Wenjiang, *Mobuqu de jiyi: Zhou Wenjiang zhandou huiyilu* [Unforgettable Stories: Combat Experience of Zhou Wenjiang] (Beijing: Zhonggong zhongyang dangshi chubanshe [CCP Central Committee's Party History Press], 2012), 211–20; CPVF 27th Army Command, *Zhongguo renmin zhiyuanjun di 27 jun kangmei yuanchao zhanzheng shi*, 20.

21. Cui and Chen, *Tao Yong jiangjun zhuan*, 393.

22. CPVF 27th Army Command, *Zhongguo renmin zhiyuanjun di 27 jun kangmei yuanchao zhanzheng shi*, 21.

23. Zhang, "Deadly Battle at Chosin," 25–26; Li, *Zhiyuanjun yuanchao jishi*, 186; PLA-AMS, "Unforgotten Korean War," 1:207.

24. Shuang, *Kaiguo diyi zhan*, 1:182.

25. Wang Shuzeng, *Zhongguo renmin zhiyuanjun zhengzhan jishi* [The True Story of the CPVF's War Experience] (Beijing: Jiefangjun wenyi chubanshe, 2001), 292; Appleman, *Escaping the Trap*, 238–39.

26. CPVF 27th Army Command, *Zhongguo renmin zhiyuanjun di 27 jun kangmei yuanchao zhanzheng shi*, 20; Montross and Canzona, *U.S. Marine Operations in Korea*, 3:270–71.

27. CPVF 27th Army Command, *Zhongguo renmin zhiyuanjun di 27 jun kangmei yuanchao zhanzheng shi*, 20.

28. Hu, *Liangjian Changjin hu*, 260.

29. Telegram from Song, Tao, and Qin to Mao, Peng, and other commanders of the CPVF Command at 10:05 P.M. on December 4, 1950, quoted in PLA-AMS, "Unforgotten Korean War," 1:194.

30. He, Feng, and Lu, *Xuezhan Changjin hu*, 115–16, 257.

31. General Smith's actual words were: "There can be no retreat when there's no rear. You can't retreat, or even withdraw, when you're surrounded. The only thing you can do is break out, and in order to do that you have to attack, and that is what we're about to do." Quoted in Russ, *Breakout*, 355.

32. In his three telegrams to Peng, Song, Tao, and Qin on December 4, Mao repeatedly asked about the battle situation at Chosin. These telegrams are in *Mao's Military Manuscripts since 1949*, 1:389–96; Zhang and Chen, *Chinese Communist Foreign Policy*, 211–12.

33. *Song Shilun Zhuan* Compilation Team, *Song Shilun Zhuan*, 285; Shuang, *Kaiguo diyi zhan*, 1:186.

34. Appendix 2, "Table of the CPVF Ninth Army Group's Formation and Equipment," in He, Feng, and Lu, *Xuezhan Changjin hu*, 299.

35. For more details on Major General Zhang Zhixiu, see *Xinghuo liaoyuan* Composition Department, *Zhongguo renmin jiefangjun jiangshuai minglu*, 3:89; and Tan, *Zhongguo renmin zhiyuanjun renwulu*, 378.

36. Zhang, *Junluu shengya*, 312–14.

37. Mao's telegram to Peng, Song, Tao, Qin, and other CPVF commanders at 1:00 A.M. on December 3, 1950, in *Mao's Military Manuscripts since 1949*, 1:385–86; Zhang and Chen, *Chinese Communist Foreign Policy*, 210–11.

38. Composition Committee, *38 xian shang de jiaofeng*, 176.

39. Zhang, *Junluu shengya*, 315–17.

40. Shuang, *Kaiguo diyi zhan*, 1:187.

41. For more details on Major General Chen Zhongmei, see *Xinghuo liaoyuan* Composition Department, *Zhongguo renmin jiefangjun jiangshuai minglu*, 3:136; and Tan, *Zhongguo renmin zhiyuanjun renwulu*, 399.

42. Telegram from Song, Tao, and Qin to the CPVF Command and the CMC at 10:05 P.M. on December 4, 1950, quoted in *Collected Military Works of Mao*, 6:238n7.

43. Peng's telegram to Song and other commanders of the 9th Army Group on December 5, 1950, quoted in PLA-AMS, "Unforgotten Korean War," 1:194n434.

44. Mao's telegram to Peng and Song at 7:00 A.M. on December 5, 1950, in *Mao's Military Manuscripts since 1949*, 1:395–96; Zhang and Chen, *Chinese Communist Foreign Policy*, 212.

45. Xinhua News Agency news release (dated December 4), drafted by Mao at 1:00 A.M. on December 5, 1950, in *Mao's Military Manuscripts since 1949*, 1:397–98; Zhang and Chen, *Chinese Communist Foreign Policy*, 213; emphasis in original.

46. Zhang, *Junluu shengya*, 315–17.

47. Ibid.

48. Captain Ma Rixiang, interview by the author in Shanghai, July 2010. Ma served as assistant political instructor of the Machine Gun Company, 1st Battalion, 231st Regiment, 77th Division, 26th Army, 9th Army Group of the CPVF, during the Battle of Chosin.

49. Quoted in PLA-AMS, "Unforgotten Korean War," 1:194.

50. Major Wu Dawei, interview by the author in Shanghai, July 2010. Wu served as a staff member at the headquarters of the 88th Division, 26th Army, 9th Army Group of the CPVF, during the Battle of Chosin. After his return to China, he was made a major in 1955.

51. He, Feng, and Lu, *Xuezhan Changjin hu*, 287–88. For more details on Senior Colonel Wu Dalin, see Tan, *Zhongguo renmin zhiyuanjun renwulu*, 286–87.

52. Major Wu, interview by the author.

53. Army Assistant Commander Zhang Zhixiu, quoted in *Song Shilun Zhuan* Compilation Team, *Song Shilun Zhuan*, 286.

54. Ibid., 285; Shuang, *Kaiguo diyi zhan*, 1:186; Montross and Canzona, *U.S. Marine Operations in Korea*, 3:283–84.

55. Taaffe, *MacArthur's Korean Generals*, 133–34.

56. Appleman, *Escaping the Trap*, 249.

57. Luan, *Xue yu huo de jiaoliang*, 139; Millett, *War for Korea*, 348.

58. He, Feng, and Lu, *Xuezhan Changjin hu*, 115–16, 257.

59. Montross and Canzona, *U.S. Marine Operations in Korea*, 3:288–90.

60. CPVF 20th Army Command, *Zhongguo renmin zhiyuanjun di 20 jun kangmei yuanchao zhanzheng shi* [Combat History of the CPVF 20th Army in the WRUSAK], PLA Twentieth Army Archives, Kaifeng, Henan, 33–34.

61. Roe, *Dragon Strikes*, 382–83.

62. Phoenix TV, "Broad View Program," *26 jun zengyuan Changjin hu* [The 26th Army Reinforces the Chosin Lake], December 24, 2010, accessed November 11, 2017, http://ucwap.ifeng.com/auto/fun/gaizhuang/news?aid=990976&rt.

63. Montross and Canzona, *U.S. Marine Operations in Korea*, 3:288–93.

64. Phoenix TV, "Broad View Program."

65. Major Wu, interview by the author.

66. He, Feng, and Lu, *Xuezhan Changjin hu*, 115–16, 256–57.

67. Appleman, *Escaping the Trap*, 264–66; Hu, *Liangjian Changjin hu*, 261.

68. Major Wu, interview by the author.

69. Lieutenant Colonel Zhi Futian, interview by the author in Shanghai, July 2010. Zhi worked as a staff member in the Political Tasks Office of the 76th Division, 26th Army, 9th Army Group of the CPVF, during the Battle of Chosin. Zhi was made a lieutenant colonel in 1955.

70. He, Feng, and Lu, *Xuezhan Changjin hu*, 115–16, 257.

71. Russ, *Breakout*, 394; Roe, *Dragon Strikes*, 383; Montross and Canzona, *U.S. Marine Operations in Korea*, 3:307.

72. Millett, *War for Korea*, 348.

73. Telegram from the 9th Army Group Command to the 20th, 26th, and 27th Armies at 11:00 P.M. on December 8, 1950, quoted in CPVF 27th Army Command, *Zhongguo renmin zhiyuanjun di 27 jun kangmei yuanchao zhanzheng shi*, 20.

74. *Song Shilun Zhuan* Compilation Team, *Song Shilun Zhuan*, 286.

75. Luan, *Xue yu huo de jiaoliang*, 139.

76. *Xinghuo liaoyuan* Composition Department, *Zhongguo renmin jiefangjun jiangshuai minglu*, 3:515; and Tan, *Zhongguo renmin zhiyuanjun renwulu*, 608–9.

77. He, Feng, and Lu, *Xuezhan Changjin hu*, 115–16, 265–67.

78. Montross and Canzona, *U.S. Marine Operations in Korea*, 3:309.

79. Appleman, *Escaping the Trap*, 297–98; Millett, *War for Korea*, 348.

80. Russ, *Breakout*, 397–98.

81. *Song Shilun Zhuan* Compilation Team, *Song Shilun Zhuan*, 286.

82. Wang, *Juezhan chaoxian*, 221–22.

83. For more details, see Tan, *Zhongguo renmin zhiyuanjun renwulu*, 462–63.

84. CPVF 20th Army Command, *Zhongguo renmin zhiyuanjun di 20 jun kangmei yuanchao zhanzheng shi*, 51–53.

85. He, Feng, and Lu, *Xuezhan Changjin hu*, 115–16, 250–51.

86. Major Yao Genlian, interview by the author in Shanghai, June 2010. Yao was assistant commander of the 3rd Battalion, 174th Regiment, 58th Division, 20th Army, 9th Army Group of the CPVF, during the Battle of Chosin. After his return to China, Yao was made a major in 1955.

87. He, Feng, and Lu, *Xuezhan Changjin hu*, 115–16, 252.

88. Major Yao Genlian, interview by the author.

89. Hu, *Liangjian Changjin hu*, 278.

90. Tan, *Zhongguo renmin zhiyuanjun renwulu*, 463.

91. He, Feng, and Lu, *Xuezhan Changjin hu*, 271.

92. Cpl. Harold L. Mulhausen (USMC, ret.), interviews by the author. See also Whitney Bryen, "Cross-section of Perspectives on War: Korean War Vet to Join Others in Sharing Stories in Norman," *Oklahoman*, November 8, 2017, 13D.

93. Luan, *Xue yu huo de jiaoliang*, 140.

94. *Song Shilun Zhuan* Compilation Team, *Song Shilun Zhuan*, 287; Hu, *Liangjian Changjin hu*, 269–70.

95. Tan, *Zhongguo renmin zhiyuanjun renwulu*, 666.

96. Hu, *Liangjian Changjin hu*, 282.

97. He, Feng, and Lu, *Xuezhan Changjin hu*, 285.

98. Captain Ma, interview by the author.

99. Montross and Canzona, *U.S. Marine Operations in Korea*, 3:328–30.

100. Captain Ma, interview by the author.

101. Appleman, *Escaping the Trap*, 311–12.

102. Captain Ma, interview by the author.

103. He, Feng, and Lu, *Xuezhan Changjin hu*, 288–89.

104. Appleman, *Escaping the Trap*, 319; Millett, *War for Korea*, 348.

105. CPVF 27th Army Command, *Zhongguo renmin zhiyuanjun di 27 jun kangmei yuanchao zhanzheng shi*, 4.

106. PLA-AMS, "Unforgotten Korean War," 1:198; Military History Institute, *Kangmei yuanchao zhanzheng shi*, 1:544.

107. Captain Wang, interview by the author; see also Wang, "Chosin Reservoir," 123.

108. Ibid.

109. Major Zhu Wenbin, interview by the author in Shanghai, June 2010. Zhu served as a staff member of the 173rd Regiment, 58th Division, 20th Army, 9th Army Group of the CPVF, during the Battle of Chosin.

110. He, Feng, and Lu, *Xuezhan Changjin hu*, 270–71.

111. Hu, *Liangjian Changjin hu*, 278–80.

112. Major Zhu, interview by the author.

113. Ibid.

114. The 173rd Regiment had captured some of the marines' supplies during its early attacks on November 27–30 at Hagaru-ri.

115. He, Feng, and Lu, *Xuezhan Changjin hu*, 277.

116. PLA-AMS, "Unforgotten Korean War," 1:194; *Song Shilun Zhuan* Compilation Team, *Song Shilun Zhuan*, 290–91.

117. *Song Shilun Zhuan* Compilation Team, *Song Shilun Zhuan*, 288–89.

118. Sandler, *Korean War*, 126; Millett, *War for Korea*, 354; Appleman, *Escaping the Trap*, 337.

119. Bevin Alexander, *Korea: The First War We Lost*, rev. ed. (New York: Hippocrene Books, 1998), 353–67.

120. Peng, "My Story," 34–35; Hong, *Kangmei yuanchao zhanzheng huiyi*, 92–93; Yang, *Zai zhiyuanjun silingbu de suiyueli*, 72–74.

121. Halberstam, *Coldest Winter*, 468–69.

122. Sandler, *Korean War*, 127.

123. Corporal Mulhausen (USMC, ret.), interviews by the author; see also Hastings, *Korean War*, 152–62; and Roe, *Dragon Strikes*, 333–43.

124. Hastings, *Korean War*, 164; Russ, *Breakout*, 433–34.

125. CPVF Command telegram to the 9th Army Group on December 15, 1950, quoted in Hu, *Liangjian Changjin hu*, 284.

126. Mao's telegram to Peng, Gao, Song, and Tao on December 17, 1950, in *Mao's Military Manuscripts since 1949*, 1:410–11; Zhang and Chen, *Chinese Communist Foreign Policy*, 216.

127. The CPVF claimed that the UNF casualties totaled 36,000 men (including 24,000 American troops). See Hong, *Hong Xuezhi Huiyilu*, 429; Du, *Zai zhiyuanjun zongbu*, 125; and Military History Research Division, *Zhongguo renmin zhiyuanjun kangmei yuanchao zhanshi*, 48. The Chinese figures, however, do not agree with the UNF Command's own casualty accounting. The U.S. 8th Army exceeded 10,000 casualties by December 3, 1950. See Millett, *War for Korea*, 347. U.S. X Corps had 8,735 battle casualties between November 27 and December 10. Mossman, *U.S. Army in the Korean War*, 147. The marines suffered 4,418 battle and 7,313 nonbattle casualties. Hastings, *Korean War*, 164.

128. Among the CPVF casualties in the Second Offensive Campaign were 50,000 non-combat dead. See Military History Research Division, *Zhongguo renmin zhiyuanjun kangmei yuanchao zhanshi*, 48; and Xu, *Diyici jiaoliang*, 60.

129. Mao Anying, Mao Zedong's older son (Mao had two sons), was Peng's Russian interpreter and secretary at the CPVF General HQ. For the death of Mao Anying, see Hong, "CPVF's Combat and Logistics," 118–21; Du, *Zai zhiyuanjun zongbu*, 94–98; Yang, *Zai zhiyuanjun silingbu de suiyueli*, 292–95; and Li, *Zhiyuanjun yuanchao jishi*, 149–53.

130. Yu, "What China Learned," 17.

Chapter 6. Recovery and Reengagement

1. Peng's telegram to Mao at 6:00 P.M. on December 8, 1950, in Ye Yumeng, *Chubing chaoxian: Kangmei yuanchao lishi jishi* [A True History of China's Entry into the Korean War] (Beijing: Shiyue wenxue chubanshe [October Literature Press], 1989), 244.

2. CMC telegram to CCP's regional bureaus, provincial committees, and metropolitan committees, and to all PLA regional commands, army groups, and army commands, drafted by Mao, December 18, 1950, in *Mao's Military Manuscripts since 1949*, 1:412–13.

3. Mao's conversation with Kim Il-sung in Beijing, December 3, 1950, quoted in Military History Research Division, *Kangmei yuanchao zhanzheng zhanshi*, 162. For more details of Kim's visit, see Li, *Zhiyuanjun yuanchao jishi*, 156–60.

4. Andrei Gromyko had a conversation with Chinese ambassador Wang Jiaxiang before the latter returned to China on December 4, 1950. In his telegram to Soviet ambassador Roshchin on December 5, Gromyko reiterated this point that China would win the war and should not negotiate with the United States at that moment. Gromyko's telegram

to Roshchin (Beijing), December 5, 1950, Archives of the President of the Russian Federation, Fond 3, Opis 65, Delo 828, List 19–21, in "New Russian Documents on the Korean War," 51–52.

5. *Chen Geng Zhuan* Compilation Team, *Chen Geng Zhuan* [Biography of Chen Geng], 580.

6. Peng's telegram to all the CPVF armies and CMC, January 4, 1951, in *Selected Military Papers of Peng*, 360–63.

7. Brian Catchpole, *The Korean War, 1950–1953* (New York: Carroll & Graf, 2000), 101–2; Millett, *War for Korea*, 384–87; Mossman, *U.S. Army in the Korean War*, 201–2.

8. CMC document, telegram to Song Shilun, Tao Yong, Chen Yi, Peng Dehuai, and others, December 17, 1950, drafted by Mao, in *Selected Military Papers of Mao*, 2:682–83.

9. *Song Shilun Zhuan* Compilation Team, *Song Shilun Zhuan*, 290; Shuang, *Kaiguo diyi zhan*, 1:189.

10. Mao's telegram to Peng, December 17, 1950, in *Mao's Manuscripts since 1949*, 1:724–25; Zhang and Chen, *Chinese Communist Foreign Policy*, 216.

11. *Song Shilun Zhuan* Compilation Team, *Song Shilun Zhuan*, 292–93.

12. Song's telegram to Peng on December 19, 1950, quoted in *Song Shilun Zhuan* Compilation Team, *Song Shilun Zhuan*, 291.

13. Peng's telegram to Mao and the CMC at 12:00 A.M. on December 20, 1950, quoted in *Mao's Military Manuscripts since 1949*, 1:415–16.

14. Mao's telegram to Peng, December 21, 1950, in *Mao's Manuscripts since 1949*, 1:731–32; Zhang and Chen, *Chinese Communist Foreign Policy*, 216–17.

15. Mao's telegram to Peng on December 13, 1950, in *Mao's Manuscripts since 1949*, 1:722–23; Zhang and Chen, *Chinese Communist Foreign Policy*, 215.

16. Mao's telegram to Song on December 30, 1950, quoted in *Song Shilun Zhuan* Compilation Team, *Song Shilun Zhuan*, 294.

17. CMC order to all PLA regional commands and copied to the CPVF and the 9th Group Army Commands, drafted by Mao, January 4, 1951, in *Collected Military Works of Mao*, 6:259.

18. CMC telegram to Peng, other CPVF commanders, and PLA military regional commands, "Certain Changes in the Rotation Plan for the CPVF in Korea, February 18, 1951," drafted by Zhou, in *Selected Military Works of Zhou*, 4:158–61.

19. Bin Yu discussed some of the PLA's tactics, such as outnumbering the enemy whenever the situation permitted in order to wipe out entire enemy units, engaging the enemy in mobile operations, and achieving surprise whenever possible in order to avoid the usually superior enemy firepower. See Yu, "What China Learned," 14.

20. Xu, "Chinese Forces and Their Casualties," 50.

21. Mao's telegram to Stalin, November 8, 1950, in "New Russian Documents on the Korean War," 48; Shen Zhihua, trans. and ed., *Chaoxian zhanzheng: Eguo dang'anguan*

de jiemi wenjian [The Korean War: Declassified Documents from Russian Archives] (Taipei: Institute of Modern History, Academia Sinica, 2015), 2:617.

22. Nie, *Nie Rongzhen huiyilu*, 2:757.

23. In Beijing, of 442 Soviet advisers, 310 chief were military advisers, 72 were economic and technology advisers, 47 were government and foreign policy advisers, and 13 were intelligence and national security advisers. Shen, *Mao Zedong, Stalin he chaoxian zhanzheng*, 371. Shen found the information in the archives of the 2nd Division, Defense Intelligence Agency, ROC Defense Ministry, Taiwan. He believes that the numbers collected by the intelligence agents in the 1950s were incomplete. See also "Filippov" (Stalin)'s telegram to Zhou, August 27, 1950, about sending Soviet military advisers, in "New Russian Documents on the Korean War," 45.

24. Hong, *Hong Xuezhi huiyilu*, 473.

25. The 20th Army of the 9th Army Group was reinforced with two artillery regiments, the 11th and 26th Regiments from the 1st Artillery Division. See Military History Research Division, *Zhongguo renmin zhiyuanjun kangmei yuanchao zhanshi*, 95; the 26th Army of the 9th Army Group was reinforced with one field artillery regiment and three antitank companies. They were the 27th Artillery Regiment and three companies of the 401st Antitank Regiment. See Tan Jingjiao et al., *Kangmei yuanchao zhanzheng* [The WRUSAK] (Beijing: Zhongguo shehui kexue chubanshe [China Social Sciences Press], 1990), 137.

26. The 27th Army of the 9th Army Group was reinforced with two field artillery regiments and three antitank companies. They were the 25th and 30th Artillery Regiments and three companies of the 401st Antitank Regiment. See Zhao, *27 Jun chuanqi*, 440–41.

27. Mao's letter to Zhou Enlai, "The Force Rotation of the CPVF Armies on the Korean Battleground," February 7, 1951, in *Mao's Military Manuscripts since 1949*, 1:462–63; Hong, *Kangmei yuanchao zhanzheng huiyi*, 184; Hong, "CPVF's Combat and Logistics," 136.

28. *Song Shilun Zhuan* Compilation Team, *Song Shilun Zhuan*, 297.

29. Song's campaign report on the Battle of Chosin at the extended conference of the 9th Army Group's Party Committee, March 8, 1951, quoted in ibid., 295.

30. Ibid., 297.

31. Ibid.

32. Yang, *Zai zhiyuanjun silingbu de suiyueli*, 128.

33. CPVF 27th Army Command, *Zhongguo renmin zhiyuanjun di 27 jun kangmei yuanchao zhanzheng shi*, 21–22.

34. Shuang, *Kaiguo diyi zhan*, 1:181.

35. The 94th Division's campaign summary, quoted in CPVF 27th Army Command, *Zhongguo renmin zhiyuanjun di 27 jun kangmei yuanchao zhanzheng shi*, 23.

36. Xiaobing Li, "Chinese Army in the Korean War, 1950–53," *New England Journal of History* 60, nos. 1–3 (2003–4): 282.

37. Hong, *Kangmei yuanchao zhanzheng huiyi*, 90–91.

38. Mao's telegram to "Filippov" (Joseph Stalin), "On the War Situation in Korea and the Rotation Plan of the CPVF," March 1, 1951, in *Selected Military Works of Mao*, 1:351; *Mao's Manuscripts since 1949*, 2:153.

39. Mao's telegram to Stalin, "On the War Situation in Korea," 1:350–51; *Mao's Manuscripts since 1949*, 2:153.

40. Mao's telegram to Peng, March 7, 1951, quoted in Military History Research Division, *Zhongguo renmin zhiyuanjun kangmei yuanchao zhanshi*, 125–26.

41. For more details on the CPVF Command meeting on March 11, 1951, see Hong, *Kangmei yuanchao zhanzheng huiyi*, 136–38; Du, *Zai zhiyuanjun zongbu*, 218–19; and Zhao Jianli and Liang Yuhong, *Fenghuo 38 xian: Diwuci zhanyi zhanshi baogao* [The Flames of Battle Raging across the 38th Parallel: Combat Report on the Fifth Campaign] (Beijing: Junshi kexue chubanshe, 2007), 291–93.

42. Peng's telegram to all the CPVF army commanders and the CMC at 5:00 P.M. on March 14, 1951, in *Selected Military Papers of Peng*, 379.

43. Peng, "Speech at the CPVF Enlarged Fifth Party Committee Conference, April 6, 1951," in ibid., 386.

44. Ibid.; Yang and Wang, *Beiwei 38 duxian*, 296.

45. Peng, "Speech at the CPVF Enlarged Fifth Party Committee Conference, April 6, 1951," in *Selected Military Papers of Peng*, 386–87.

46. Ibid.

47. Yang, *Zai zhiyuanjun silingbu de suiyueli*, 128.

48. Military History Institute, *Kangmei yuanchao zhanzheng shi*, 2:192–93.

49. Peng's telegram to Mao, April 10, 1951, in *Mao's Manuscripts since 1949*, 2:239n2.

50. Mao's telegram to Peng, April 13, 1951, in ibid., 2:239.

51. Peng's telegram to all CPVF armies and the CMC, April 18, 1951, in *Selected Military Papers of Peng*, 391.

52. Hong, *Kangmei yuanchao zhanzheng huiyi*, 152, 154; Military History Research Division, *Zhongguo renmin zhiyuanjun kangmei yuanchao zhanshi*, 131.

53. Du, *Zai zhiyuanjun zongbu*, 238–39; Cui and Chen, *Tao Yong jiangjun zhuan*, 396; Tan, *Kangmei yuanchao zhanzheng*, 137.

54. Li Ying et al., *40 Jun zai chaoxian* [The 40th Army in Korea] (Shenyang: Liaoning renmin chubanshe, 2010), 188; Yang and Wang, *Beiwei 38 duxian*, 313; Military History Research Division, *Zhongguo renmin zhiyuanjun kangmei yuanchao zhanshi*, 131; Li, *Zhiyuanjun yuanchao jishi*, 293; Wang, *Juezhan chaoxian*, 301; Chu, *Chaoxian zhanzheng neimu quangongkai*, 289.

55. Colonel Wang Po, PLA Logistics Academy, interview by the author in Beijing, July 1994. See also Zhou, *Kangmei yuanchao zhanzheng houqinshi jianbianben*, 25–29.

56. The CMC's instruction on April 16, 1951, quoted in Hong, "CPVF's Combat and Logistics," 132.

57. Zhou, *Kangmei yuanchao zhanzheng houqinshi jianbianben*, 87–88; Hong, "CPVF's Combat and Logistics," 135.

58. Hong, *Kangmei yuanchao zhanzheng huiyi*, 137; Military History Research Division, *Zhongguo renmin zhiyuanjun kangmei yuanchao zhanshi*, 129.

59. Shu Guang Zhang, "Command, Control, and the PLA's Offensive Campaigns in Korea, 1950–1951," in Ryan, Finkelstein, and McDevitt, *Chinese Warfighting*, 110–11, 113.

60. Peng's telegram to all the CPVF army commanders and the CMC at 5:00 P.M. on March 14, 1951, in *Selected Military Papers of Peng*, 379.

61. Yang, *Zai zhiyuanjun silingbu de suiyueli*, 125; Li et al., *40 jun zai chaoxian*, 188–94; Tan, *Kangmei yuanchao zhanzheng*, 138–39.

62. Wu, *Chaoxian zhanchang 1000 tian*, 603–6; Li et al., *40 Jun zai chaoxian*, 200; Catchpole, *Korean War*, 120. For more information on Lieutenantt General Wu, see *Xinghuo liaoyuan* Composition Department, *Zhongguo renmin jiefangjun jiangshuai minglu*, 1:292–93; and Tan, *Zhongguo renmin zhiyuanjun renwulu*, 291–92.

63. Li et al., *40 Jun zai chaoxian*, 188–89; Military History Research Division, *Zhongguo renmin zhiyuanjun kangmei yuanchao zhanshi*, 138–39; Shuang, *Kaiguo diyi zhan*, 1:369–70.

64. Zhao and Liang, *Fenghuo 38 xian*, 53; Luan, *Xue yu huo de jiaoliang*, 205.

65. Li et al., *40 Jun zai chaoxian*, 194–202; Wang Shuzeng, *Yuandong chaoxian zhanzheng* [The Korean War in the Far East] (Beijing: Jiefangjun wenyi chubanshe, 2000), 2:705–7.

66. Wang Hechuan, *Zhongguo dadi shang de jufeng: 40 jun zhengzhan jingli* [The Hurricane over China: War Experience of the 40th Army] (Beijing: Jiefangjun wenyi chubanshe, 2004), 331–34.

67. Wu, *Chaoxian zhanchang 1000 tian*, 414–15; Tan, *Kangmei yuanchao zhanzheng*, 139; Li et al., *40 Jun zai chaoxian*, 203.

68. Du, *Zai zhiyuanjun zongbu*, 238–39; Luan, *Xue yu Huo de Jiaoliang*, 205–6.

69. History Research Division, *Zhongguo renmin zhiyuanjun kangmei yuanchao zhanshi*, 131; Millett, *War for Korea*, 431.

70. Colonel Wang, interview by the author; Zhou, *Kangmei yuanchao zhanzheng huoqinshi jianbianben*, 75.

71. Du, *Zai zhiyuanjun zongbu*, 229–31; Zhao and Liang, *Fenghuo 38 xian*, 53.

72. NCO Han Shunzhou, interview by the author in Beijing, July 2010. Han served in the 3rd Battalion, 241st Regiment, 81st Division, 27th Army 9th Army Group of the CPVF. See also Tan, *Kangmei yuanchao zhanzheng*, 137; and Zhao, *27 Jun chuanqi*, 443.

73. Telegram from Song Shilun and other commanders of the 9th Army Group to the commanders of all its armies and divisions at 2:30 P.M. on April 23, 1951, quoted in PLA-AMS, "Unforgotten Korean War," 411.

74. Han, interview by the author; Zhao, *27 Jun chuanqi*, 443–44.

75. Ridgway, *Korean War*, 171–72; Mossman, *U.S. Army in the Korean War*, 389; Donald Knox, *The Korean War: Uncertain Victory* (New York: Harvest/HBJ Book, 1988), 170–71.

76. Xu, *Mao Zedong yu kangmei yuanchao zhanzheng*, 212; Wang Yongping, "Our Understanding of the Lessons and Experience of the Fifth Offensive Campaign," in Chen, *Kangmei yuanchao zhanzhenglun*, 258.

77. Yang and Wang, *Beiwei 38 duxian*, 314–15; Zhao and Liang, *Fenghuo 38 xian*, 57.

78. Captain Wang, interview by the author.

79. Li et al., *40 Jun zai chaoxian*, 202–3; Military History Research Division, *Zhongguo renmin zhiyuanjun kangmei yuanchao zhanshi*, 95, 97.

80. Han, interview by the author; Tan, *Kangmei yuanchao zhanzheng*, 133.

81. After the Korean Armistice in 1953, the PLA reorganized its services into a Soviet-style structure. As part of his effort to reform the PLA, Peng Dehuai, the first defense minister of the PRC, established a Soviet-style system of military ranks in 1955, when 10 marshals, 10 grand generals, 57 generals, 175 lieutenant generals, and 800 major generals were granted by the PLA. The ranks mentioned in this work are awarded in 1955 unless an endnote provides further information on the officer.

82. Nie, "Beijing's Decision to Intervene," 52–53.

83. PLA-AMS, "Unforgotten Korean War," 422–23; Zhao and Liang, *Fenghuo 38 xian*, 59; Mossman, *U.S. Army in the Korean War*, 383–85.

84. Nie, "Beijing's Decision to Intervene," 52–53; Yang Qinghua, "Establish and Develop the CPVF's Logistics Conception," in Chen, *Kangmei yuanchao zhanzhenglun*, 347.

85. Hong, *Kangmei yuanchao zhanzheng huiyi*, 137; Military History Research Division, *Zhongguo renmin zhiyuanjun kangmei yuanchao zhanshi*, 129.

86. General Wu Ruilin, *Wu Ruilin huiyilu* [Memoirs of Wu Ruilin] (Beijing: Zhongguo dang'an chubanshe [China's Archival Publishing], 1995), 3:143–45; Yang, *Zai zhiyuanjun silingbu de suiyueli*, 132.

87. Yang, *Zai zhiyuanjun silingbu de suiyueli*, 133; Military History Research Division, *Zhongguo renmin zhiyuanjun kangmei yuanchao zhanshi*, 98.

88. Li et al., *40 Jun zai chaoxian*, 203–4, 212; PLA-AMS, "Unforgotten Korean War," 422–23.

89. Official Chinese statistics show a total of 80,000–85,000 casualties in the Spring Offensive Campaign from April 22 to June 10, 1951. An estimated half of the total took place during the first stage of the campaign on the western front on April 22–29. See Military History Research Division, *Zhongguo renmin zhiyuanjun kangmei yuanchao zhanshi*, 152; and Tan, *Kangmei yuanchao zhanzheng*, 159. See also the other statistics in Korean Institute of Military History, ROK Ministry of Defense, *The Korean War* (Seoul: Korean Institute of Military History, 1998), 2:5; and Sandler, *Korean War*, 142.

90. Peng's telegram to Mao and the CMC, copied to Kim Il-sung, April 26, 1951, quoted in Wang et al., *Peng Dehuai zhuan*, 466.

91. "Agree Your Operation Plan and Force Deployment of the Fifth Campaign," CMC telegram to Peng, April 28, 1951, drafted by Zhou Enlai, in *Selected Military Works of Zhou*, 4:193–95.

92. Peng pointed out the "limited results" of the first stage of the Spring Offensive Campaign in his telegram to Mao and the CMC, April 26, 1951. His telegram was included in the notes of the CMC reply to Peng; see ibid., 4:195.

93. Peng's telegram to the CMC and all the CPVF armies, May 6, 1951, in *Selected Military Papers of Peng*, 392–93.

94. Yang and Wang, *Beiwei 38 duxian*, 323; Zhao and Liang, *Fenghuo 38 xian*, 176; Luan, *Xue yu huo de jiaoliang*, 209–11.

95. Peng and Deng Hua's telegram to the CMC, all CPVF army groups, and Northeast Military Region at 10:00 P.M. on May 6, 1951, in *Selected Military Papers of Peng*, 392–95.

96. Du, *Zai zhiyuanjun zongbu*, 244; Tan, *Kangmei yuanchao zhanzheng*, 147; Wang, *Yuandong chaoxian zhanzheng*, 2:722–23.

97. Yang, *Zai zhiyuanjun silingbu de suiyueli*, 134; He Zongguang, *Wo zai chaoxian zhanchang: 1950–1953* [I Was There: The Korean Battleground, 1950–1953] (Beijing: Changzheng chubanshe [Long March Publishing House], 2011), 253–54; China National Military Museum, ed., *Kangmei yuanchao zhanzheng fengyunlu* [The Operational Files of the WRUSAK], 195–96.

98. Korean Institute of Military History, *Korean War*, 2:663, 665.

99. Ridgway, *Korean War*, 175; Millett, *War for Korea*, 443.

100. Peng's telegram to Song Shilun and Kim Woong at 1:00 A.M. on May 17, 1951, quoted in PLA-AMS, "Unforgotten Korean War," 437–38.

101. China National Military Museum, ed., *Kangmei yuanchao zhanzheng fengyunlu*, 196; Tan, *Kangmei yuanchao zhanzheng*, 147; Military History Research Division, *Zhongguo renmin zhiyuanjun kangmei yuanchao zhanshi*, 103.

102. "Citation to the 178th Regiment of the 20th Army for Cutting Off Enemy Retreat," signed by Peng, Deng Hua, and Pak Il-yu on May 17, 1951, in PLA-AMS, "Unforgotten Korean War," 434n786.

103. Composition Committee, *38 xian shang de jiaofeng*, 325–27; Zhao and Liang, *Fenghuo 38 xian*, 171.

104. Jongnam Na, "Making Cold War Soldiers: The Americanization of the South Korean Army, 1945–55" (Ph.D. diss., University of North Carolina, 2006), 97.

105. The ROK 8th Regiment of the 7th Division lost the 6th and 10th Companies in the battle. See Gu Cheng et al., trans. and eds., *Kangmei yuanchao zhanzheng: Dijun shiliao* [WRUSAK: ROK Army Archives] (Harbin: Heilongjiang chaoxian minzu

chubanshe [Heilongjiang Korean Ethnic Minority Publishing], 1988–90), 2:125–26; and Na, "Making Cold War Soldiers," 92.

106. Shuang, *Kaiguo diyizhang*, 1:385; Military History Research Division, *Zhongguo renmin zhiyuanjun kangmei yuanchao zhanshi*, 103–4.

107. Han Shunzhou, interview by the author.

108. Zhao, *27 jun chuanqi*, 446; Tan, *Kangmei yuanchao zhanzheng*, 148–49; Luan, *Xue yu huo de jiaoliang*, 212.

109. Military History Research Division, *Zhongguo renmin zhiyuanjun kangmei yuanchao zhanshi*, 103–4; Composition Committee, *38 xian shang de jiaofeng*, 327–28; Li, *Zhiyuanjun yuanchao jishi*, 310–11.

110. Ridgway, *Korean War*, 175.

111. Korean Institute of Military History, *Korean War*, 2:675.

112. "Citation to NKPA V Corps' 1st Regiment and CPVF 27th Army's 81st Regiment on Cutting Off Enemy Retreat," signed by Peng, Deng, and Pak on May 18, 1951, quoted in PLA-AMS, "Unforgotten Korean War," 435.

113. Gu et al., *Kangmei yuanchao zhanzheng dijun shiliao*, 2:128; Composition Committee, *38 xian shang de jiaofeng*, 327.

114. "Citation to NKPA V Corps' 1st Regiment and CPVF 27th Army's 81st Regiment," in PLA-AMS, "Unforgotten Korean War," 435.

115. Zhao and Liang, *Fenghuo 38 xian*, 179; Shuang, *Kaiguo diyizhan*, 1:385–86.

116. Military History Research Division, *Zhongguo renmin zhiyuanjun kangmei yuanchao zhanshi*, 103–5; Tan, *Kangmei yuanchao zhanzheng*, 148–49; Mossman, *U.S. Army in the Korean War*, 468.

117. Ridgway, *Korean War*, 176.

118. Korean Institute of Military History, *Korean War*, 2:691.

119. Tan, *Kangmei yuanchao zhanzheng*, 149; Military History Research Division, *Zhongguo renmin zhiyuanjun kangmei yuanchao zhanshi*, 103; Shuang, *Kaiguo diyizhan*, 1:385–86.

120. Yang, *Zai zhiyuanjun silingbu de suiyueli*, 134; Li, *Zhiyuanjun yuanchao jishi*, 312; Shuang, *Kaiguo diyizhan*, 1:386.

121. Hong, *Kangmei yuanchao zhanzheng huiyi*, 47; Yang, *Zai zhiyuanjun silingbu de suiyueli*, 31–34.

122. Hong, *Hong Xuezhi huiyilu*, 476–77; Tan, *Kangmei yuanchao zhanzheng*, 149; Xu Yaguang, "The Difficult Withdrawal to the North," in Ge Chumin, *Laozhanshi yishi*, 86–87. NCO Xu Yaguang served as a company officer in the 101st Regiment, 34th Division, 12th Army, 3rd Army Group of the CPVF, during the Fifth Offensive Campaign in April–June 1951.

123. Du, *Zai zhiyuanjun zongbu*, 244–45; Luan, *Xue yu huo de jiaoliang*, 212; Mossman, *U.S. Army in the Korean War*, 448–50; Clark C. Munroe, *The Second U.S. Infantry Division in Korea, 1950–1951* (Tokyo: Toppan Printing, 1954), 131–35.

124. The 12th Army had been under the command of the 3rd Army Group since it entered Korea in March 1951. The army was reassigned to the command of the 9th Army Group just for the second stage of the Spring Offensive Campaign at the CPVF commanders meeting on May 6, 1951. See Yan Xinning, *Wei Jie zhongjiang* [Lieutenant General Wei Jie] (Beijing: Jiefangjun wenyi chubanshe, 2005), 37–38.

125. Du, *Zai zhiyuanjun zongbu*, 244–45; Zhao and Liang, *Fenghuo 38 xian*, 178–79.

126. For more details on the battle at Bunker Hill, see "Hill 800 (Bunker Hill)," in Gugeler, *Combat Actions in Korea*, 166–82; Munroe, *Second U.S. Infantry Division*, 132–36; and Catchpole, *Korean War*, 136. See also Military History Research Division, *Zhongguo renmin zhiyuanjun kangmei yuanchao zhanshi*, 104.

127. Hong, *Hong Xuezhi huiyilu*, 476; Tan, *Kangmei yuanchao zhanzheng*, 150.

128. Du, *Zai zhiyuanjun zongbu*, 246; Xu, "Difficult Withdrawal to the North," 87–89; Tan, *Kangmei yuanchao zhanzheng*, 152; Military History Research Division, *Junqi piaopiao*, 1:135–36.

129. Zhao and Liang, *Fenghuo 38 xian*, 188–89; Shuang, *Kaiguo diyizhang*, 1:395.

130. Chang Buting (POW), interview by the author. Chang was captured by the UNF during the Spring Offensive Campaign in May 1951. He did not go back to China, but instead went to Taiwan, after the Korean Armistice in 1953.

131. *Chen Geng Zhuan* Compilation Team, *Chen Geng Zhuan*, 580.

Conclusion

1. Chen Hui, "Tracing the 180,000 Martyrs of WRUSAK," in Zhang, *Kangmei yuanchao*, 127; Xu, "Chinese Forces and Their Casualties," 56–57; Li, *Zhiyuanjun yuanchao jishi*, 13; Shuang, *Kaiguo diyi zhan*, 2:836–37. The UNF intelligence statisticians put Chinese losses far higher: 1.5 million casualties in all categories including killed in action, died of wounds and disease, missing in action, and wounded in action. For example, see Walter G. Hermes, *Truce Tent and Fighting Front: U.S. Army in the Korean War* (1966; reprint, Washington, D.C.: Office of the Chief of Military History and U.S. Government Printing Office, 1988), 477–78.

2. The Chinese official number was 26,000 POWs held by the UNF. See Foreign Affairs to Chinese chargé d'affaires in Pyongyang (Gan Yetao), "[Zhou Enlai's] Speech (Draft) at the Third Anniversary of the Korean War, June 24, 1953," in "Premier Zhou Enlai's Approvals and Instructions on North Korean Telegrams and Documents, 1953," File#106–00034–01 (1), 24–25 (31 pp.), Foreign Ministry Archives, Beijing.

3. Xu, *Diyici jiaoliang*, 308–10.

4. Military History Research Division, *Zhongguo renmin zhiyuanjun kangmei yuanchao zhanshi* [Combat History of the CPVF in the WRUSAK], 233–34.

5. For example, see Mao's conclusion at the Second Plenary Session of the CCP Seventh Central Committee, March 13, 1949, and his speech, "Address to the Preparatory

Meeting of the New Political Consultative Conference," in *Selected Works of Mao*, 4:1464, 1470.

6. Ellis Joffe, *The Chinese Army after Mao* (Cambridge, Mass.: Harvard University Press, 1987), 1.

7. Gries, *China's New Nationalism*, 56.

8. Peng, "China's Military Experience in the Past Four Years and the Fundamental Issues for Our Future Military Development," speech at an enlarged CMC meeting in December 1953, in *Selected Military Papers of Peng*, 468–69.

9. I borrow this term from Thomas J. Christensen's research on grand strategy and Sino-American relations. But the "useful adversary" here describes a learning curve of the CPVF in Korea through its engagements with the UN/U.S. forces. See Christensen, *Useful Adversaries: Grand Strategy, Domestic Mobilization, and Sino-American Conflict, 1947–1958* (Princeton, N.J.: Princeton University Press, 1996), 1–2.

10. The Soviet Union delivered its weapons to China for sixteen infantry divisions in 1951, and for forty-four divisions in 1952–54. Xu, "Purchase of Arms from Moscow," 53.

11. Peng, "China's Military Experience," 474–76.

12. Ming-Yen Tsai, *From Adversaries to Partners: Chinese and Russian Military Cooperation after the Cold War* (Westport, Conn.: Praeger, 2003), 25–27.

13. Nie, *Nie Rongzhen huiyilu*, 2:745–46; Xu, "Chinese Forces and Their Casualties," 54; Li, "China's Intervention and the CPVF Experience in the Korean War," in Wilkinson, ed., *The Korean War: International Perspectives*, 136–37.

14. CPVF 27th Army Command, *Zhongguo renmin zhiyuanjun di 27 jun kangmei yuanchao zhanzheng shi*, 6.

15. Military History Research Division, *Zhongguo renmin zhiyuanjun kangmei yuanchao zhanshi*, 395–96.

16. Han et al., *Dangdai Zhongguo jundui de junshi gongzuo* [Contemporary Chinese Military Affairs] (Beijing: Zhongguo shehui kexue chubanshe [China Social Sciences Press], 1989), 2:86; Military History Research Division, *Zhongguo renmin zhiyuanjun kangmei yuanchao zhanshi*, 458.

17. Xia Guang, "From Naval School to Naval Academy," in *Haijun: huiyi shiliao* [The Navy: Memoirs and Historical Records] (Beijing: Haichao chubanshe [Ocean Wave Publishing], 1994), ed. PLA Navy History Compilation Committee, 2:631–32.

18. *Song Shilun Zhuan* Compilation Team, *Song Shilun Zhuan*, 426–30.

19. Jurgen Domes, *Peng Te-huai: The Man and the Image* (London: C. Hurst, 1985), 71.

20. Ryan, Finkelstein, and McDevitt, "Patterns of PLA Warfighting," in *Chinese Warfighting*, 15.

21. Military History Research Division, *Junqi piaopiao*, 1:293.

22. Among the recent publications in China on the Vietnam War are Guo Jinliang, *Qinli Yuezhan* [Vietnam War in My Eyes] (Beijing: Jiefangjun wenyi chubanshe

[PLA Literature Publishing], 2005); Military History Research Division, PLA-AMS, *Meiguo qinyue zhanzhengshi* [War History of the U.S. Invasion of Vietnam] (Beijing: Junshi kexue chubanshe, 2004); Luo Xuanyou, *Zhongyue taihai zhanzheng zhengzhan jishi* [The History Records of the Sino-Vietnam and Taiwan Strait Wars] (Urumqi: Xinjiang renmin chubanshe [Xinjiang People's Press], 2004); Chen Pai, *Yuezhan qinliji* [My Personal Experience in the Vietnam War] (Zhengzhou: Henan renmin chubanshe [Henan People's Press], 1997); Wang Xiangen, *Yuanyue kangmei shilu* [True Stories of Aiding Vietnam and Resisting America] (Beijing: Guoji wenhua chubanshe [International Cultural Publishing], 1990).

23. John L. Gaddis, Foreword in Qiang Zhai, *China and the Vietnam War, 1950–1975* (Chapel Hill: University of North Carolina Press, 2000), x.

24. Han et al., *Dangdai Zhongguo jundui de junshi gongzuo*, 1:643–44; Military History Research Division, *Zhongguo renmin zhiyuanjun kangmei yuanchao zhanshi*, 582.

25. Yang Kuisong, "From the Zhenboa Island Incident to Sino-American Rapprochement," *Dangshi yanjiu ziliao* [Party History Research Materials], no. 12 (1997): 7–8; Thomas Robinson, "The Sino-Soviet Border Conflicts of 1969: New Evidence Three Decades Later," in Ryan, Finkelstein, and McDevitt, *Chinese Warfighting*, 198–216.

26. Chen Jian and Xiaobing Li, "China and the End of the Global Cold War," in *The Cold War: From Détente to the Soviet Collapse*, ed. Malcolm Muir Jr. (Lexington: Virginia Military Institute Press, 2006), 120–32.

27. Military History Research Division, PLA Academy of Military Science, *Zhongguo renmin jiefangjun de qishinian, 1927–1997* [Seventy Years of the PLA, 1927–1997] (Beijing: Junshi kexue chubanshe, 1997), 559.

28. Lushun Naval Command, PLA Navy, "Document Collection on Lin Biao and Li Zuopeng's Criminal Activities of Attacking the Party and Betraying the PLA, October 1971," in *Political Files against the Lin-Li Group (1971–1972)*, Lushun Naval Base Archives, 242–45.

29. Cui and Chen, *Tao Yong jiangjun zhuan*, 447, 449.

30. Lushun Naval Command, "Collective Documents," 56.

31. Military History Research Division, *Zhongguo renmin jiefangjun de qishinian*, 559.

32. Among the publications on Marshal Lin Biao, in Chinese and in English, are Huang Yao and Yan Jingtang, *Lin Biao yisheng* [Lin Biao's Life] (Beijing: Jiefangjun wenyi chubanshe [PLA Literature Publishing], 2004); Wang Zhaojun, *Shui shale Lin Biao* [Who Killed Lin Biao] (Taipei: Shijie chubanshe [Global Publishing], 1994); Michael Y. M. Kau, ed., *The Lin Biao Affair: Power Politics and Military Coup* (White Plains, N.Y.: International Arts and Science Press, 1975); and Martin Ebon, *Lin Piao: The Life and Writings of China's New Ruler* (New York: Stein and Day Publishers, 1970).

33. There have been several lines of speculation about the causes of Lin's plane crash, including a Chinese missile attack, running out of fuel, or simply an accident. See

Gao Wenqian, *Wannian Zhou Enlai* [Zhou Enlai's Later Years] (Hong Kong: Mingjing chubanshe [Bright Mirror Publishing], 2003), 350–55; Huang and Yan, *Lin Biao yisheng*, 490–507; and Ye Yonglie, *Gaoceng jiaoliang* [Struggle at the Top] (Urumqi: Xinjiang renmin chubanshe [Xinjiang People's Press], 2004), 369–76.

34. For the details of the arrest of the "Gang of Four," see Deng Rong, *Deng Xiaoping and the Cultural Revolution* (Beijing: Foreign Languages Press, 2002), 436–43.

35. Deng became the figurehead of the second generation of the CCP's political and military leadership. See Cheng Li, *China's Leaders: The New Generation* (Lanham, Md.: Rowman & Littlefield, 2001), 7–9.

36. Deng, "Emancipate the Mind, Seek Truth from Facts, and Unite as One in Looking to the Future, December 13, 1978," speech as the closing session of the CCP Central Conference. This speech was prepared for the Third Plenary Session of the CCP Eleventh Central Committee. In fact, this speech served as the keynote address for the Third Plenary Session. See *Selected Works of Deng Xiaoping*, 2:150–63; and CCP Central Committee, "Communiqué of the Third Plenary Session of the CCP Eleventh Central Committee," adopted on December 22, 1978. The party document is included in Research Department of Party Literature, CCP Central Committee, ed., *Major Documents of the People's Republic of China—Selected Important Documents since the Third Plenary Session of the Eleventh CCP Central Committee* (Beijing: Foreign Languages Press, 1991), 20–22.

37. Warren I. Cohen, *America's Response to China: A History of Sino-American Relations*, 5th ed. (New York: Columbia University Press, 2010), 206–7.

38. Deng Xiaoping, "Streamline the Army and Raise Its Combat Effectiveness," speech at an enlarged meeting of CMC Standing Committee on March 12, 1980, in *Selected Works of Deng Xiaoping*, 2:284–87.

39. Deng's comments photocopied in Song, *Hujiang Song Shilun*, 233.

40. Xi Jinping's speech at the "Sixtieth Anniversary Celebration of the CPVF's Participation in the War to Resist the U.S. and Aid Korea," *Renmin ribao*, October 26, 2010.

Glossary of Names and Terms

Anti-Japanese War (1937–45): On July 7, 1937, Japanese Imperial Army attacked the Chinese troops at the Marco Polo Bridge, southwest of Beijing. This event marked the beginning of the resistance of the Republic of China against Japan's invasion, or the Anti-Japanese War. The ROC government established the united front, including the Chinese Communist forces, to defense the country. In 1937–39, almost all of north, central, and southeast China fallen into the enemy's hands. After Japan's attack at Pearl Harbor in 1941, China began to receive the Allied support and American aid. On August 15, 1945, Japan surrendered unconditionally to the Allies. The price in Chinese lives for resisting Japanese aggression was very high. The total military deaths were over 3 million, and the civilian death toll was estimated at 10 million. Nevertheless, the CCP forces increased from 50,000 men in 1937 to 1.27 million regular troops and 2.6 million militias in 1945.

Cai Qunfan: Chief of staff of the CPVF 60th Division of the Twentieth Army in the Battle of Chosin. Cai joined the CCP New Fourth Army during the Anti-Japanese War, and became a guerrilla commander, political commissar, regiment commander, division deputy chief of staff, and chief of staff of the PLA 60th Division during the Chinese Civil War. After return to China, Cai became assistant commander of the 60th Division, Chief of the Operation Division of the Nanjing Regional Command, and deputy chief of staff of Shanghai Garrison Command. He was granted a colonel in 1955 and a senior colonel in 1965.

Chen Yi: One of the most brilliant military leaders of the CCP. He participated in the Nanchang Uprising on August 1, 1927, and served as party representative of the 1st Division and then commander of the 12th Division of the Fourth Red

Army. During the Anti-Japanese War, Chen was vice commissar in 1939, then deputy commander and chief staff in 1940, and acting commander of the New Fourth Army in 1941. He became commander of the East China Field Army in 1947. A year later, he was commander and political commissar of the Third Field Army, totaling 1 million troops, which took over Nanjing, Shanghai, and many cities in southeast China in the Chinese Civil War. After the founding of the PRC, Chen was mayor of Shanghai, vice premier of the PRC and vice chairman of the CMC in 1954. He became one of the ten marshals in 1955. In 1958, Chen became the Minister of Foreign Affairs. Mao purged him in 1966 during the Cultural Revolution.

Chen Zhongmei: Commander of the 76th Division of the Twenty-Sixth Army in the Battle of Chosin. Chen was a company political instructor, battalion political commissar, and regimental deputy commander and commander during the Anti-Japanese War. He became a divisional chief of staff, assistant commander, and commander of the PLA 78th and later the 76th Division during the Chinese Civil War. After return to China, Chen was promoted to the chief of staff and assistant commander of the Twenty-Sixth Army. He was made a major general in 1955, and served as deputy commander of the Shandong Provincial Command in the 1960s.

Chinese Civil War (1946–49): The Chinese Nationalist (GMD) government and the Chinese Communist forces fought after WWII for the control of the country. The first phase began on June 26, 1946, when Jiang Jieshi launched an all-out offensive campaign against the CCP-held regions. After his failure, Jiang changed from broad assaults to attacks on key targets from March 1947 to August 1948, as the second phase of the war. The third phase of the civil war, from August 1848 to October 1949, was a CCP offensive from rural areas against Jiang's defenses in urban areas. Nearly all of Jiang's troops, more than 7 million, were wiped out. Jiang had to remove the seat of his government from the mainland to Taiwan. The CCP forces, renamed the PLA in 1948, increased from 1.7 million in 1945 to 5.1 million in 1949. On October 1, 1949, Mao Zedong, Chairman of the CCP, proclaimed the founding of the People's Republic of China in Beijing.

CMC: The Central Military Commission of the Chinese Communist Party (CCP)'s Central Committee is the highest command of China's armed forces with Mao Zedong as its chairman from 1938 to 1976 and with defense minister and joint chiefs as its vice chairmen after 1949.

CPG: The Central People's Government was established by the CCP in October 1949 after the CCP won the Chinese Civil War on mainland China. It served as the national government with Mao Zedong, the CCP chairman, as its president until 1954 when the First National People's Congress (NPC) passed the Constitution and elected Mao as the president of the People's Republic of China (PRC).

Cultural Revolution (1966–76): A political movement launched by Mao, who used mass organizations such as the millions involved in the Red Guards to publicly attack his political rivalries in the party, government, and army such as Vice President Liu Shaoqi and Secretariat General of the CCP Deng Xiaoping in 1966–68. More than 80,000 PLA officers were accused and purged in 1967–69. Among them, 1,169 died of torture or starvation or were executed. Then, in 1970, Marshal Lin Biao, China's Defense Minister, became a new political target of Mao. On September 13, 1971, Lin and his family were killed in a plane crash in Mongolia. After Lin's death, another top-down purge and shakeup began in 1972. The Cultural Revolution became an extensive purge for ten years, in which an estimated 100 million people were killed, injured, or persecuted and victimized.

Dai Kelin: Commander of the 59th Division of the Twentieth Army in the Battle of Chosin. Dai joined the Red Army in 1929 and the CCP in 1930. He served as a platoon, company, and battalion commander of the Red Army. Then, Dai became a regiment and brigade commander in the Anti-Japanese War. In the Chinese Civil War, he was appointed as a chief of staff and assistant division commander. When the war ended in 1949, Dai was commander of the 59th Division. After his return to China, Dai was appointed as assistant commander of the PLA Twentieth Army and then the Twenty-Seventh Army. In the 1960s, he became the assistant commander of the PLA Zhejiang Provincial Military Command. Dai was made a senior colonel in 1955 and a major general in 1964.

Deng Hua: First assistant commander of the CPVF in 1951–52 and commander in chief of the CPVF in 1953. As one of the most experienced commanders in the Fourth Field Army in the Chinese Civil War, Deng had been commander of the 15th Army Group and 13th Army Group. In July 1950, he had also commanded the NEBDA before it became Peng's most trusted CPVF commander in 1950–52. Deng was later chief delegate of the CPVF at the Truce Talks in 1951–52. Returning from Korea, Deng was promoted to regional commander in 1954, rank of general in 1955, and deputy Chief of the PLA General Staff in 1956.

Gao Gang: A member of the CCP Central Committee and Politburo, secretary general of the CCP Northeast Bureau, commander and political commissar of the PLA's Northeast Military Region, and chair of the Northeast People's Government of the PRC in 1949–53. He was purge by Mao and committed suicide in August 1954.

GMD: Guomindang (or Kuomintang, KMT), the Chinese Nationalist Party, established in August 1912 by Sun Yat-sen in Nanjing, becoming the dominant political party from 1927 to 1949 on mainland China and from 1950 to 2000 and 2008 to 2016 in Taiwan (Republic of China).

Hao Liang: Political commissar of the 174th Regiment of the 58th Division. Hao joined the Eighth Route Army in 1938, and became a platoon and company commander in 1939–45. Hao served as battalion political commissar and regiment deputy political commissar during the Chinese Civil War. He was killed in the Battle of Chosin in the air raid on December 9, 1950.

He Jinnian: Joined the CCP in 1928 and the Red Army in 1932, He served as a company, battalion, regiment, and division commander and political commissar in the Red Army. During the Anti-Japanese War, He became a brigade and division commander in the Eighth Route Army. During the Chinese Civil War, He was appointed as the commander of the PLA Forty-Eighth Army, assistant commander of the Fifteenth Army Group, and assistant commander of the Northeast Regional Command. In the Korean War, he became the commander of the Railway Transportation and Engineering Headquarters of the CPVF in 1951. After his return to China from Korea, He became the assistant commander of the PLA Armored Corps and major general in 1955.

Hong Xuezhi: Assistant commander of the CPVF in 1950–53. Hong joined the CCP armed forces when he was sixteen. Then, he became an experienced commander of the Heilongjiang Provincial Command, the Sixth Army of the Northeastern Field Army, and Forty-Third Army of the Fourth Field Army in the Chinese Civil War. In 1949–50, he served as the chief of staff of the 15th Army Group and assistant commander of the 13th Army Group. In charge of CPVF operation, logistics, and security, Hong had successfully protected the CPVF HQ and had personally saved Peng's life twice during UNF air raids when Peng refused to leave his office for a shelter in the cave. Hong became Chief of the PLA Department of General Logistics (DGL) after his return from Korea. He was the only Chinese commander who was promoted to general twice, in 1955 and in 1988.

Hu Qianxiu: Chief of staff of the 58th Division of the Twentieth Army in the Battle of Chosin. Hu joined the Red Army in 1929 and the CCP in 1931. He became a squad and platoon leader in the Red Army, and was promoted to a company, battalion, and regiment commander in 1937–45. He served as deputy chief of staff of the PLA 59th Division and chief of staff of the 58th in the Chinese Civil War. Hu was killed in the Battle of Chosin in the air raid on December 9, 1950.

Huang Chaotian: Commander of the 58th Division of the Twentieth Army in the Battle of Chosin. Huang joined the Red Army in 1929 and the CCP in 1933. After the Long March, he served as a platoon, company, and battalion commander of the Red Army. During the Anti-Japanese War, Huang became a regiment commander and brigade chief staff. Then he was appointed as assistant commander of the 32nd Division, and assistant Command and commander of the 58th Division in the Chinese Civil War. After his return to China, Huang became the Chief Staff and assistant commander of the Twentieth Army. He was made a major general in 1955 and commander of the Jiangsu Provincial Command in the 1960s.

Lin Biao: One of the most brilliant military leaders of the CCP and the defense minister of the PRC in 1959–71. He participated in the Nanchang Uprising in August 1927, and became a battalion, regiment, and division commander in the Red Army in 1927–31. He rose quickly through the ranks because of his success in combat and loyalty to Mao. Lin was commander of the Red Fourth Army and then the President of the Red Army University. During WWII, Lin commanded the Eighth Route Army's 115th Division. At the beginning of the Chinese Civil War, Lin was appointed commander and political commissar of all the CCP forces in the northeast. In 1948, the CCP reorganized its troops into the PLA and established four field armies. Lin became the commander of the Fourth Field Army, totaling 800,000 troops. His successful campaigns against the GMD forces brought about an early victory for the CCP in the war and made him one of the top national leaders. He became one of the ten marshals in 1955, and China's defense minister. During the Cultural Revolution, Lin became the second most powerful leader in the country, next to Mao, who made Lin his successor in 1969. Two years later, however, Lin was accused of leading a military clique against Mao, and Lin and his family members were killed in a plane crash in Mongolia on September 13, 1971.

Liu Haotian: Political commissar of the Twenty-Seventh Army of the CPVF 9th Army Group in the Battle of Chosin. Liu joined the CCP in 1931 and Red

Army in 1932. He participated in the Long March and served as commander of a squad, platoon, company, and political commissar of battalion in the Red Army. During the Anti-Japanese War, Liu became deputy director of the political section of the 2nd Brigade, 115th Division, Eighth Route Army. During the Chinese Civil War, Liu was appointed as a brigade and division political commissar, and later political commissar of the Twenty-Seventh Army of the PLA. After his return to China, Liu was granted lieutenant general in 1955 and became commander of the East China Sea Fleet of the PLA Navy in the 1960s.

Long March (1934–35): A CCP effort to save the Red Army by moving its main strength away from the GMD-controlled central region and to develop a new strategic initiative in a remote northwest region. In October 1934, its First Front Army left Jiangxi and led the way to northwest. Other armies followed and traveled through eleven provinces for 8,000 miles, crossing perpetually snowcapped mountains and trackless grasslands while engaging many battles against the GMD troops. When the Red Army arrived in northern Shaanxi in October 1935, it shrank from 80,000 to 30,000 men. Thereafter, Mao made Yan'an the new capital of the CCP in 1935.

Mao Anying: Mao Zedong's older son (Mao had two sons), Peng Dehuai's Russian interpreter and secretary at the CPVF General HQ. He was killed in a U.S. air raid on November 25, 1950.

Mulhausen, Harold L.: U.S. Marine corporal assigned to a 3.5-inch rocket section in A Company, 1st Battalion, 7th Regiment, 1st Marine Division, in Korea in November 1950, just in time to participate in the Battle of Chosin. His unit held its defensive positions at Yudam-ni and Hagaru-ri. Then, Mulhausen survived the retreat from the Chosin Reservoir to Hamhung and become a member of "The Chosin Few."

Nie Rongzhen: One of Mao's closest working colleagues and trusted generals. He joined the CCP in 1922 and went to the Soviet Union for further education in the military and defense industry in 1924–25. On August 1, 1927, he was the CCP representative to the Eleventh Army. Nie became a deputy director of the Political Department in the Red Army HQ in the late 1920s and political commissar of the Red Army's 1st Army Group in the Long March. He was the political commissar of the 115th Division of the Eighth Route Army and commander of the North China Military Region in 1937–45. Then, Nie served as the second secretary of the CCP's Northern China Bureau and commanded the PLA's Northern Military Region. In 1948–49, he worked closely with Mao on a daily basis after the Communist leadership moved from Yan'an, the remote Communist capital in the northwest. Nie successfully protected the CCP HQ and PLA high command by defeating the GMD attacks and personally saved Mao's life once in an air raid when Mao refused to leave his bedroom for a shelter. He became acting Chief of the PLA General Staff in 1950 and one of the ten marshals in 1955.

Peng Dehuai: Commander in chief of the CPVF in Korea in 1950–53. As one of the PLA's most dedicated and experienced generals, he had worked closely with Mao since the Long March. Peng enlisted at seventeen in the Hunan Army (*xiangjun*) of the warlords, and attended Hunan Military Academy. He served as a GMD officer and became a brigade commander before defecting. In 1928, Peng joined the CCP, and then commanded the Fifth Army of the Chinese Red Army. His revolutionary fervor and military aggressiveness gained Mao's attention and favor by 1930. Peng served as assistant commander of the Eighth Route Army, acting Secretary General of the CCP North Bureau, and Vice Chairman and Chief of General Staff of the Central Revolutionary Military Committee in 1937–45. Then, he commanded the Eighteenth Army Group, the Northwestern Field Army, and the First Field Army in 1945–49. Peng became deputy commander of the PLA in 1949. After the Korean War, Peng was the first Defense Minister of the PRC and became one of the ten marshals of the PLA in 1955. Before long, however, Mao dismissed Peng from all posts in 1959, accusing him of leading an "anti-Party clique" or a "military club" against Mao's policy. In the Cultural Revolution, Peng was arrested and imprisoned in 1967.

Peng Deqing: Commander of the Twenty-Seventh Army of the CPVF 9th Army Group in the Battle of Chosin. Peng joined the Red Army in 1926 and the CCP in 1930. He served as a guerrilla company commander and later a battalion political commissar in the Red Army. Peng became a company political instructor, battalion political commissar, and chief of the political section of regiment and brigade in the New Fourth Army in 1937–45. During the Chinese Civil War, he was appointed as a brigade and division political commissar, chief of staff, and commander. Later he became assistant commander of the Twenty-Second and Twenty-third Armies, and commander of the PLA Twenty-Seventh Army. After his return to China, Peng became the assistant commander of the East China Sea Fleet of the PLA Navy. He was granted major general in 1955. He served as Vice Minister and Minister of the Transportation Ministry of the PRC in the 1960s and 1970s.

Peng Fei: Assistant commander and chief of staff of the Twentieth Army of the CPVF 9th Army Group in the Battle of Chosin. Peng joined the Red Army in 1934 and the CCP in 1936. After the Long March, he became a platoon and company commander in the Red Army, rising to a battalion and regiment chief of staff in the Anti-Japanese War and assistant commander of the 59th Division and commander of the 60th Division during the Chinese Civil War. After returned to China, Peng was appointed as assistant commander and Chief Staff of the Thirty-first Army. Peng was made a senior colonel in 1955 and a major general in 1964. In the 1960s, he became deputy Chief Staff of the Fuzhou Regional Command.

Peng Hui: Assistant commander of the 80th Division of the Twenty-Seventh Army in the Battle of Chosin. He joined the CCP and the Eighth Route Army in 1937, and became a squad, platoon, company, and battalion commander in the Anti-Japanese War. Peng was promoted to a regimental deputy commander, chief of staff, commander and a division chief of staff and deputy commander in the Chinese Civil War. After the Korean War, he was promoted to the chief of staff and then assistant commander of the Twenty-Seventh Army. Xiao was made a senior colonel in 1955.

Political instructor: A CCP representative serves in each PLA company and shares the leadership with the captain. The company political instructor leads the party branch as its secretary, guides the political training and education, recruits party members, and guarantees the company following the party line and operational orders.

Political commissar: A CCP representative serves at each PLA battalion, regiment, division, and army and shares the leadership with the commander of the unit. Followed the model of the Soviet Red Army, the CCP established the principle of the party's absolute leadership over the army in the 1930s by having party representation in the Red Army all the way down to the company level. The party representatives were renamed political commissars in 1931. The CCP leaders always emphasize the party must control the gun, and the gun must never control the party.

Rao Huitan: Commander of the 80th Division of the Twenty-Seventh Army in the Battle of Chosin. Rao joined the Red Army in 1930 and the CCP in 1933. He became a squad, platoon, and company commander in the Red Army, and served as battalion and regimental chief of staff and commander in the New Fourth Army in 1938–45. He was assistant commander and commander of the 80th Division in 1946–49. After the Battle of Chosin, Rao Huitan was promoted to the Chief Staff and assistant commander of the Twenty-third Army. On February 21, 1953, he was killed in the front in Central Korea.

Red Guard: Mostly college and high school students who were mobilized and empowered by Mao Zedong in the early years (1966–68) of the Cultural Revolution to criticize his political rivalries such as Liu Shaoqi and Deng Xiaoping. An estimated 30 million young people joined the Red Guards, and they became the driving force for the Cultural Revolution.

ROC: The Republic of China founded by Sun Yat-sen in January 1, 1912, established its national government in Nanjing under the leadership of Jiang Jieshi in 1927. After Jiang lost the Chinese Civil War to the Communist Army, he removed the seat of the ROC government from the mainland China to Taiwan in 1949.

Song Shilun: Commander and political commissar of the CPVF 9th Army Group in the Korean War. Song joined the CCP in 1927 and the Red Army in 1929. He served as commander and political commissar of CCP guerrilla teams in Hunan, and division and army chief of staff in the Red Army. In 1937–45, Song became regiment and division commander in the Eighth Route Army, and was promoted to commander and political commissar of the 9th Army Group in 1948. In April 1949, the 9th with other groups launched the attack and crossed the Yangzi River by sending the GMD defenders into a headlong retreat. Then, Song successfully took over Shanghai, the largest city in China, by May. After his return from Korea, Song was made general in 1955, and became president of the PLA Academy of Military Sciences (AMS) in 1957–82.

Su Yu: One of the most experienced generals in the PLA. Su participated in the CCP's Nanchang Uprising and joined the Red Army in 1927. During the Anti-Japanese War, he led his division to establish the CCP military base in southern provinces. In the Chinese Civil War, Su became assistant commander of the East China Command in 1947 and then the Third Field Army in 1948–49. After the founding of the PRC in 1949, he served in numerous positions including the commander of the NEBDA in July 1950 and Chief of the PLA General Staff. Su made one of the ten grand generals in 1955.

Sun Ruifu: Commander and political commissar of the 81st Division of the Twenty-Seventh Army in Korea. Sun joined the CCP in 1937 and the Eighth Route Army in 1938. He became a company, battalion, and regiment commander in 1940–45. Sun eventually served as a brigade and divisional commander in the Chinese Civil War. After the Battle of Chosin, he was promoted to assistant commander of the Twenty-Seventh Army. After his return to China, Sun was appointed as commander of the Twenty-Seventh Army. In the 1960s, he became assistant commander of the Anti-aircraft Artillery Force of the PLA Air Force, and assistant commander of Beijing Regional Command Air Force. Sun became a major general of the PLAAF in 1963.

Tao Yong: Assistant commander of the CPVF 9th Army Group in the Korean War. Tao joined the Red Army in 1929 and the CCP in 1931. He served as a commander of squad, platoon, company, battalion, regiment, and division in the Red Army. During the Anti-Japanese War, he became a regiment commander and divisional commander and political commissar of the New Fourth Army. In the Chinese Civil War, he was appointed as a divisional commander and political commissar, commander of the Twenty-Third Army and later assistant commander of the 9th Army Group. After his return to China, Tao became commander of the East Sea Fleet of the PLA Navy, assistant commander of the PLA Navy, and assistant commander of the Nanjing Regional Command. He was ranked lieutenant general of the PLAN in 1955. Tao was accused and committed suicide during the Cultural Revolution.

United Front: A political and military coalition established between the Chinese Communist Party (CCP) and the Nationalist Party (Guomindang, GMD) to oppose Japanese aggression against China in 1937–45. The United Front received Allied support but collapsed in 1946.

Wu Dalin: Commander of the 88th Division of the Twenty-Sixth Army in the Battle of Chosin. Wu joined the Red Army in 1932 and the CCP in 1933. He became a squad, platoon, and company commander in the Red Army. During the Anti-Japanese War, Wu served as company, battalion, and regiment commander in the Eighth Route Army. During the Chinese Civil War, he became an assistant brigade commander, brigade commander, assistant division commander, and the commander of the 88th Division. After his return to China, Wu became commander of the PLA Jinzhou Metropolitan Command, and was made a senior colonel in 1955.

Wu Donglai: Chinese army private who served in the 3rd Company, 172nd Regiment, 58th Division, Twentieth Army, 9th Army Group of the CPVF, in Korea from 1950 to 1953. His unit attacked the Marines at Hagaru-ri in late November and then participated in the pursuit of the Marines all the way to Hamhung in early December.

Wu Xinquan: Commander of the CPVF Thirty-Ninth Army in the Korean War. After joined the Red Army and the CCP in 1930, he was promoted from a squad and company commander to a battalion and regiment political commissar in the Red Army. Wu participated in the Long March. During the Anti-Japanese War, he became political commissar of the 687th and 688th

Regiments of the 115th Division, Eighth Route Army. In the Chinese Civil War, he served as commander and political commissar of the 6th Division of the Northeastern Command, assistant commander and commander of the Thirty-Ninth Army. After his return to China, Wu became chief of staff of the Shenyang Regional Commands and assistant commander of the PLA Artillery Force. He was ranked lieutenant general in 1955.

Xiao Jinghai: Commander and political commissar of the 79th Division of the Twenty-Seventh Army in the Battle of Chosin. Xiao joined the CCP and its Eighth Route Army in 1938. During the Anti-Japanese War, Xiao served as a company, battalion, and regiment deputy commander and commander. In the Chinese Civil War, he became a brigade and division chief of staff, deputy commander, and then commander and political commissar of the 79th Division. After his return to China, Xiao was sent to study at the Russian Academy of Military Sciences in the Soviet Union in 1954–57. After his graduation, he was appointed as the Department Chair of Foreign Military Studies, PLA Academy of Military Sciences (AMS). Xiao was made a senior colonel in 1955 and a major general in 1961. In the 1960s, he became assistant commander of the PLA Lanzhou Military Region.

Xu Fang: Deputy political commissar of the 59th Division of the Twentieth Army in the Battle of Chosin. Xu joined the Eighth Route Army and the CCP in the Anti-Japanese War, and became a battalion and regiment political commissar, and Director of the Political Department of the 60th Division in the Chinese Civil War. After returned to China, Xu Fang was appointed as political commissar of the 59th Division. In the 1960s, he became the Director of the Political Department of the Logistics Division of Nanjing Regional Command. Xu was made a colonel in 1955 and a senior colonel in 1960.

Yan Chuanye: Commander of the 238th Regiment of the 80th Division, Twenty-Seventh Army, in the Battle of Chosin. Yan joined the Communist forces in 1939 and the CCP in 1940. He became an assistant captain, company political instructor, and assistant battalion commander in 1940–45, and a battalion political commissar, regiment chief of staff, and commander of the 235th and then 238th Regiment in 1946–49. After the Battle of Chosin, Yan Chuanye was promoted to the deputy chief of staff of the 80th Division. After his return to China, Yan became assistant commander and Chief Staff of the 79th Division in 1954 and the 81st Division in 1958. After he became a colonel in 1955, Yan was promoted to commander of the 81st Division in 1963 and the 80th Division in 1964. He became chief of staff of the Twenty-Seventh Army in 1967 and assistant Army commander in 1969. Yan served as commander of the Twenty-Seventh Army from 1970 to 1983.

Yang Yizhi: A first lieutenant and a platoon leader of 3rd Company, 1st Battalion, 237th Regiment, 79th Division, Twenty-Seventh Army of the 9th Army Group. He and his platoon entered Korea in mid-November 1950 and participated in the Battle of Chosin. He was captured by the UNF during the CPVF Fifth Campaign in May 1951. After the Korean Armistice was signed in July 1953, he decided to go to Taiwan rather than return to China.

Zhan Da'nan: Assistant commander of the Twenty-Seventh Army of the CPVF 9th Army Group in the Battle of Chosin. Zhan joined the Red Army in 1931 and the CCP in 1936. He became a company, battalion, and regiment commander and political commissar in the Eighth Route Army in 1937–49, and rising to commander of the 80th Division in the Chinese Civil War. Before the Battle of Chosin, Zhan became assistant commander of the Twenty-Seventh Army. After his return to China, Zhan was appointed as commander of the Twenty-Eighth Army, Gansu Provincial Military Command, and made a major general in 1955. In the 1960s, he became the governor of Gansu, assistant commander of the PLA Lanzhou Regional Command, and assistant commander of the Nanjing Regional Command.

Zhang Renchu: Commander of the Twenty-Sixth Army of the CPVF 9th Army Group in the Korean War. Zhang joined the Red Army in 1927 and the CCP in 1928. He served as a squad, platoon, company, battalion, and regiment commander in the Red Army, and participated in the Long March. Zhang became deputy commander and commander of the 686th Regiment of the 115th Division, and commander of the Tenth Brigade of the Shandong Command in 1937–45. He was commander of the Twenty-Sixth Army in 1948–50. After his return to China, Zhang became assistant commander of the Ji'nan Regional Command and a lieutenant general in 1955.

Zhang Yingbuo: Political commissar of the 80th Division of the Twenty-Seventh Army in the Battle of Chosin. Zhang joined the CCP in 1934 and became an assistant captain and company political instructor in the Red Army. He served as battalion and regiment political commissar in the Anti-Japanese War, and political commissar of the 91st, 92nd, 81st, and 80th Divisions through the Chinese Civil War and the Korean War. After returning to China, Zhang Yingbuo was promoted deputy political commissar of the provincial military commands of Gansu and Shaanxi. He was made senior colonel in 1955.

Zhang Yixiang: Commander and political commissar of the Twentieth Army of the CPVF 9th Army Group in the Korean War. Zhang joined the Red Army in 1929 and the CCP in 1932. He served as a squad, platoon, company, battalion, and regiment commander in the Red Army, and participated in the Long March. He became assistant commander and commander of the 14th and 16th Regiments and assistant commander of the 5th Brigade of the New Fourth Army in 1937–45. In the Chinese Civil War, he became assistant commander, commander, and political commissar of the Twentieth Army. After returned to China from Korea, he became chief of staff of the Fuzhou Military Region Command and commander of the PLA 2nd Artillery (Strategic Missile) Force. He was ranked lieutenant general in 1955.

Zhang Zhixiu: Chief of staff of the Twenty-Sixth Army of the CPVF 9th Army Group in the Battle of Chosin. Zhang became a soldier of the Red Army in 1928, and joined the CCP in 1934. Then, he was a squad, platoon, company, battalion, and regiment commander in the Red Army. Zhang served as battalion and regimental commander and brigade and divisional chief of staff in the New Fourth Army against the Japanese invasion. He was promoted to commander of the 80th Division and assistant commander of the Twenty-Sixth Army in the Chinese Civil War. After his return to China, Zhang became commander of the Twenty-Sixth Army and later the Sixty-Eighth Army. He was made a major general in 1955, and served as assistant commander and commander of the Kunming Military Region and governor of Yunnan Province in the 1970s.

Zhongnanhai: Translated as "middle and southern seas." A palace of the emperors and empresses within the Forbidden City in the center of Beijing, it became the home of Mao, Zhu, Zhou, and several other top CCP leaders after 1949. Most of the important CCP, PRC, and PLA meetings, such as the Politburo, were and still are held there.

Zhou Wenjiang: Assistant commander of 2nd Battalion, 177th Regiment, 59th Division, Twentieth Army, in the Battle of Chosin. Zhou joined the Chinese Communist armed forces in 1944 and the CCP in 1945. During the Civil War, he became a squad, platoon, and company commander. After his return to China, Zhou became a battalion, regiment, and division assistant commander and commander. He was promoted a major in 1955, and appointed as assistant commander of the Henan Provincial Command in the 1960s.

Zhu Qixiang: Deputy political commissar of the 58th Division of the Twentieth Army in the Battle of Chosin. Zhu joined the New Fourth Army and the

CCP in 1939. During the Anti-Japanese War, he became a company political instructor, battalion and regiment political commissar. During the Chinese Civil War, he was appointed as director of the Political Department of the 58th Division and the division's deputy political commissar. After the Battle of Chosin, Zhu was promoted to political commissar of the 58th Division. After he returned to China, he was appointed as the commander of the 58th Division, chief of staff of the Twentieth Army, assistant commander of the Twenty-Seventh Army, and commander and political commissar of the Sixtieth Army. In the 1960s, he became commander and political commissar of the Artillery Force of Wuhan Regional Command. Zhu was made a senior colonel in 1955 and a major general in 1964.

Selected Bibliography

Chinese-Language Sources

Archives, Manuscripts, and Collected Military Papers

Archives of the PRC Ministry of Foreign Affairs. *Foreign Relations of the People's Republic of China.* 1949–58. Archives Section of the General Office, Beijing.

Archives of the ROC Ministry of Defense. *Programs and Budget for the Communist POWs from the Korean War.* File Nos. 00012390–00056703. The Center for Military Archives, Defense Ministry, Taipei.

Archives of the ROC Ministry of Foreign Affairs. *Anti-Communist Chinese POWs from the Korean War: Plans, Arrangements, and Reports.* Files of the North American Bureau, nos. 411, 417, and 422. Files of the Asia-Pacific Bureau, nos. 005, 013, and 021. Archival Center of the Foreign Affairs Ministry, Taipei.

———. *Negotiations and Settlements for the Anti-Communist Chinese POWs from the Korean War.* File nos. 172-3 and 172-4. National Archives, Taipei.

CCP Central Archives, comp. *Zhonggong zhongyang wenjian xuanji, 1921–1949* [Selected Documents of the CCP Central Committee, 1921–1949]. 18 vols. Beijing: Zhonggong zhongyang dangxiao chubanshe [CCP Central Party Academy Press], 1989–92.

CCP Central Archives, Central Archival and Manuscript Research Division, and CCP Organization Department, comps. *Zhongguo gongchandang zuzhishi ziliao, 1921–1997* [Documents of the CCP Organization's History, 1921–1997]. 14 vols. Beijing: Zhonggong dangshi chubanshe [CCP Central Committee's Party History Press], 2000.

Chen Yi. *Chen Yi junshi wenxuan* [Selected Military Papers of Chen Yi]. Beijing: Jiefangjun chubanshe [PLA Press], 1996.

CPVF Twentieth Army Command. *Documents of the War to Resist the U.S. and Aid Korea (WRUSAK), 1950–1953.* In PLA Twentieth Army Archives. PLA Twentieth Army Headquarters, Kaifeng, Henan.

———. *Zhongguo renmin zhiyuanjun di 20 jun kangmei yuanchao zhanzheng shi* [Combat History of the CPVF Twentieth Army in the WRUSAK]. PLA Twentieth Army Archives. Kaifeng, Henan.

CPVF Twenty-Seventh Army Command. *Collection of the Orders, Instructions, and Documents for All Operations and Battles in Korea, 1950–1952.* PLA Twenty-Seventh Army Archives, Shijiazhuang, Hebei.

———. "The Instruction on Tactic Issues on Fighting the U.S. and ROK Armies, November 13, 1950." In *The Collection of the Army Instructions, Orders, and Documents in Korea (1950–1954),* PLA Twenty-Seventh Army Archives, Shijiazhuang, Hebei: Twenty-Seventh Army Headquarters, 110-8.

———. *Zhongguo renmin zhiyuanjun di 27 jun kangmei yuanchao zhanzheng shi* [Combat History of the CPVF Twenty-Seventh Army in the WRUSAK] (April 1954). PLA Twenty-Seventh Army Archives. Shijiazhuang, Hebei.

Defense Ministry, Republic of China. *Guojun houqin shi* [Logistics History of the GMD Armed Forces]. 8 vols. Taipei: Guofangbu shizheng bianyiju [Bureau of History and Political Records of the Defense Ministry], 1992.

Gu Cheng, et al., trans. and eds. *Kangmei yuanchao zhanzheng: Dijun shiliao* [WRUSAK: ROK Army Archives]. 5 vols. Harbin, Heilongjiang: Heilongjiang chaoxian minzu chubanshe [Heilongjiang Korean Ethnic Minority Publishing], 1988–90.

He Long. *He Long junshi wenxuan* [Selected Military Papers of He Long]. Beijing: Jiefangjun chubanshe, 1989.

Huang Xiuhuan, ed. *Zhanhou waijiao shiliao huibian: Hanzhan yu fan'gong yishi pian* [Collected Archives of the Postwar Diplomacy: The Korean War and the Anti-Communist POWs]. 3 vols. Taipei: Guoshiguan [National Archives Printing], 2005–7.

Liu Bocheng. *Liu Bocheng junshi wenxuan* [Selected Military Papers of Liu Bocheng]. Beijing: Jiefangjun chubanshe, 1992.

Liu Shaoqi. *Jianguo yilai Liu Shaoqi wengao, 1949–1955* [Liu Shaoqi's Manuscripts since the Founding of the State, 1949–1955]. 7 vols. Beijing: Zhongyang wenxian chubanshe [CCP Central Archival and Manuscript Press], 2008.

Lushun Naval Command, PLA Navy. "Document Collection on Lin Biao and Li Zuopeng's Criminal Activities of Attacking the Party and Betraying the PLA, October 1971." In *Political Files against the Lin-Li Group (1971–1972),* Lushun Naval Base Archives, Lushun, Liaoning.

Mao Zedong. *Jianguo yilai Mao Zedong junshi wengao* [Mao Zedong's Military Manuscripts since the Founding of the PRC]. 3 vols. Beijing: Junshi kexue chubanshe [Military Science Press] and Zhongyang wenxian chubanshe, 2010.

———. *Jianguo yilai Mao Zedong wengao, 1949–1976* [Mao Zedong's Manuscripts since the Founding of the State, 1949–1976]. 13 vols. Beijing: Zhongyang wenxian chubanshe, 1989–93.

———. *Mao Zedong junshi wenji* [Collected Military Works of Mao Zedong]. 6 vols. Beijing: Junshi kexue chubanshe, 1993.

———. *Mao Zedong junshi wenxun: Neibuben* [Selected Military Papers of Mao Zedong: Internal Edition]. 2 vols. Beijing: Jiefangjun zhanshi chubanshe [PLA Soldiers Press], 1981.

———. *Mao Zedong wenxun* [Collected Works of Mao Zedong]. 8 vols. Beijing: Renmin chubanshe [People's Press], 1999.

———. *Mao Zedong xuanji* [Selected Works of Mao Zedong]. 5 vols. Beijing: Renmin chubanshe, 1977.

National Committee of Chinese People to Support World Peace against American Invasion. *Chaoxian tingzhan tanpan wenti* [The Issues of the Korean Truce Negotiations]. 2 vols. Beijing: Shijie zhishi chubanshe [World Knowledge Publishing], 1951–52.

———, ed. *Zhandou zai Changjin hupan* [War-fighting around the Chosin Lake]. Beijing: Renmin chubanshe, 1951.

Nie Rongzhen. *Nie Rongzhen junshi wenxuan* [Selected Military Papers of Nie Rongzhen]. Beijing: Jiefangjun chubanshe, 1992.

Peng Dehuai. *Peng Dehuai junshi wenxuan* [Selected Military Papers of Peng Dehuai]. Beijing: Zhongyang wenxian chubanshe, 1988.

Shen Zhihua, trans. and ed. *Chaoxian zhanzheng: Eguo dang'anguan de jiemi wenjian* [The Korean War: Declassified Documents from Russian Archives]. 3 vols. Taipei: Institute of Modern History, Academia Sinica, 2015.

Xinhuashe [New China News Agency]. *Xinhuashe wenjian ziliao huibian* [A Collection of Documentary Materials of the New China News Agency]. Beijing: Xinhua chubanshe [New China Publishing House], n.d.

Xu Xiangqian. *Xu Xiangqian junshi wenxuan* [Selected Military Papers of Xu Xiangqian]. Beijing: Jiefangjun chubanshe, 1992.

Yang Yiming. *Beihan zhanchang guilai* [I Returned from the North Korean Battlefield]. Hong Kong: Ziyou chubanshe [The Freedom Press], 1953.

Zhiyuanjun yiri Compilation Committee. *Zhiyuanjun yiri* [Daily Life of the CPVF Soldiers]. 3 vols. Beijing: Renmin wenxue chubanshe [People's Literature Press], 1956–57.

Zhonggong zhongyang Nanjing jiu: Zhonggong lishi ziliao [The Nanjing Bureau of the CCP Central Committee: CCP Historical Documents]. Beijing: Zhonggong zhongyang dangshi chubanshe, 1990.

Zhou Enlai. *Zhou Enlai junshi wenxun* [Selected Military Works of Zhou Enlai]. 4 vols. Beijing: Renmin chubanshe, 1997.

Zhu De. *Zhu De junshi wenxuan* [Selected Military Papers of Zhu De]. Beijing: Jiefangjun chubanshe, 1986.

Zhu Yulin. *Zhu Yulin riji, 1950–1953* [Diary of Zhu Yulin, 1950–1953]. Diary entries from Chen Shuang, "A Touchable War Memory: A Newly Discovered Combat Diary of a CPVF Officer." *Shu Cheng* [Book City] (November 2010): 5–18.

Books, Articles, and Other Published Works

Ba Tanshan. "Nisuo buzhidao de chaoxian zhanzheng: Bingxue Changjin hu" [The Korean War You Don't Know: Snow and Blood in the Chosin Lake]. Accessed April 24, 2017, http://www.360doc.com/content/11/0525/00/2984805-119180423.shtml.

Bo Yibo. *Ruogan zhongda juece yu shijian de huigu* [Recollections of Certain Important Decisions and Events]. 2 vols. Beijing: Zhonggong zhongyang dangxiao chubanshe, 1991.

CCP Central Archival and Manuscript Research Division. *Dang de wenxian* [Party Archives and Documents] (2000–1).

———. *Mao Zedong nianpu, 1893–1949* [A Chronological Record of Mao Zedong, 1893–1949]. 3 vols. Beijing: Zhongyang wenxian chubanshe, 1993.

———. *Mao Zedong zhuan, 1893–1976* [Biography of Mao Zedong, 1893–1976]. 2 vols. Beijing: Zhongyang wenxian chubanshe [CCP Archival and Manuscript Press], 1996.

———. *Zhou Enlai nianpu, 1949–1976* [A Chronological Record of Zhou Enlai, 1949–1976]. 3 vols. Beijing: Zhongyang wenxian chubanshe, 1997.

———. *Zhu De nianpu, 1886–1976* [A Chronological Record of Zhu De, 1886–1976]. Beijing: Renmin chubanshe, 1986.

CCP Party History Research Division. *Zhongguo gongchandang lishi dashiji, 1919–1987* [Major Historical Events of the CCP, 1919–1987]. Beijing: Renmin chubanshe, 1990.

Chai Chengwen. *Banmendian tanpan jishi* [The True Stories of the Panmunjom Negotiations]. Beijing: Shishi chubanshe [Current Affairs Press], 2000.

Chen Fu and Zhu Jinhui. "Army Commander Liao Zhengguo Recalls the Battle of the Chosin Lake." *Zhiwang kangjian* [Digital Library], 226–35, accessed September 17, 2017, http://www.cnki.com.cn.

Chen Geng Zhuan Compilation Team. *Chen Geng Zhuan* [Biography of Chen Geng]. Beijing: Dangdai zhongguo chubanshe [Contemporary China Press], 2007.

Chen Guanren. *Bingtuan silingyuan* [PLA Commanders of the Army Groups]. Beijing: Zhonggong dangshi chubanshe, 2015.

Chen Pai. *Yuezhan qinliji* [My Personal Experience in the Vietnam War]. Zhengzhou: Henan renmin chubanshe [Henan People's Press], 1997.

Chen Shuang. "A Touchable War Memory: A Newly Discovered Combat Diary of a CPVF Officer." *Shu Cheng* [Book City] (November 2010): 5–19.

Chen Wenhan. "Brave Battle Fighting of Heroic Tang Yun." In *Zhongguo renmin zhiyuanjun 20 jun kangmei yuanchao yingmo ji'nianji* [Memorial Collection of the Heroes of the CPVF 20th Army in the WRUSAK]. Shanghai: The PLA Twentieth Army Headquarters, 1953.

———. "The Heroic Story of Comrade Tang Yun." In *Zhongguo renmin zhiyuanjun 20 jun kangmei yuanchao yingmo ji'nianji* [Memorial Collection of the Heroes of the CPVF 20th Army in the WRUSAK]. PLA Twentieth Army Archives (1953), Kaifeng, Henan, 62–71.

Chen Wenhan and Zhao Yongtian. *Banmendian tanpan* [The Panmunjom Negotiations]. 2nd ed. Beijing: Jiefangjun chubanshe, 1992.

Chen Zhonglong, ed. *Kangmei yuanchao zhanzheng lun* [On the WRUSAK]. Beijing: Junshi wenyi chubanshe [Military Literature Press], 2001.

China National Military Museum, ed. *Kangmei yuanchao zhanzheng fengyunlu* [The Operational Files of the WRUSAK]. Beijing: Huacheng chubanshe [Huacheng Publishing], 1999.

———, ed. *Kangmei yuanchao zhanzheng jishi* [A Chronological Record of the WRUSAK]. Beijing: Jiefangjun chubanshe, 2008.

Chinese Military Advisory Group (CMAG) Compilation Team, comp. *Zhongguo junshi guwentuan yuanyue kangfa shilu: Dangshiren de huiyi* [The Records of the Chinese Military Advisory Group in the War to Aid Vietnam and Resist France: Personal Accounts of the Veterans]. Beijing: Zhonggong dangshi chubanshe [CCP Party History Press], 2002.

Chu Yun. *Chaoxian zhanzheng neimu quangongkai* [Declassifying the Korean War]. Beijing: Shishi chubanshe [Current Affairs Publishing], 2005.

Composition Committee. *38 xian shang de jiaofeng: Kangmei yuanchao zhanzheng jishi* [The War-fighting over the 38th Parallel: The True Records of the WRUSAK]. Beijing: Jiefangjun wenyi chubanshe, 2010.

Cui Xianghua and Chen Dapeng. *Tao Yong jiangjun zhuan* [Biography of General Tao Yong]. Beijing: Jiefangjun chubanshe, 1989.

Deng Feng. "Kangmei yuanchao yanjiu zongshu, 1996–2006" [Korean War History Research in China, 1996–2006]. Paper presented at the International Cold War Conference, Changchun, Jilin, July 14–17, 2006.

———. *Lengzhan chuqi dongya guoji guanxi yanjiu* [International Relations in East Asia during the Early Cold War Era]. Beijing: Jiuzhou chubanshe [Jiuzhou Press], 2015.

Du Ping. *Zai zhiyuanjun zongbu: Du Ping huiyilu* [At the CPVF General HQ: Memoirs of Du Ping]. Beijing: Jiefangjun chubanshe, 1989.

Feng Xianzhi and Li Jie. *Mao Zedong yu kangmei yuanchao* [Mao Zedong and the Resistance against the U.S. and Assistance to Korea]. Beijing: Zhongyang wenxian chubanshe, 2000.

Gao Wenqian. *Wannian Zhou Enlai* [Zhou Enlai's Later Years]. Hong Kong: Mingjing chubanshe [Bright Mirror Publishing], 2003.

Ge Chumin, ed. *Laozhanshi yishi* [Personal Stories of the Veterans]. Beijing: Zhongguo duiwai fanyi chuban gongsi [China Outreach and Translation Publishing Company], 2000.

Guo Baoheng and Hu Zhiyuan. *Chipin hanjiang nanbei: 42 jun zai chaoxian* [Fighting over the Han River: The Forty-Second Army in Korea]. Shenyang: Liaoning renmin chubanshe, 1996.

Guo Jinliang. *Qinli Yuezhan* [Vietnam War in My Eyes]. Beijing: Jiefangjun wenyi chubanshe [PLA Literature Publishing], 2005.

Guo Zhigang. "Foreign Military Assistance after the Founding of the New Republic." In Military History Research Division, PLA-AMS, *Junqi piaopiao*, 1:145–61.

Han Huaizhi, et al. *Dandai Zhongguo jundui de junshi gongzuo* [Contemporary Chinese Military Affairs]. 2 vols. Beijing: Zhongguo shehui kexue chubanshe [China Social Sciences Press], 1989.

He Chuwu, Feng Ming, and Lu Hongyu. *Xuezhan Changjin hu* [The Bloody Battle at the Chosin Lake]. Chongqing, Sichuan: Chongqing chubanshe [Chongqing Publishing House], 2014.

He Zongguang. *Wo zai chaoxian zhanchang, 1950–1953* [I Was There: The Korean Battleground, 1950–1953]. Beijing: Changzheng chubanshe [Long March Publishing House], 2011.

Hong Xuezhi. *Hong Xuezhi Huiyilu* [Memoirs of Hong Xuezhi]. Beijing: Jiefangjun chubanshe, 2007.

———. *Kangmei yuanchao zhanzheng huiyi* [Recollections of the WRUSAK]. Beijing: Jiefangjun wenyi chubanshe [PLA Literature Press], 1990.

Hu Haibo. *Liangjian Changjin hu: Dierci zhanyi zhanshi baogao* [Waving the Sword at the Chosin Lake: The Combat Report on the Second Campaign]. Beijing: Junshi kexue chubanshe, 2007.

Hu Haibo and Yu Hongjun. *Genzhe Mao Zedong da tianxia* [Follow Mao Zedong to Seize the State Power]. Changsha: Hunan renmin chubanshe [Hunan People's Press], 2009.

Hu Ruiping and Li Tao. *Zhongguo renmin zhiyuanjun zhengzhan chuanqi* [Important Battles of the CPVF]. Beijing: Changzheng chubanshe [Long March Press], 2016.

Hu Zhaocai. *Chaoxian zhanzheng, 1950–1953* [The Korean War, 1950–1953]. Beijing: Taihai chubanshe [Taihai Publishing House], 2017.

Huang Yao and Yan Jingtang. *Lin Biao yisheng* [Lin Biao's Life]. Beijing: Jiefangjun wenyi chubanshe, 2004.

Jiang Tingyu. *Jiedu kangmei yuanchao zhanzheng* [Understanding the War to Resist the U.S. and Aid Korea]. Beijing: Jiefangjun chubanshe, 2011.

Jiang Yonghui. *38 jun zai chaoxian* [The Thirty-Eighth Army in Korea]. 2nd ed. Shenyang: Liaoning renmin chubanshe [Liaoning People's Press], 2009.

Li Changjiu and Shi Lujia, eds. *Zhongmei guanxi erbainian* [History of Sino-American Relations]. Beijing: Xinhua chubanshe [New China Press], 1984.

Li Feng. *Juezhan chaoxian* [The Showdown in Korea]. Beijing: Zhongguo chuban jituan [China Publishing Group], 2017.

Li Qingshan. *Zhiyuanjun yuanchao jishi* [The CPVF Records of Aiding Korea]. Beijing: Zhonggong dangshi chubanshe, 2008.

Li Ying, et al. *40 jun zai chaoxian* [The 40th Army in Korea]. Shenyang: Liaoning renmin chubanshe, 2010.

Li Zhuang. "CPVF Combat around the Chosin Lake." In National Committee of Chinese People to Support World Peace against American Invasion, *Zhandou zai Changjin hupan*, 7–13.

Lin Wei. "Hand Combat in the Snow." In National Committee of Chinese People to Support World Peace against American Invasion, *Zhandou zai Changjin hupan*, 14–20.

Liu Shufa. *Chen Yi nianpu, 1901–1972* [A Chronological Record of Chen Yi, 1901–1972]. Beijing: Renmin chubanshe, 1995.

Luan Kechao. *Xue yu huo de jiaoliang: Kangmei yuanchao jishi* [The Contest: Blood vs. Fire: The Records of Resisting America and Aiding Korea]. Beijing: Huayi chubanshe [China Literature Publishing House], 2008.

Luo Xuanyou. *Chaoxian zhanzheng: Zhengzhan jishi* [The Korean War: The Battle Records]. Beijing: Jiefangjun wenyi chubanshe, 2007.

———. *Zhongyue taihai zhanzheng zhengzhan jishi* [The History Records of the Sino-Vietnam and Taiwan Strait Wars]. Urumqi: Xinjiang renmin chubanshe [Xinjiang People's Press], 2004.

Military History Institute, PLA Academy of Military Science. *Kangmei yuanchao zhanzheng shi* [History of the WRUSAK]. 3 vols. 3rd ed. Beijing: Junshi kexue chubanshe, 2014.

Military History Research Division, PLA Academy of Military Science, ed. *Junqi piaopiao: Xinzhongguo 50 nian junshi dashi shushi* [PLA Flag Fluttering: Facts of China's Major Military Events in the Past Fifty Years]. 2 vols. Beijing: Jiefangjun chubanshe, 1999.

———, ed. *Meiguo qinyue zhanzhengshi* [War History of the U.S. Invasion of Vietnam]. Beijing: Junshi kexue chubanshe, 2004.

———, ed. *Zhongguo renmin jiefangjun de qishinian, 1927–1997* [Seventy Years of the PLA, 1927–1997]. Beijing: Junshi kexue chubanshe, 1997.

———, ed. *Zhongguo renmin zhiyuanjun kangmei yuanchao zhanshi* [Combat History of the CPVF in the WRUSAK]. Beijing: Junshi kexue chubanshe, 1990.

National Defense University's War History Series Compilation Team. *Zhongguo renmin zhiyuanjun zhanshi jianbian* [A Concise History of CPVF War-Fighting]. Beijing: Jiefangjun chubanshe, 1992.

Ni Gongluan. "The Iron Division: The 60th Division in Resisting the U.S. and Aiding Korea." In *Ji'nin Li Xiannian tongzhi danchen 100 zhunian huiyi wenxian* [Conference Proceedings for the 100th Anniversary of Comrade Li Xiannian's Birthday], 341–78. Beijing, June 2009.

Nie Rongzhen. *Nie Rongzhen huiyilu* [Memoir of Nie Rongzhen]. 2 vols. Beijing: Jiefangjun chubanshe, 1984.

Niu Jun. *Lengzhan yu xin zhongguo waijiao de yuanqi, 1949–1955* [The Cold War and Origin of Diplomacy of People's Republic of China, 1949–1955]. Rev. ed. Beijing: Shehui kexue wenxian chubanshe [Archival and Manuscript Materials of Social Sciences Publishing], 2013.

Noboru Kojima. *Chosen Senso* [The Korean War]. Tokyo: Bungeishun, 1977. Translated by Zhou Xiaoyin, et al. as *Zui hanleng de dongtian* [The Coldest Winter]. Chongqing, Sichuan: Chongqing chubanshe, 2015.

Peng Dehuai Biography Compilation Team. *Peng Dehuai zhuan* [Biography of Peng Dehuai]. Beijing: Dangdai zhongguo chubanshe [Contemporary China Press], 2006.

———. *Yige zhanzheng de ren* [A Real Man]. Beijing: Renmin chubanshe, 1994.

Peng Renlong. "A Few Stories about Resisting the U.S. and Aiding Korea." In Ge Chumin, *Laozhanshi yishi*, 443–46.

Phoenix TV. "Broad View Program." *26 jun zengyuan Changjin hu* [The Twenty-Sixth Army Reinforces the Chosin Lake], December 24, 2010. Accessed November 11, 2017, http://ucwap.ifeng.com/auto/fun/gaizhuang/news?aid=990976&rt.

Qi Dexue. *Kangmei yuanchao gaoceng juece* [The Top Decisions on Resisting the U.S. and Aiding Korea]. Shenyang: Liaoning renmin chubanshe, 2017.

———. *Ni buliaojie de chaoxian zhanzheng* [The Korean War You Don't Know]. Shenyang: Liaoning renmin chubanshe, 2011.

———. "Several Issues on the Resisting U.S. and Aiding Korea War." In *Zhonggong dangshi yanjiu* [CCP Party History Research] 1 (1998): 57–83.

Qu Zhongyi. "The Battle of Sinhung-ni: Annihilation of an Entire Regiment of the U.S. Seventh Division." In National Committee of Chinese People to Support World Peace against American Invasion, *Zhandou zai Changjin hupan*, 28–34.

Shen Xingyi. *14000 ge renzheng: Hanzhan shiqi "fan'gong yishi" zhi yanjiu* [14,000 Witnesses: The Anti-Communist POWs in the Korean War]. Taipei: National Archives Press, 2013.

Shen Zhihua. *Lengzhan zai yazhou: Chaoxian zhanzheng yu zhongguo chubing chaoxian* [The Cold War in Asia: The Korean War and Chinese Intervention in Korea]. Beijing: Jiuzhou chubanshe, 2013.

———. *Mao Zedong, Stalin he chaoxian zhanzheng* [Mao Zedong, Stalin, and the Korean War]. Guangzhou: Guangdong renmin chubanshe [Guangdong People's Press], 2004.

Shuang Shi. *Kaiguo diyi zhan: Kangmei yuanchao zhanzheng quanjing jishi* [The First War since the Founding of the State: The Complete Story of the War to Resist the U.S. and Aid Korea]. 2 vols. Beijing: Zhonggong dangshi chubanshe, 2004.

Song Chongshi. *Hujiang Song Shilun* [A Tiger General: Song Shilun]. Beijing: Zhishi chanquan chubanshe [Intellectual Rights Publishing], 2013.

Song Liansheng. *Kangmei yuanchao zai huishou* [Revisit the Resistance of the U.S. and Assistance of Korea]. Kunming: Yunnan renmin chubanshe [Yunnan People's Press], 2002.

Song Shilun Zhuan Compilation Team, PLA Academy of Military Science. *Song Shilun Zhuan* [Biography of Song Shilun]. Beijing: Junshi kexue chubanshe, 2007.

Su Changjie, Wang Qinjun, and Jiang Xiangqin. *Jinlu: 27 jun zhandou lichen* [Mighty Military Force: The Combat History of the PLA Twenty-Seventh Army]. Beijing: Jiefangjun wenyi chubanshe, 2004.

Tan Jingjiao, et al. *Kangmei yuanchao zhanzheng* [The WRUSAK]. Beijing: Zhongguo shehui kexue chubanshe, 1990.

Tan Zheng. *Zhongguo renmin zhiyuanjun renwulu* [Veterans' Profile of the Chinese People's Volunteer Force]. Beijing: Zhonggong dangshi chubanshe, 1992.

Tao Wenzhao. *Zhongmei guanxishi, 1949–1972* [PRC-U.S. Relations, 1949–1972]. Shanghai: Shanghai renmin chubanshe [Shanghai People's Press], 1999.

Wang Hechuan. *Zhongguo dadi shang de jufeng: 40 jun zhengzhan jingli* [The Hurricane over China: War Experience of the Fortieth Army]. Beijing: Jiefangjun wenyi chubanshe, 2004.

Wang Jun. *Changjin Hu* [The Chosin Lake]. Changsha: Hunan wenyi chubanshe [Hunan Literature Publishing], 2011.

Wang Ping. "Opening the Path of Attacks." In National Committee of Chinese People to Support World Peace against American Invasion, *Zhandou zai Changjin hupan*, 53–57.

Wang Shuzeng. *Juezhan chaoxian: Chaoxian zhanchang shi wojun tong meijun jiaoliang de lianbingchang* [The Showdown in Korea: The Battleground for a Competition between the Chinese Army and American Army]. Beijing: Jiefangjun wenyi chubanshe, 2007.

———. *Yuandong chaoxian zhanzheng* [The Korean War in the Far East]. 2 vols. Beijing: Jiefangjun wenyi chubanshe [PLA Literature Press], 2000.

———. *Zhongguo renmin zhiyuanjun zhengzhan jishi* [The True Story of the CPVF's War Experience]. Beijing: Jiefangjun wenyi, 2001.

Wang Xiangen. *Yuanyue kangmei shilu* [True Stories of Aiding Vietnam and Resisting America]. Beijing: Guoji wenhua chubanshe [International Cultural Publishing], 1990.

Wang Yan et al. *Peng Dehuai zhuan* [Biography of Peng Dehuai]. Beijing: Dangdai zhongguo chubanshe [Contemporary China Publishing], 1993.

Wang Yang. "Bloody Attack at Sinhung-ni and Destruction of 'Polar Bear.'" In *Wenshi jinhua* [The Essence of Historical Literature] 166, no. 3 (2004): 44–51.

Wang Yongping. "Our Understanding of the Lessons and Experience of the Fifth Offensive Campaign." In Chen Zhonglong, *Kangmei yuanchao zhanzhenglun*, 257–65.

Wang Zhaojun. *Shui shale Lin Biao* [Who Killed Lin Biao]. Taipei: Shijie chubanshe [Global Publishing], 1994.

Wu Ruilin. *Kangmei yuanchao zhong de 42 jun* [The Forty-Second Army in the WRUSAK]. Beijing: Jincheng chubanshe [Golden City Publishing], 1995.

———. *Wu Ruilin huiyilu* [Memoirs of Wu Ruilin]. Beijing: Zhongguo dang'an chubanshe [China's Archival Publishing], 1995.

Wu Xinquan. *Chaoxian zhanchang 1000 tian: 39 jun zai chaoxian* [One Thousand Days on the Korean Battleground: The Thirty-Ninth Army in Korea]. Shenyang: Liaoning renmin chubanshe, 1996.

Xia Guang. "From Naval School to Naval Academy." In *Haijun: Huiyi shiliao* [The Navy: Memoirs and Historical Records]. Edited by PLA Navy History Compilation Committee. Beijing: Haichao chubanshe [Ocean Wave Publishing], 1994.

Xia Jicheng. "The True Story of the U.S. Tasking Team's Surrender." *Dajiang nanbei* [North and South of the Great River] 10 (2010): 203–8.

Xiao Jinguang. *Xiao Jinguang huiyilu* [Memoirs of Xiao Jinguang]. Beijing: Jiefangjun chubanshe, 1988.

Xinghuo liaoyuan Composition Department, comp. *Zhongguo renmin jiefangjun jiangshuai minglu* [Marshals and Generals of the PLA]. 3 vols. Beijing: Jiefangjun chubanshe, 1987–92.

Xinhua News Agency. "So Much about the Best American Division." In National Committee of Chinese People to Support World Peace against American Invasion, *Zhandou zai Changjin hupan*, 35–43.

Xu Yaguang. "The Difficult Withdrawal to the North." In Ge Chumin, *Laozhanshi yishi*, 86–90.

Xu Yan. *Diyici jiaoliang: Kangmei yuanchao zhanzheng de lishi huigu yu fansi* [The First Encounter: A Historical Retrospective of the WRUSAK]. Beijing: Zhongguo guangbo dianshi chubanshe [China's Radio and Television Press], 1990.

———. *Junshijia Mao Zedong* [Mao Zedong as a Military Leader]. Beijing: Zhongyang wenxian chubanshe, 1995.

———. *Mao Zedong yu kangmei yuanchao zhanzheng* [Mao Zedong and the War to Resist the U.S. and Aid Korea]. 2nd ed. Beijing: Jiefangjun chubanshe, 2006.

Yan Xinning. *Wei Jie zhongjiang* [Lieutenant General Wei Jie]. Beijing: Jiefangjun wenyi chubanshe, 2005.

Yang Di. *Zai zhiyuanjun silingbu de suiyueli: Xianwei renzhi de zhenshi qingkuang* [My Years at the CPVF General HQ: Untold True Stories]. Beijing: Jiefangjun chubanshe, 1998.

Yang Feng'an and Wang Tiancheng. *Beiwei 38 duxian: Peng Dehuai yu chaoxian zhanzheng* [The North Latitude 38th Parallel: Peng Dehuai and the Korean War]. Beijing: Zhongyang wenxian chubanshe, 2009.

Yang Guoyu. *Dangdai Zhongguo haijun* [Contemporary Chinese Navy]. Beijing: Zhongguo shehui kexue chubanshe, 1987.

Yang Kuisong. "From the Zhenboa Island Incident to Sino-American Rapprochement." *Dangshi yanjiu ziliao* [Party History Research Materials], no. 12 (1997): 1–15.

Yang Qinghua. "Establish and Develop the CPVF's Logistics Conception." In Chen Zhonglong, *Kangmei yuanchao zhanzhenglun*, 345–52.

Yao Youzhi and Li Qingshan. *Zhiyuanjun yongcuo qiangdi de 10 da zhanyi* [The Ten Major Battles of the CPVF against a Strong Enemy]. Shenyang: Baishan chubanshe [White Mountain Publishing], 2009.

Ye Fei. *Ye Fei huiyilu* [Memoirs of Ye Fei]. Beijing: Jiefangjun chubanshe, 1988.

Ye Yonglie. *Gaoceng jiaoliang* [Struggle at the Top]. Urumqi: Xinjiang renmin chubanshe, 2004.

Ye Yumeng. *Chubing chaoxian: Kangmei yuanchao lishi jishi* [A True History of China's Entry into the Korean War]. Beijing: Shiyue wenxue chubanshe [October Literature Press], 1989.

Yu Huachen. "Comrade Wei Guoqing in the War to Aid Vietnam and Resist France." In CMAG Compilation Team, *Zhongguo junshi guwentuan yuanyue kangfa shilu*, 32–105.

Zhang Guanghua. "The Secret Records of China's Important Decisions to Assist Vietnam and Resist France." In CMAG Compilation Team, *Zhongguo junshi guwentuan yuanyue kangfa shilu*, 17–31.

Zhang Xiaowu and Li Xianming. "On the Reasons Why the CPVF Failed to Annihilate the American Divisions in the Battle of the Changjin Lake." *Gaige yu kaifang* [The Reform and Opening] 13 (2015): 82–84.

Zhang Xingxing, ed. *Kangmei yuanchao: 60 nianhou de huimou* [Resist the U.S. and Aid Korea: Retrospective after 60 Years]. Beijing: Dangdai zhongguo chubanshe [Contemporary China Press], 2011.

Zhang Yong. "Deadly Battle at Chosin." In National Committee of Chinese People to Support World Peace against American Invasion, *Zhandou zai Changjin hupan*, 21–27.

Zhang Zhixiu. *Junluu shengya* [My Military Career in the Chinese Army]. Beijing: Jiefangjun chubanshe, 1998.

Zhao Jianli and Liang Yuhong. *Fenghuo 38 xian: diwuci zhanyi zhanshi baogao* [The Flames of Battle Raging across the 38th Parallel: Combat Report on the Fifth Campaign]. Beijing: Junshi kexue chubanshe, 2007.

Zhao Yihong. *27 jun chuanqi* [The Legacy of the Twenty-Seventh Army]. Jilin: Jilin renmin chubanshe [Jilin People's Press], 1995.

Zhongguo xueshu zazhi dianzi faxing, 1994–2016. China Academic Journal Electronic Publishing House, 1994–2016. http://www.cnki.net.

Zhou Enlai Military Record Compilation Team, comp. *Zhou Enlai junshi huodong jishi* [The Records of Zhou Enlai's Military Affairs]. Beijing: Zhongyang wenxian chubanshe, 2000.

Zhou Maofang. "Unforgettable Years of the War." In Ge Chumin, *Laozhanshi yishi*, 481–92.

Zhou Wenjiang. *Mobuqu de jiyi: Zhou Wenjiang zhandou huiyilu* [Unforgettable Stories: Combat Experience of Zhou Wenjiang]. Beijing: Zhonggong zhongyang dangshi chubanshe, 2012.

Zhou Zhong. *Kangmei yuanchao zhanzheng huoqinshi jianbianben* [A Concise History of the Logistics in the WRUSAK]. Beijing: Jindun chubanshe [Golden Shield Press], 1993.

English-Language Sources

Alexander, Bevin. *Korea: The First War We Lost*. Rev. ed. New York: Hippocrene Books, 1998.

Appleman, Roy E. *East of Chosin: Entrapment and Breakout in Korea, 1950*. College Station: Texas A&M University Press, 1990.

———. *Escaping the Trap: The US Army X Corps in Northeast Korea, 1950*. College Station: Texas A&M University Press, 1990.

———. *South to the Naktong, North to the Yalu (June–November 1950): U.S. Army in the Korean War*. Washington, D.C.: Office of the Chief of Military History and U.S. Government Printing Office, 1961.

Bernstein, Thomas P., and Hua-yu Li. *China Learns from the Soviet Union, 1949–Present*. Lanham, Md.: Lexington Books, 2010.

Black, Jeremy. *Rethinking Military History*. London: Routledge, 2004.

Blair, Clay. *The Forgotten War: America in Korea, 1950–1953*. New York: Times Books, 1987.

Catchpole, Brian. *The Korean War, 1950–1953*. New York: Carroll & Graf, 2000.

Chang, Gordon H. *Friends and Enemies: The United States, China, and the Soviet Union*. Stanford, Calif.: Stanford University Press, 1990.

Chen Jian. *China's Road to the Korean War: The Making of the Sino-American Confrontation*. New York: Columbia University Press, 1994.

———. *Mao's China and the Cold War*. Chapel Hill: University of North Carolina Press, 2001.

Chen Jian and Xiaobing Li. "China and the End of the Global Cold War." In *The Cold War: From Détente to the Soviet Collapse*, ed. Malcolm Muir Jr., 120–31. Lexington: Virginia Military Institute Press, 2006.

Christensen, Thomas J. *Useful Adversaries: Grand Strategy, Domestic Mobilization, and Sino-American Conflict, 1947–1958*. Princeton, N.J.: Princeton University Press, 1996.

Cohen, Warren I. *America's Response to China: A History of Sino-American Relations*. 5th ed. New York: Columbia University Press, 2010.

Compilation Committee of ROC History. *A Pictorial History of the Republic of China*. 2 vols. Taipei: Modern China Press, 1981.

Cornell, Brian R. "The Origins of the Human Wave Phenomenon in Chinese Military History and the Korean War (1950–1953)." Term Paper for Graduate Seminar: Non-Western Military History, *MMH Seminar 4*. Norwich, Vt.: Norwich University, 2011.

Deng Rong. *Deng Xiaoping and the Cultural Revolution*. Beijing: Foreign Languages Press, 2002.

Deng Xiaoping. *Selected Works of Deng Xiaoping*. 3 vols. Beijing: Foreign Languages Press, 1994.

Domes, Jurgen. *Peng Te-huai: The Man and the Image*. London: C. Hurst, 1985.

Drury, Bob, and Tom Clavin. *The Last Stand of Fox Company: A True Story of U.S. Marines in Combat*. New York: Grove, 2009.

Du Ping. "Political Mobilization and Control." In Li, Millet, and Yu, *Mao's Generals Remember Korea*, 61–105.

Ebon, Martin. *Lin Piao: The Life and Writings of China's New Ruler*. New York: Stein and Day Publishers, 1970.

Elleman, Bruce A. *Modern Chinese Warfare, 1795–1989*. London: Routledge, 2001.

Fairbank, John K., Rosemary Foot, and Frank A. Kierman Jr., eds. *Chinese Ways in Warfare*. Cambridge, Mass.: Harvard University Press, 1974.

Finkelstein, David M. *Washington's Taiwan Dilemma, 1949–1950: From Abandonment to Salvation*. Fairfax, Va.: George Mason University Press, 1993.

Goulden, Joseph C. *Korea: The Untold Story of the War*. New York: Times Books, 1982.

Graff, David A., and Robin Higham, eds. *A Military History of China*. Extended ed. Lexington: University Press of Kentucky, 2012.

Gries, Peter Hays. *China's New Nationalism: Pride, Politics, and Diplomacy.* Berkeley: University of California Press, 2004.

Gugeler, Russell A. *Combat Actions in Korea.* Washington, D.C.: Center of Military History, U.S. Army, 1987.

Halberstam, David. *The Coldest Winter: America and the Korean War.* New York: Hyperion, 2007.

Hanson, Victor Davis. *Carnage and Culture: Landmark Battles in the Rise of Western Power.* New York: Anchor Books, 2002.

Hastings, Max. *The Korean War.* New York: Simon & Schuster, 1987.

He Di. "The Last Campaign to Unify China: The CCP's Unrealized Plan to Liberate Taiwan, 1949–1950." In Ryan, Finkelstein, and McDevitt, *Chinese Warfighting,* 73–90.

Hermes, Walter G. *Truce Tent and Fighting Front: U.S. Army in the Korean War.* 1966, reprint, Washington, D.C.: Office of the Chief of Military History and U.S. Government Printing Office, 1988.

Hong Xuezhi. "The CPVF's Combat and Logistics." In Li, Millet, and Yu, *Mao's Generals Remember Korea,* 106–39.

Joffe, Ellis. *The Chinese Army after Mao.* Cambridge, Mass.: Harvard University Press, 1987.

Kau, Michael Y. M., ed. *The Lin Biao Affair: Power Politics and Military Coup.* White Plains, N.Y.: International Arts and Science Press, 1975.

Kaufman, Burton I. *The Korean Conflict.* Westport, Conn.: Greenwood Press, 1999.

———. *The Korean War: Challenges in Crisis, Credibility, and Command.* 2nd ed. New York: McGraw-Hill, 1997.

Keegan, John. *A History of Warfare.* New York: Knopf, 1993.

Kennedy, Andrew B. "Military Audacity: Mao Zedong, Liu Shaoqi, and China's Adventure in Korea." In *History and Neorealism,* ed. Ernest May, Richard Rosecrance, and Zara Steiner, 201–27. Cambridge: Cambridge University Press, 2010.

Kinard, Jeff. "Human Wave Attacks." In *The Encyclopedia of the Korean War.* 2nd ed. Edited by Spencer C. Tucker, 1:343–44. Santa Barbara, Calif.: ABC-CLIO, 2010.

Knox, Donald. *The Korean War: Uncertain Victory.* New York: Harvest/HBJ Book, 1988.

Korean Institute of Military History, ROK Ministry of Defense. *The Korean War.* 3 vols. Seoul: Korean Institute of Military History, 1998.

Leckie, Robert. *Conflict: The History of the Korean War.* New York: Da Capo Press, 1996.

Lee, Jong Kan (NKPA, ret.). "A North Korean Officer's Story." In Peter and Li, *Voices from the Korean War,* 76–84.

Lei Yingfu. "The Establishment of the Northeast Border Defense Army, July 1950." Translated and Edited by Xiaobing Li, Don Duffy, and Zujian Zhang. *Chinese Historians* 7, nos. 1–2 (Spring and Fall 1994): 123–62.

Li, Cheng. *China's Leaders: The New Generation.* Lanham, Md.: Rowman & Littlefield, 2001.

Li, Xiaobing. *China's Battle for Korea: The 1951 Spring Offensive Campaign.* Bloomington: Indiana University Press, 2014.

————. "China's Intervention and the CPVF Experience in the Korean War." In *The Korean War at Fifty: International Perspectives*. Edited by Mark F. Wilkinson. Lexington, Va.: Virginia Military Institute Press, 2004, 130–49.

————. "Chinese Army in the Korean War, 1950–53." *New England Journal of History* 60, nos. 1–3 (2003–4): 276-92.

————. *A History of the Modern Chinese Army*. Lexington: University Press of Kentucky, 2007.

————. "Truman and Taiwan: A U.S. Policy Change from Face to Faith." In Matray, *Northeast Asia and the Legacy of Harry S. Truman*, 119–44.

Li, Xiaobing, and Hongshan Li, eds. *China and the United States: A New Cold War History*. Lanham, Md.: University Press of America, 1998.

Li, Xiaobing, Allan R. Millett, and Bin Yu, trans. and eds. *Mao's Generals Remember Korea*. Lawrence: University Press of Kansas, 2001.

Luthi, Lorenz M. *The Sino-Soviet Split: Cold War in the Communist World*. Princeton, N.J.: Princeton University Press, 2008.

Lynn, John A. *Battle: A History of Combat and Culture*. New York: Basic Books, 2008.

MacArthur, Douglas. *Reminiscences*. New York: McGraw-Hill, 1964.

MacKenzie, S. P. "Period of Mobile Warfare." In Matray and Boose, *Ashgate Research Companion to the Korean War*, 371–82.

Mao Zedong. *Mao Zedong on Diplomacy*. Beijing: Foreign Languages Press, 1998.

————. *Selected Works of Mao Tse-tung*. 4 vols. Beijing: Foreign Languages Press, 1977.

"Mao's Dispatch of Chinese Troops to Korea: Forty-six Telegrams, July–October 1950." Translated and Edited by Xiaobing Li, Xi Wang, and Chen Jian. *Chinese Historians* 5, no. 1 (Spring 1992): 63–88.

"Mao's Telegrams during the Korean War, October–December 1950." Translated by Xiaobing Li and Glenn Tracy. *Chinese Historians* 5, no. 2 (Fall 1992): 65–85.

Matray, James I., ed. *Northeast Asia and the Legacy of Harry S. Truman: Japan, China, and the Two Koreas*. Kirksville, Mo.: Truman State University, 2012.

Matray, James I., and Donald W. Boose Jr., eds. *Ashgate Research Companion to the Korean War*. London: Ashgate, 2014.

Millett, Allan R. *Their War for Korea: American, Asian, and European Combatants and Civilians, 1945–1953*. Washington, D.C.: Brassey's, 2002.

————. *The War for Korea, 1950–1951: They Came from the North*. Lawrence: University Press of Kansas, 2010.

Montross, Lynn, and Nicholas A. Canzona. *U.S. Marine Operations in Korea, 1950–1953*. Vol. 3, *The Chosin Reservoir Campaign*. Washington, D.C.: Marine Corps Headquarters, 1957.

Mossman, Billy C. *U.S. Army in the Korean War: Ebb and Flow, November 1950–July 1951*. Washington, D.C.: U.S. Army Center of Military History and U.S. Government Printing Office, 1990.

Mulhausen, Harold L. "The Chosin Reservoir: A Marine's Story." In Peters and Li, *Voices from the Korean War*, 98–116.

Munroe, Clark C. *The Second U.S. Infantry Division in Korea, 1950–1951.* Tokyo: Toppan Printing, 1954.

Na, Jongnam. "Making Cold War Soldiers: The Americanization of the South Korean Army, 1945–55." Ph.D. diss., University of North Carolina, 2006.

"New Russian Documents on the Korean War." In Archives of the President of the Russian Federation. Translated and Edited by Kathryn Weathersby. *Bulletin: Cold War International History Project* 6–7 (Winter 1995–96): 30–125. Washington, D.C.: Wilson International Center for Scholars.

Nie Rongzhen. "Beijing's Decision to Intervene." In Li, Millet, and Yu, *Mao's Generals Remember Korea,* 38–60.

O'Dowd, Edward C. *Chinese Military Strategy in the Third Indochina War: The Last Maoist War.* London: Routledge, 2007.

Parker, Geoffrey, ed. *The Cambridge History of Warfare.* New York: Cambridge University Press, 2008.

Peng Dehuai. "My Story of the Korean War." In Li, Millet, and Yu, *Mao's Generals Remember Korea,* 30–38.

Peters, Richard, and Xiaobing Li. *Voices from the Korean War: Personal Stories of American, Korean, and Chinese Soldiers.* Lexington: University Press of Kentucky, 2004.

PLA Academy of Military Science. "The Unforgotten Korean War: Chinese Perspective and Appraisals." 3 vols. Unpublished manuscript written by PLA officer-historians and sponsored by the Office of Net Assessment, Office of the U.S. Secretary of Defense, 2006.

Qing, Simei. "The US-China Confrontation in Korea: Assessment of Intention in Time of Crisis." In Matray, *Northeast Asia and the Legacy of Harry S. Truman,* 93–118.

Research Department of Party Literature, CCP Central Committee, ed. *Major Documents of the People's Republic of China—Selected Important Documents since the Third Plenary Session of the Eleventh CCP Central Committee.* Beijing: Foreign Languages Press, 1991.

Ridgway, Matthew B. *The Korean War.* Garden City, N.Y.: Doubleday, 1967.

Robinson, Thomas. "The Sino-Soviet Border Conflicts of 1969: New Evidence Three Decades Later." In Ryan, Finkelstein, and McDevitt, *Chinese Warfighting,* 198–216.

Roe, Patrick C. *The Dragon Strikes: China and the Korean War, June–December, 1950.* Novato, Calif.: Presidio Press, 2000.

Russ, Martin. *Breakout: The Chosin Reservoir Campaign, Korea, 1950.* New York: Penguin Books, 1999.

Ryan, Mark A., David M. Finkelstein, and Michael A. McDevitt, eds. *Chinese Warfighting: The PLA Experience since 1949.* Armonk, N.Y.: M. E. Sharpe, 2003.

Sandler, Stanley. *The Korean War: No Victors, No Vanquished.* Lexington: University Press of Kentucky, 1999.

Sawyer, Ralph. *The Seven Military Classics of Ancient China.* New York: Basic Books, 2007.

Scobell, Andrew. *China's Use of Military Force: Beyond the Great Wall and the Long March.* Cambridge: Cambridge University Press, 2003.

Shen Zhihua. "China Sends Troops to Korea: Beijing's Policy-making Process." In *China and the United States: A New Cold War History*, ed. Xiaobing Li and Hongshan Li, 13–47. Lanham, Md.: University Press of America, 1998.

Shen Zhihua and Danhui Li. *After Leaning to One Side: China and Its Allies in the Cold War*. Stanford, Calif.: Stanford University Press, 2011.

Shen Zhihua and Yafeng Xia. *Mao and the Sino-Soviet Partnership, 1945–1959: A New History*. Lanham, Md.: Lexington Books, 2017.

Sheng, Michael M. *Battling Western Imperialism: Mao, Stalin, and the United States*. Princeton, N.J.: Princeton University Press, 1997.

Simmons, Edwin H. *Frozen Chosin: U.S. Marines at the Changjin Reservoir*. Washington, D.C.: History and Museums Division, U.S. Marine Corps, 2002.

Spurr, Russell. *Enter the Dragon: China's Undeclared War against the U.S. in Korea, 1950–1951*. New York: Newmarket Publishing, 1988.

Steed, Brian. *Armed Conflict: The Lessons of Modern Warfare*. New York: Ballantine Books, 2003.

Stueck, William W. *The Korean War: An International History*. Princeton, N.J.: Princeton University Press, 1995.

Sunzi. *The Art of War*. In Sawyer, *Seven Military Classics of Ancient China*, 157–86.

Taaffe, Stephen. *MacArthur's Korean Generals*. Lawrence: University Press of Kansas, 2016.

Thompson, William R. "The Military Superiority Thesis and the Ascendancy of Western Eurasia." *Journal of World History* 10, no. 1 (Spring 1999): 143–78.

Tsai, Ming-Yen. *From Adversaries to Partners: Chinese and Russian Military Cooperation after the Cold War*. Westport, Conn.: Praeger, 2003.

U.S. Department of State. *Foreign Relations of the United States: China, Korea, Vietnam, and Indochina, 1945–1972*. 8 vols. Washington, D.C.: Government Printing Office, 1982–89.

van de Ven, Hans, ed. *Warfare in Chinese History*. Boston: Brill Academic, 2000.

Wang Xuedong. "The Chosin Reservoir: A Chinese Captain's Story." In Peters and Li, *Voices from the Korean War*, 117–26.

Weintraub, Stanley. *A Christmas Far from Home: An Epic Tale of Courage and Survival during the Korean War*. New York: Da Capo Press, 2014.

———. *MacArthur's War: Korea and the Undoing of an American Hero*. New York: Free Press, 2000.

Westad, Odd Arne, ed. *Brothers in Arms: The Rise and Fall of the Sino-Soviet Alliance, 1945–1963*. Stanford, Calif.: Stanford University Press, 1998.

Xu Xiangqian. "The Purchase of Arms from Moscow." In Li, Millet, and Yu, *Mao's Generals Remember Korea*, 139–47.

Xu Yan. "Chinese Forces and Their Casualties in the Korean War." Trans. Xiaobing Li. *Chinese Historians* 6, no. 2 (Fall 1993): 45–64.

Yu, Bin. "What China Learned from Its 'Foreign War' in Korea." In Li, Millet, and Yu, *Mao's Generals Remember Korea*, 9–29.

Zhai, Qiang. *China and the Vietnam War, 1950–1975*. Chapel Hill: University of North Carolina Press, 2000.

Zhang, Shuguang, and Jian Chen, eds. *Chinese Communist Foreign Policy and the Cold War in Asia: New Documentary Evidence, 1944–1950*. Chicago: Imprint Publications, 1996.

Zhang, Shu Guang. "Command, Control, and the PLA's Offensive Campaigns in Korea, 1950–1951." In Ryan, Finkelstein, and McDevitt, *Chinese Warfighting*, 91–122.

———. *Deterrence and Strategic Culture: Chinese-American Confrontations, 1949–1958*. Ithaca, N.Y.: Cornell University, 1992.

———. *Mao's Military Romanticism: China and the Korean War, 1950–1953*. Lawrence: University Press of Kansas, 1995.

Zhou Baoshan. "China's Crouching Dragon." In Peters and Li, *Voices from the Korean War*, 85–96.

Zubok, Vladislav, and Constantine Pleshakov. *Inside the Kremlin's Cold War: From Stalin to Khrushchev*. Cambridge, Mass.: Harvard University Press, 1996.

Index

air defense, 4, 5, 11

Almond, Edward M. "Ned," 31, 42, 43, 97, 113; on CPVF, 94; orders of, 96, 102

ammunition of Chinese forces, 36, 50–51, 67, 95, 135, 145; annual needs for the war, 135, 141; shortage of, 63, 67, 76, 95, 128, 130, 142, 152; Soviet supply, 135

Amtal-dong, 149

Andong, 34, 37

Anti-Japanese War, 8, 63. *See also* World War II

artilleries of Chinese forces, 10, 32, 35, 67, 135, 155, 156; 75 mm, 50, 67; 92 mm, 90; 92 mm rocket launchers, 67; antiaircraft artilleries (AAA), 5, 156, 159; barrage of, 99, 101, 147; failed shells, 67; firepower of, 127; howitzers, 67, 90, 143; lack of, 6, 67, 95, 143; manufacturing of, 10, 156; rotation of, 156; Russian-made, 156; shells of, 50, 67, 90, 94, 95, 145; transportation of, 47; weather impact on, 67

artillery battalions, 47, 116

artillery divisions, 134, 156

artillery regiments: 11th Regiment, 147; 25th Regiment, 147; 26th Regiment, 147; 28th Regiment, 147

Asia, 2, 13, 14, 23

Barr, David G., 43, 96

Beijing, 5, 13, *17*, 20, *26*, 28, 33, 130; and Taiwan, 22; meetings in, 16, 21, 29, *104*; support to North Korea, 15, 137

Bi Zheyang, 91

Britain, 30; Embassy of, 82

British forces, 82, 139, 146, 156; 27th Brigade, 35, 37, *55*, 139; 29th Brigade, 139, 208; cruisers of, 20; destroyers of, 20; mine-sweepers, 20; POWs of, 82; Royal Marines, 81

Cai Qunfan, 81, 124

Cai Zhengguo, *45*

Canadian forces, 156

CCP (Chinese Communist Party), 79, 157–58; armed forces, 6, 18, 22, 63, 79; Central Committee, 11, 132, 161; controls PLA, 79, 157, 160; documents of, 167nn44–45; leaders of, 1, 11, 22, 23; Party Center, 20–21, 158

CCP Central Military Commission (CMC), 21, 29, 134, 144, 156, 161; and 9th Army Group, 50, 119, 131, 137; approvals by, 20, 25, 146; decisions of, 25, 27, 153, 156; documents of, 11; meetings of, 15, 24, 27; orders from, 15, 22, 25, 31, 34, 38, 131

CCP Politburo, 11, 161; meetings of, 7, 23, 25–26, 29–30